MARKET WOMEN

MARKET WOMEN

BLACK WOMEN ENTREPRENEURS: PAST, PRESENT, AND FUTURE

Cheryl A. Smith

Foreword by Laurent Parks Daloz

Westport, Connecticut
London

Library of Congress Cataloging-in-Publication Data

Smith, Cheryl A., 1945–
    Market women : black women entrepreneurs—past, present, and future /
Cheryl A. Smith ; Foreword by Laurent Parks Daloz.
        p. cm.
    Includes bibliographical references and index.
    ISBN 0-275-98379-X (alk. paper)
    1. African American women executives. 2. African American
    businesspeople. 3. Businesswomen—United States. I. Title.
    HD6054.4.U6S65 2005
    338'.04'08996073—dc22   2004028379

British Library Cataloguing in Publication Data is available.

Library of Congress Catalog Card Number: 2004028379
ISBN: 0-313-36183-5
ISBN: 978-0-313-36183-8

First published in 2005

Praeger Publishers, 88 Post Road West, Westport, CT 06881
An imprint of Greenwood Publishing Group, Inc.
www.praeger.com

Printed in the United States of America

The paper used in this book complies with the
Permanent Paper Standard issued by the National
Information Standards Organization (Z39.48-1984).

10 9 8 7 6 5 4 3 2 1

This work is dedicated to my ancestors,
unknown and known:

The Josephs, the Watsons, and the Smiths,
especially my mother Florence, the memory of
my father, Leonard, and my Uncle O. J. Watson
And to my descendant, my daughter Akiba,
who has lived up to the meaning of her name, growing
more precious as time goes on.

Contents

Foreword

Conducting research on ethical development at a prestigious business school, Senior Research Associate Sharon Parks asked her young adult subjects a curious and provocative question: "If the purpose of medicine is health, and the purpose of law is justice, what is the purpose of business?" The question would often cause an awkward pause in the conversation as these privileged, highly success oriented students struggled for an adequate answer. "Well," said one, "the answer that comes to mind is *to make money*, but it must be more than that."

Ask that question of the entrepreneurs in this important book—bankers, publishers, laundry workers, journalists, real-estate developers, dressmakers, shopkeepers, educators—and the answers come back very different indeed, and without a lot of hesitation: to care for and educate our children, to build a stronger community among our people, to provide a sense of self-worth, to build a world that works for all. This conviction that economic success brings with it the responsibility to share that success with others is deeply rooted in the Black American experience. "Lifting as we climb" was a prominent slogan among successful African American women over a century ago. Then, as now, it flew squarely in the face of the prevailing ethic of radical individualism and unrestrained material success.

The women whom we meet here have never bought into the latter ideology. Black in a racist world, female in a sexist society, they have paid firsthand the terrible cost of mindless condescension, social shunning, illegal maneuvering, economic boycotts, and stark exploitation. In telling their stories, Cheryl Smith could have ignored all this. She could have written a book about gallant entrepreneurs, celebrating the extraordinary "character" of her heroines as they transcended all difficulties and triumphed alone. The message could have been the kind our culture loves: work hard, protect your interests, and you will defeat your enemies and make it against all odds. Indeed, these women do work hard and they do have character—extraordinary character. Their determination, perseverance, resilience, independence, and sheer grit shine through every page.

To her credit, however, Smith is telling a larger story, a truer story. This is the story of women called to the "triple duty" of work, family, and social justice. In a culture that relentlessly tears work from family, it is the story of the tireless struggle to stay whole; in a society rife with discriminatory policies and racist practices, it is the story of fierce commitment to justice; in a culture that measures success by material acquisition, it is the story of a deep spiritual conviction that what matters in life is not measured by bread alone.

The unifying metaphor is that of a quilt embracing in a single fabric the luminous stories of a host of previously unrecognized entrepreneurs. And just as the elements of a great quilt create a coherent pattern, so do the stories of this important book collectively tell a powerful alternative tale to the established economic mythology. In the face of that mythology, it is economic heresy to suggest that the purpose of business might be more than simply a growing bottom line for the benefit of the shareholders. It is economic heresy to suggest that cooperation might be a more adequate motivation for entrepreneurs than competition. It is economic heresy to include moral and social outcomes as a part of one's definition of "success." But these women have committed all these heresies and more, and they now constitute the fastest-growing group of entrepreneurs in the country. Before our eyes, as we read, terms we took for granted take on new meanings. "Success" must include the betterment of the community, not the individual alone; "capital" must be measured in terms that include the growth of connections among people rather than simply the accumulation of material assets; "entrepreneur" means someone who creates wealth that benefits all and harms none. Again and again, we witness how earnings are used creatively to form networks, strengthen social organizations, further racial and gender justice, and change the conditions that unfairly favor those who have over those who have not.

Our times are hungry for tales like these. In our quest for a better answer for Sharon Parks's disturbing question, in pursuit of what she calls "a more adequate economic imagination," we will do well to read carefully the stories that Cheryl Smith has so powerfully offered here. "Yes," comes the answer to that perplexed young business school student, "there is more to the purpose of business than making money, and it has been in our midst all along." We owe a debt of gratitude to Cheryl Smith for raising this welcome and sorely needed alternative at this time in our nation's history.

Laurent Parks Daloz

Preface

On September 11, 2001, life as we knew it changed forever. The attack on the World Trade Center in New York City and on the Pentagon in Washington, DC, using commercial airliners as weapons, rocked the world to its core. For some of us born and bred in the United States, terrorism, war, and the destruction of life and property came home for the first time since the Civil War. The loss of life, of a sense of security, and of trust was gone forever. Yet while I watched the coverage from Massachusetts, a truly U.S. paradigm seemed to prevail in the national media coverage of this tragedy: the continued focus on victims and heroes privileged by race, gender, and class.

As a native New Yorker watching the coverage from Boston, I felt compelled to visit my home and traveled to Ground Zero. Like others, I was shaken by the extent of the destruction of an edifice and streets I knew so well; like others I was in search of answers and comfort and found none. However, I did find some of the stories I knew were missing. On arriving at the closest open subway stop to Ground Zero, I immediately saw pictures and posters of those missing in the towers that told a very different story than that seen in the national nightly news. Although many posters were seeking people who worked in brokerage firms and financial industries, just as many if not more were about people who worked in the restaurants, in the offices, and in the departments that serviced the complex. Poignant posters included a brother and sister from Guyana, workers in the Windows of the World restaurant who were missing; the African chef from the same restaurant; and the Puerto Rican and Dominican food service, janitorial, and clerical workers. The police, firefighters, medical and National Guard personnel on duty were as varied and myriad as the city itself. The people who visited Ground Zero the week after the attack, regardless of their color, class, or ethnicity, were draped in red, white, and blue flags of every type and shape in a show of unity and mutual support. Yet the different portrayal of the victims and the heroes of this global tragedy reflects the ongoing racial, economic, and gender discrimination experienced on a daily basis by many citizens even in this most tragic of events. The fact that marginalization continues to manifest itself even as we call for unity of all "Americans" provides an even greater impetus for me to tell the stories, reclaim the history, and make visible those who have been invisible. The untold stories of those lives lost and affected resonated with me, an African/American/Caribbean woman, and with the work I am trying to do in writing this book. The main purpose of the book is to tell the stories of those uncounted heroines, both past and present, whose work contributed to the wealth and well-being of this nation. In doing so I hope to present lessons and strategies that enhance a more inclusive, respectful society, one in which issues of social justice, economic equity, and historical truth are present for the greater good.

Cambridge, Massachusetts
October 2001

When I wrote this preface in 2001, the world was one way. Now, in 2004, it is another. Yet, as the saying goes, "the more things change, the more they stay the same." Rapid changes and events occurred in our global village that have become generational markers for us all: A war was manufactured and fought for oil and money; corporate greed and venality was brought to light; the shuttle *Columbia* exploded, with déjà vu images of the *Challenger* disaster; new health threats arose across the world, with SARS competing for attention with AIDS. Underlying these events is continuity and constancy: The rich are getting richer and the poor poorer.

Against this backdrop of change and continuity, the lived experiences of successful Black women entrepreneurs take on a special significance. Black women continue to be barely visible in the news, the media, and the economy. For example, Black women make up one of the largest segments of the new volunteer military forces, yet they are rarely, if ever, seen or portrayed in the coverage of the war. An example is the media's differential treatment of two women who were injured and captured in the war in Iraq. Jessica Lynch, a White, blue-eyed blonde, was made an icon in and by the media, to even her own chagrin. In stark contrast, Shoshana Johnson, a corn-rowed Black woman who was shot, captured, beaten, and held in captivity for 22 days, was essentially ignored. There were no books written about her, no made-for-TV movies. Recognition and reward came from within the wider Black community and her hometown. In a like manner, Black women, defined as women of African descent, are on the rise in business and entrepreneurship in every industry and in many countries, yet this group of contributors to the global economy, who have prevailed in spite of the double yoke of racism and sexism, are often unacknowledged. They, like the women in this book, have important lessons to offer.

The guiding principle of this book is Sankofa, the wisdom of learning from the past. The concept is depicted by the African Adinkra symbol, presented as a stylized bird looking in two directions. We learn from the past by knowing our history, the stories of those who came before us. We capture the present through our own stories, which add to that history for those who come after us. The history of ancient African and early African American Market Women, along with the stories of the present-day entrepreneurs profiled in this book, provide a sense of connection and continuity across time and place. As we will see, these modern-day Market Women present an approach to doing business in a way that transcends greed and atomistic asset accumulation. Their extensive social capital networks of support, grounded in an African tradition of family, spirituality, and community, provide collaborative strategies for survival and success useful for the common good. Finally, their warrior's will, sense of humor, and demand for excellence provide role models and guidelines for all those seeking success, regardless of the area of endeavor, race, ethnicity, or gender. It is my hope that their history, their stories, and their efforts will be recognized for the value they have added to our communities, nation, and world.

Cambridge, Massachusetts
June 2004

*Sankofa, African Adinkra Symbol, meaning
"the wisdom of learning from the past."
Courtesy of Adolph H. Agbo.*

Acknowledgments

I t takes a "village" to complete a book. I would like to acknowledge and thank those members of my "village" who have helped along the way. There are several "houses" in the village, and I would like to mention some of them.

First and foremost, this book honors the memory of Maria Padilla-Orasel, Director of Minority and Women's Business Services at Empire State Development and the Entrepreneurial Assistance Program, who left us too soon. Her unwavering commitment to microenterprise development on a local, regional, and national basis, particularly for women and people of color, had an effect on the field in a significant way. A scholarship has been established in her name by the Association for Enterprise Opportunity, where she was on the board of directors, in recognition of her contributions and great good work. On a personal level, her enthusiastic support and sponsorship of the Market Women project and her integrity, honesty, and friendship are missed. I would also like to acknowledge members of her staff who assisted in the data gathering and thank them for their cooperation in this project, specifically Marion Samuels-Ramsey and Joyce Chandler-Smith. Thanks also go to my Entrepreneurial Assistance Program teaching partner and buddy, S. Edward Rutland of Jupiter Marketing, whose humor and knowledge made our work together memorable. Special recognition goes to former fellow directors of the Entrepreneurial Assistance Program centers throughout New York State, whose assistance in referring and encouraging their successful clients to participate in the study was invaluable.

I would also like to express my appreciation to Dr. M. Vicki Wachsman, president and chief executive officer of Black Women Enterprises, Inc.; Rosetta Caban, assistant director of the York College Small Business Development Center; and Maria Salcedo, counseling director of the

American Women's Economic Development Corporation, for their support and assistance in organizing the focus groups from their organizations. Their support provides examples of strong and weak ties in action, contributing to the connections among and between entrepreneurs and organizations.

This book evolved out of my dissertation research at Teachers College, Columbia University, so I would also like to acknowledge the members of that "house." First, I would like to thank my dissertation sponsor, Dr. Jeanne Bitterman, for her ongoing guidance and encouragement. Next, I would like to thank my other committee member, Dr. J. Phillip Thompson, for taking on a completely unknown student and adding immeasurably to this work. I would also like to take this opportunity to thank other members of the Teachers College and Columbia University community whose comments strengthened the study: Drs. Victoria J. Marsick, Kathleen McLoughlin, Dawn Person, Katherine Wilcox, and Rita McGrath. I would also like to express my appreciation to the American Association of University Women's Educational Foundation for awarding me their American Dissertation Fellowship.

Core members of the Teachers College "house" include my study and dissertation group members, Vicki Breitbart, Ann Martin, Colleen Aalsburg Wiessner, Althea Neilson, Faith Schottenfeld, and Nancy Lloyd Pfhal, who were there from the very beginning. Special thanks go to my Caribbean sister Althea, who brought me a gift from Jamaica—a picture of Market Women that hangs in a place of honor in my home. I would also like to thank Dr. Clement Hill II, whose consistent encouragement while working on his own dissertation inspired my own.

Words cannot express my deep gratitude to Laurent "Larry" Daloz, who wrote the definitive book on mentoring of adults and who taught me at Teachers College. He was the first to tell me I was a writer and the first to suggest I write a book. He has been a consistent writing mentor to me over the years, offering full and steadfast support of my efforts. We made a deal—if I wrote and published the Market Women book, he would write the foreword. We both kept our promises. Thank you, Larry.

Thanks also go to my recently built "house" of scholars and colleagues at Lesley University: Dr. Phyllis C. Brown, my friend, colleague, and technology mentor, who has increased not only my enthusiasm for but also my skills in the use of technology and multimedia; my office mate and friend the Rev. Dr. Marjorie Jones, who brings not only intellectual collaboration but also spirituality to our work together; Dr. Arlene Dallafar, whose sharing of her work with women entrepreneurs from Iran has given me an insight into the global experiences of women in business; Dr. Rosemary Knickles, whose resources on multicultural aspects of health added new and important insights to the work; and to Dr. Aziza Braithwaite Bey, whose commissioned sketch and doll of Hapshetsut highlighted in the book provide a visual image of the ancient African queen and leader. Particular thanks goes to my former Lesley colleague and constant friend, John De Cuevas—wine aficionado, jazz lover, and trustee of the Baker Foundation. My appreciation also to the Board of the Baker Foundation for awarding me the grant that enabled me to write the proposal for this book.

I would also like to thank research librarians whose knowledge, patience, and courtesy never fail to impress me. Some who have been particularly helpful are the librarians at the Ludcke library and Kresge Media Center at Lesley University, headed by Patricia Payne, Kathy Holmes, and Marie Gannon; Heather Gretzinger McMorrow of the Center for Academic Technology for her assistance in enhancing some of the images in the book; Sharon Butler at the Schomburg Center for Black Culture and Research; and Jacalyn Blume of the Schlesinger Library for the History of Women at the Radcliffe Institute at Harvard University.

The next "house" is my home, where my extended family of blood and fictive kin live: Faye Hines, my sister by choice and function, business partner and Market Woman, whose helpful insights and urging made me work harder and better, and her son, my nephew Jumaane; my sister Martha Sanchez, and her daughter, my niece Candice; my childhood sister Claudia Harris, godmother to my daughter and her children, my godson Eric and niece Colette; Dorothy Harris, my "social work" sister and other godmother to my daughter and her daughter Nova and a host of other family and friends, who provided me with places to rest and write, meals, and most important, love and support as I worked: Phillis and Leititia Thompson, Catherine Clark-Nelson, Patricia Jones, and Sandra Grymes. To them I say simply "Thank You."

The newest "house" in the village is Greenwood Publishing Group/ Praeger Publishers, where the editors live. They are Hilary Claggett, who first expressed enthusiastic interest in the book and passed that enthusiasm on to Nick Philipson, my editor. Nick's infectious laugh, solid support, and keen editing skills have made the book happen. He also got excited when he recognized the Sankofa symbol while on vacation—a decided plus! Thank you, Nick. Keep laughing!

Finally, I would like to thank the Market Women of the past for their courage and inspiration and those of the present for their time, honesty, and trust. This is your story!

Introduction

ful Market Women of ancient Africa. The prevailing myth in
nd, in fact, in many other parts of the world is that people of the
iaspora, especially women, have no entrepreneurial history, no
role models, and no traditions in this field. Nothing could be
om the truth! This belief is based on tradition and unexamined
ns and, as such, must be replaced with information rooted in the
riences of women of African descent in America.

a Market Woman. With my business partner Faye Hines, I de-
wned, and operated a business in Antigua, West Indies, called
st Cottages. We chose the name Cape Coast to symbolize the
n between women of the Diaspora in Africa, the Caribbean, and
d States. Cape Coast Castle in Ghana was a "slave castle" in
usands of enslaved Africans were held and then packed into ships
iddle Passage to the "New World." We visited Cape Coast Castle,
to the dungeons, saw the shackles, and slipped on the rocks the
fricans had to navigate when forced onto the small boats that
to the ships. We stood in the dark for frightening, heartbreaking
hen the lights went out, giving us the tiniest sense of what might it
e felt like to be captured and held there. We also saw the altars
e "ancestors" who had been stolen away and poured libations to
nories, participating in a ceremony that ensured they were not
—and that we were not forgotten in the Motherland. The con-
were strong and clear and empowering.

et Women in Accra, Ghana. Original photograph courtesy of
Cheryl A. Smith © 1975.

the pow
America
African
skills, n
further
assump
lived ex
I an
veloped
Cape C
connect
the Uni
which t
for the l
walked
chained
took th
seconds
might h
left for
their m
forgotte
nection

Introduc

Black women are a prism though which t
and sex are first focused and then refrac
transform these rays into a spectrum of
which illuminates the experience of all m

—Margaret B. Wilkers
A Shi

The sun rose slowly. The sky lightened
hot as they began their work. Stalls
selling fruits and vegetables, fish, fow
soup, and other prepared foods. "Lap" b
backs, "knee" babies clung to their skirts. Tl
swirling vista of color, movement, and sou
oranges as the brown and black women
garments and gaileys bent over their equall
out to each other and their children. The
their day.

Ma

A Different Vi

The term "Market Women" often evoke
above. However, it can also be interpreted
smart, savvy entrepreneurial women of the pr
the stage for positioning the accomplishmen
Black women entrepreneurs along a continu

When we got to Antigua and began the business, we experienced many of the issues faced by Market Women and used many of the strategies employed to conduct a successful business. First of all, we were foreigners and women and as such were not taken seriously until we were a proven success. In the beginning of the business, negotiations had to be handled by our Antiguan male lawyer, who convinced others to "let the girls have this land." The "girls" ended up with prime beachfront property that we developed into a thriving cottage resort and full-service restaurant. Along the way we hired and trained local staff, creating more than 20 jobs. Yet we could not both leave the business at the same time—one of us had to stay on-site at all times to ensure that the business ran smoothly—which sometimes created time poverty.

We tapped into our support systems of family and friends, selling shares to them to start the business; they bought the shares based on their trust in us. My mother worked in the business, handling our reservations from the United States; other family and friends helped with referrals and baby-sitting. We operated with a set of values that made connections with community and people. We made strategic alliances with other small hotel owners and the Tourist Board, run by a Black woman. We were for the most part ignored by White male managers of the large hotels, even though we were active members of the hotel association, but we made other good connections with like-minded business owners on the island. We connected with the local village in many ways, including sponsoring a Carnival troupe for a number of years.

Closer to home, we treated our employees with respect and recognition of their work and talents, helping them get additional training and promoting from within to management positions. We gave no-interest loans, hired their relatives, and participated in their family celebrations. They in turn connected with the business, feeling that it was theirs as well and worked as a team to ensure that it prospered. The staff connected with our families as well, including spoiling our children shamelessly. We made a conscious decision to buy our goods from as many local merchants as possible, including local farmers such as our own employees, who also had small patches of "ground"; fishermen; local bakeries; and vegetable peddlers. One of the most formidable Market Women I have ever met was a vegetable seller I bought from at least once a week for ten years: She never budged in her prices, rarely smiled, and only occasionally threw an extra onion or potato in my basket in recognition that I was a good customer. She ruled her corner of the market, used her profits to send her sons to schools in the United States, including sending one to medical school. For me, she was a Market Woman personified, one who had formidable marketing, negotiating, and money management skills reminiscent of the women in Ancient Africa.

As an adult and entrepreneurship educator, I have taught literally hundreds of entrepreneurs, many of whom were women of color. I was drawn to this work because of my own entrepreneurship and was able to combine my experiences with my teaching and counseling skills. The women were able to connect with me because I had "been there and done that." In working with them, I have been continually impressed by their strength, resiliency, integrity, and will in the face of racism and sexism as it affected their business ownership and management. As a scholar–practitioner in both entrepreneurship and adult education, I also knew that their stories were largely absent from the literature and research in both fields.

I have traveled in Africa and in the Caribbean, where I witnessed firsthand the entrepreneurship skills of the Market Women in those regions. These travels and observations enabled me to understand the effect they had on their families and their communities because of the contributions they made to the economy. I saw commonalities in business activities in Africa, the Caribbean, and the United States among women of African descent. I experienced and understood the value of Black women's businesses, whether formal or informal, legal or underground, in the survival and support of their families and communities. I knew there was a connection between the Market Women of ancient Africa and the Market Women of the Diaspora and sought to find it. It became my personal and professional mission and passion to correct the record and reclaim the history of this traditionally invisible assemblage of women.

A Different Kind of Story Quilt

One of the ways I teach and learn is through metaphor, so when I began to write this book, I searched for a fitting metaphor for the work. The first that came to mind was weaving—connecting strands of stories and history. Then, several things happened that changed my mind. One of my students, a middle-aged White woman whose hobby was quilting, wrote a thesis that presented solid historical research of the life of a little-known Black woman quilter, Harriet Powers. My student introduced me to this woman who lived in the Civil War and Reconstruction eras of U.S. history and who made and sold quilts decorated with African symbols. One of the two surviving pieces of her work is displayed in the Boston Museum of Fine Arts. The following summer I went to South Africa and was stopped dead in my tracks as I stood before a recently made quilt that told the story of the AIDS epidemic ravishing the country. The similarities between that quilt and Harriet Powers's in terms of style, colors, symbols, and form were riveting!

A little later, two African American students, one of whom was an actor in a play, written by the above-mentioned student, that told Harriet's story, and the other, who was married to a Ghanaian and lived in Ghana, worked quite independently on quilts that they made as part of their own course work. The first created a story quilt telling the tale of the Underground Railroad, the second told a tale of modern Africa using ancient quilting techniques. My student from Ghana had also brought me a gift of a hand-carved Sankofa symbol. When we looked at this work together, the three of us decided to present it all to our learning community in an event in which we all had an opportunity to share our work. I presented the Sankofa symbol first, explaining its meaning—the wisdom of learning from the past. The two students then presented their quilts, clarifying the links and emphasizing that this completely unplanned offering was symbolic of the unbroken thread that connected ancient African women to those living in the present, wherever they were.

I thus determined that quilting was a more fitting and meaningful organizing metaphor for the book. I began to look at the work of quilters such as Faith Ringgold, an internationally renowned African American artist specializing in story quilts. I knew that to tell the stories of Market Women of African descent, past and present, my task was to become a quilter, patching together untold tales of the history, battles, and successes of this group of unrecognized, unappreciated, and underestimated women. I wanted to create a verbal story quilt that told the stories of Black female entrepreneurs in the United States, beginning in Africa. Thus, the framing metaphor for the book is a quilt, and the primary image is the Sankofa symbol. Together they provide a guide and a process for creating this book.

The first step in the process was to challenge the dominant myths by uncovering the history and traditions of entrepreneurship among Black women, untangling and discarding the pieces that were tattered and destructive while keeping the good ones. Critical review and analysis of appropriate literature provided the basis for the first step. The second step was to access the narratives of present-day Market Women to present a fuller story involving their struggles, their strategies, and their successes. I did so by interviewing 19 Black women entrepreneurs in depth, capturing the stories of their lives and business experiences in their own voices. The themes that emerged became the threads that connected the pieces of the quilt and include history, gender, race, ethnicity, spirituality, family, personality, balance, success, power, wealth, community, class, learning, capital, and culture. The final step was to reconnect all the sections, patching together the old with the new, creating new patterns for a whole cloth that is inclusive and encompassing, leaving an unfinished hem so that other patches can continue to be added.

This written story quilt must include all whose voices have been left out of history and whose contributions to society in general and to the economy in particular have been ignored, misconstrued, or trivialized. By doing so, I believe that "Gifts from the Margin"—lessons, role models, and strategies provided by Black women entrepreneurs—can serve to inspire and sustain all who are seeking to accomplish goals and achieve success.

PART I

The Past: The Historical Perspective

Soup House Interior, 1876; Black woman serving soup to patrons both Black and White. Courtesy of the Schlesinger Library, Radcliffe Institute, Harvard University.

CHAPTER 1

Setting the Stage: Background and Context

The chief business of the American people is business.

—Andrew Carnegie

The room was filled with women chatting, murmuring, and laughing. They were dressed in power suits or soft dresses with jackets, with a few in business casual clothing. They were eating lunch, and the clink of the silverware and glasses and conversations slowly subsided as a diminutive woman, the keynote speaker, made her way to the dais. She smiled, waited for the introduction, and began her speech.

She was Pamela Thomas-Graham, an African American woman who is a triple Harvard degree holder, the first Black woman to be a partner at McKinsey & Company (a major multinational consulting firm), and the chief executive officer of CNBC. She is also a mystery writer (The Ivy League Series), a wife and mother of three children, including twins born just months before this speaking engagement. The women, mostly White, middle-aged, middle-class professionals, listened carefully, and asked questions of this woman who "had it all" about how she balanced work and home life, moved through the corporate world, and maintained her sense of self. She enthralled them with her wit, charm, and grace while giving concrete advice and suggestions. She is the new face of business in the United States today.

The keynote luncheon described above took place at a conference entitled "Women, Money, and Power," sponsored by the Radcliffe Institute of Advanced Study in November 2002. The conference also launched a watershed museum exhibit, "Enterprising Women" which documented and celebrated two hundred fifty years of women's entrepreneurial activities in the United States. The color and gender of the speaker, the very title of the conference, and the existence of the exhibit speak volumes about how the world of business, entrepreneurship, and economic development is finally beginning to acknowledge the effect of women, especially women of color, in the United States. Such acknowledgment was not always present and did not come lightly.

The Present-Day Economic Context

The economic climate of the early and mid-1990s in the United States was characterized by financial uncertainty and insecurity for the majority of its citizens. The economic "recovery" and rapid growth reported by government and industry in the past ten years has benefited a relatively small percentage of the population and has yet to "trickle down" in any significant manner to the general public. In the closing days of the twentieth century, Cornel West accurately analyzed the decade of the 1990s as being characterized by inequality of wealth, crystallization of a market society, and impoverishment of public life illustrated by corporate greed, a meanness of spirit, and the fact that 1 percent of the population holds 38 percent of the wealth of the country.[1] Many of those holding that wealth are entrepreneurs.

Interestingly, one of the most visible female entrepreneurs, Martha Stewart, was recently convicted of insider trading and fraud. In her stockbroker days, she became "one of the boys"—taking on their values and ways of doing business even as she exploited the "cult of domesticity" to build a multimillion dollar empire. Some say her gender brought her down. Regardless of gender, color, or class, however, the loss of trust in corporate America and the increasing unease with government economic policy has led to a search for meaning and values as people, communities, and the nation at large try to survive the country's new realities.

In this period of economic upheaval and imbalance, traditional economic theories, business behavior, and definitions of success must be questioned and reevaluated by scholars, practitioners, politicians, and entrepreneurs. One of the complications of doing business in the new millennium is dealing with the larger issue of economic justice and the inclusion of the "have nots" in a rapidly changing economic landscape. To meet the challenges of doing business in a visibly unethical, increasingly diverse, and technology- driven global marketplace, alternative strategies for conducting business must be sought by new and established businesses, both large and small.[2]

The world is rapidly becoming a global village, united in this postmodern information age by mass media, technology, and cheap transportation. In addition, the U.S. population is becoming browner, older, and more sophisticated. Wage work as we know it is rapidly disappearing, and those who do it and control its economic institutions are increasingly female and people of color. To remain competitive in the global economy, American business must become aware of the diversity that is its strength and to use it. To do so effectively, however, business must acknowledge the effect of race, gender, and culture on business behavior. It must also recognize and celebrate the past and present contributions of those on the "margin" to take advantage of the contributions they have made, are making, and will make in the future.

By looking at those who have successfully applied a different style of doing business and of accumulating and using capital, educators, policy makers, and funders may discover lessons about learning and business strategies that can be applied more effectively in the present and future. For example, people of color, women, non-elite Whites, immigrants, and others who have been on the edge of the American economic system have traditionally employed small business ownership for personal, family, and community survival, often using creative methods and approaches to start, maintain, and grow businesses.[3] However, positive discussions of the activities and contributions of some groups have essentially been absent from literature, either popular or scholarly. "But women's business has always been part of America's business. Whether they inherited or initiated their businesses, whether they marketed to women or the general public, enterprising women have contributed to the vitality of the nation from its inception to the present."[4]

The Numbers

One of the measures of economic development is the level of entrepreneurial activity in any given community or nation. Although the level of entrepreneurial activity in the United States has increased since the 1950s, the demographic profile of recognized entrepreneurs has changed dramatically. Demographic and statistical evidence points to the fact that women and minorities account for the largest segment of new business owners in the last decade, driving the economic growth of the country. Women are opening new businesses at a rate four times that of men, and women of color open businesses at a rate three times faster than that of White women.[5] Thus, Black women are part of the largest and fastest-growing group of new business owners in the country, yet their activities in the economic sphere and their place on the economic landscape have essentially gone unnoticed.

One of the reasons for this omission may be that purely quantitative, "formal" measures of economic activity are traditionally used to determine entrepreneurial success, such as level of sales and profits and size of the business measured in number of locations, and number of employees. Because individuals on the "margins" of the economy have had differential access to capital, markets, and networks, resulting in smaller sales figures and profits, they have been deemed unsuccessful, unproductive, or unimportant in the national economic picture. In addition, the motivations for starting a business, the goals for the business, and the use of the business by many "lifestyle entrepreneurs" may and often do differ from traditional entrepreneurs held up as exemplars.

Black women, regardless of their abilities, motivations, or accomplishments in business have faced both inter- and intraracial and sexual discrimination, rendering them one of the most unseen groups in the mainstream economy. Thus, information that is cognizant of the particular circumstances of Black women within the mainstream economy is vital to the development and survival of minority- and women-owned businesses—the fastest-growing segment of the economy. Furthermore, because prevailing wisdom about Black women and entrepreneurship indicates that they have no history or few skills in this area, it is also essential that their past and present contributions to their communities, to the larger economy, and to society be documented and used. "In their business activities, black women have sustained a commercial cultural tradition of self-help that has distinguished the economic lives of black women in America for almost 400 years."[6]

The Other Contexts

Any discussion of Black women's lived experiences must be conducted in a way that takes into account their economic, political, social, cultural, historical, and gender realities. Many academics, especially Black women, have been concerned with the inclusion of the truth about Black women's lives in mainstream economics, social science, history, higher and adult education, anthropology, and literature. For example, Leith Mullings, a Black feminist anthropologist and historian, importantly points out that "women of color, and particularly African-American women, are the focus of well-elaborated, strongly held, highly contested ideologies concerning race and gender."[7] Those stereotypes, constructed in the beginning of the Antebellum era, are supported by several images, all negative, that took hold in slavery days and are among the most enduring to this day: "Jezebel," "Mammy," and "Sapphire." One of the most pernicious modern versions is that of the strong, dominating, and emasculating matriarch, felt by some as having a strength that destroyed Black men—and thus Black families.

Deborah Grey White, a Black woman historian who researched the lives of enslaved women in the plantation South, discovered that female bond-women, in their need to survive the horrific conditions of chattel slavery, formed close-knit cooperative networks in which female cooperation and interdependence were facts of life.[8] She pointed out the truth that Black women did what women have done since time immemorial—made themselves a bulwark against the destruction of their families: "Slave women did what pioneer Americans did on the frontier: they mustered their reserves, persevered and helped each other survive."[9] However, the negative stereotypes have become common wisdom, obscuring and practically obliterating the true nature of Black women's economic lives, both past and present.

The New, True Images

Women of African descent have a long tradition of entrepreneurial activity, skill, and success, beginning with the powerful Market Women of ancient Africa.[10] This tradition has provided for the retention and adaptation of entrepreneurial marketing skills over time and place and advanced the success of several Black women entrepreneurs in both the slave and free communities in the Colonial and Antebellum eras of American history, throughout the eighteenth, nineteenth, and twentieth centuries to the present day. The tradition continues today and is illustrated in part by the profiles of highly successful women, usually appearing in the issues of *Black Enterprise* and *Essence* magazines—Black owned and operated publications. The types of businesses owned and operated by the women highlighted include retail and service businesses as well as those in businesses not usually associated with women—especially Black women—such as communications, engineering, and international business.

There are certainly more books and articles on this topic now than when I began my research nine years ago. Biographies such as A'Leila Bundle's wonderful story of her great-grandmother Madame C. J. Walker, solidly researched and well-written books about Black women's work as managers and professionals in the corporate world, and timely scholarly research about Black women and work, written by Black women have raised our visibility in the economic sphere.[11] This discovery was a pleasant surprise but does not mitigate the fact that there is still a dearth of information about Black women entrepreneurs in the academic or public view, those relatively well-known historical figures such as Madame C. J. Walker and present-day celebrity figures such as Oprah Winfrey notwithstanding.

Across the spectrum of American history, Black women dominated certain sectors of the economy, engaging in entrepreneurial activities that were at times informal and often clandestine. "Habits of survival" were retained informally as those "people teach these habits...to each other, often by example."[12] Becoming visibly successful was often dangerous and deadly for people of color in the United States, as evidenced by the riots of the 1830s, when Black-owned businesses were burned; the Trail of Tears forced march of the Cherokees from their successful towns; and the burning of Black Wall Street in Tulsa, Oklahoma. To survive the violence perpetrated by jealous Whites, Black people and people of color went about doing their business quietly. Given that history, even some successful modern-day entrepreneurs, both male and female, prefer not to be interviewed about their businesses or their successes. Yet, women, especially women of color, continue to open businesses at a rate greater than anyone else in the country.

The prevailing social, political, and economic conditions in history and in the present continue to provide motivation for Black women to choose entrepreneurship as a vehicle for freedom, economic survival, and empowerment. There are many "success stories" of historical Black women who became successful business owners, although only a few historical figures became so successful they achieved national recognition. A few stories were documented in some form, but most were unknown except to family and friends within the Black community. Because their enterprises were not documented in written form and were usually unknown to the power structure, the firmly incorporated myth that Blacks, and especially women, had no entrepreneurial history prevailed. However, Walker's research has proven otherwise:

> The Antebellum Black businesswomen were entrepreneurs whose business activities were characterized by ingenuity, creativity and innovativeness....[They] participated in business while having to contend with slavery, racism and sexism...they no doubt had developed a formidable business acumen.[13]

which has been passed on to their descendents.

The Uniqueness of Black Women's Experiences

The significance of the documentation of the lives and successes of Black women entrepreneurs in history and in the present is based on the assumption that their stories, still largely untold, will inspire and sustain new entrepreneurs, especially women of color, providing role models and mentors, both known and unknown. Women of the African diaspora in the United States are unique. Black women's uniqueness is related to the fact that they "share with White women a similar experience of what it means to be female in a sexist society and with Black men what it means to be Black in a racist society."[14] In addition, Black women have been historically viewed as an "inferior" sex of an "inferior" race.[15]

These women are barely noticed in history because until recently, history was written by White men, and Black history was written by Black men.[16] African American women also share the experience of being women of color in a White male–dominated society but are different even from other women of color in that we were brought here and suffered under chattel slavery for centuries. Thus, as pointed out by Mullings, "women of color engender unique consciousness, informed not only by the double consciousness and second sight of the veil but also by the triple consciousness of being at the forefront of race, class and gender conflict."[17] Gender is not always unifying.

Popular writers and scholars concerned with the experiences of Black women in the United States, analyzed from their unique "standpoint" and from the perspective of the "center" rather than the " margin," have identified the strengths and strategies employed by Black women that have enabled them to battle and in some cases prevail against the Goliath of the hegemony of White male dominance in U.S. culture.[18]

I see this book as doing battle against those deeply held beliefs that ignore and denigrate Black women. Writing it is both race and legacy work in the tradition of Black women, bringing to light old and constructing new knowledge. By examining the existing literature in many disciplines, bringing to the surface the buried treasure of Black women's economic history and connecting this history to the lived experiences of a small group of modern-day entrepreneurs, I am creating new knowledge.

The perceptions of the study groups' business histories, types of learning experiences, and definitions of success were explored. I felt the experiences and behavior of successful Black women entrepreneurs would contribute a unique group perspective—one that is not usually found in either scholarly or popular literature but that is critical in the present-day context of economic upheaval and imbalance among various segments of U.S. society. I also intended to illuminate the linkages between the larger issues of economic justice and power in an increasingly diverse and rapidly changing world.

The major findings of my exploratory study were the generation of themes relating to Black women, entrepreneurship, learning, and success, and their perceived relationship to each other. The outstanding finding was the breadth and depth of social capital networks of the participants, which seemed to be a thread that was interwoven throughout both their learning and their success, linking their learning and business activities. Relationships with others were evident and paramount in the women's learning and entrepreneurial ventures, expressed clearly and powerfully in their own voices.

Other major themes identified were the pervasiveness of spirituality in the women's lives, which they felt enhanced their success, and the importance of achieving balance not only between their business and personal lives but in their inner lives as well. Other themes were the business strategies these women employed and how they were learned, the personal characteristics of the entrepreneurs, the perceived effect of race and gender on entrepreneurial activities, and their own definitions of success. The combination of formal and informal strategies was an apparent major factor in success. The findings on the effect of race and gender on entrepreneurial success suggested that the Black women in the study, although having much in common with women entrepreneurs in general, found race to be a more compelling factor in their lives and their businesses than gender. The findings support other studies which concluded that Black women entrepreneurs indeed had and continue to have different issues than those of White women.[19] In contrast, the more compelling finding seems to be that the intersection of race and gender is critical in measuring success in the entrepreneurship and economic activity of Black women entrepreneurs. A related question raised is the presence of the themes among other groups of entrepreneurs, especially other women of color, White women, and men.

In their own words, the participants identify the factors that contributed to who and how they are as successful Black businesswomen. More importantly, I felt the study would highlight Black women's self-definition, which they have used as a strategy for empowerment, to be shared with others who have traditionally been defined as the "other" by those dominant in mainstream society. One of the ways Black women and other groups have been controlled has been by being defined by others and their vision of what we should be. This definition of how we are or how we are wanted to be is used to maintain the status quo. I hope that these redefinitions will help correct that situation. As pointed out by Jill Nelson, a Black woman writer and journalist who described how she "became a grown-up" Black woman, "Those who don't define themselves are doomed to be defined by others, erased, or as is the case with black women, both."[20] These Black women and others like them did neither.

A related purpose of this book is to explore and expand the conventional definitions of success, drawing on some of the newer and more expansive definitions emerging in the literature and from the entrepreneurs themselves.[21] The overall conclusions drawn from the research suggest that these Black women entrepreneurs may in fact have distinctive life experiences that have affected their business activities and learning strategies. Their views of the world, and their ways of acting in and on it, although displaying many commonalities with entrepreneurs in general, possess some unique aspects resulting from the intersection of race, gender, and class in their lives. These include their spirituality, their concern for balance, their integrity, their will, their coping mechanisms, and their connections with others—notably their mothers and their "sisters," their communities, and the larger society. For these women, Black women's history and culture have positively affected their business activities. Their ways of doing business, anchored by centuries-old cultural traditions, offer alternative models of business development and expanded definitions of success, wealth, and power.

Limitations

Although understanding the value of the information obtained, I acknowledge the fact that these findings only describe the thoughts, feelings, and experiences of a small group of women, that the conclusions drawn may not be applicable to all Black women, nor are they limited to them. However, the basic assumption underlying my work is that the examination of this group of successful Black female entrepreneurs has worth and value and can provide useful lessons for all entrepreneurs, educators, and learners, regardless of race, ethnic group, or gender. I also assume that enough of their distinctive "stories" have not been told outside of Black history classes, historically Black educational institutions, and popular literature targeted to the African American market. Their history and stories need to be integrated into mainstream literature as well as into their respective academic disciplines. I also believe that entrepreneurship is a viable means of achieving financial self-sufficiency for individuals, communities, and nations and that entrepreneurship education, history, and research can contribute to that empowerment process. Finally, I assume that entrepreneurial skills can be learned and that lessons learned from shared life stories can provide an effective means of teaching and strengthening those skills.

When people in social settings asked about the topic of the book, I was initially surprised when one of the responses I received, especially from some Black women, was "Is there anyone I would know in the book?" Because I interviewed unknown women, I doubt they would yet be known in the larger world, much like their unsung predecessors. I predict some will become well-known, well-heeled, and well-respected by any measure. Those who do not may choose to remain lifestyle entrepreneurs, seeking a different outcome, or they may choose to close their businesses. Yet, like some historians of old as well as of the present, I seek to make them visible by telling their stories, connecting them to the hidden work of their entrepreneurial ancestors. There are many more stories to be told, much more history to be reclaimed, and many more unknown entrepreneurs to be recognized and encouraged for our story quilt to be completed.

Anyone who has ever lived among women of African descent knows that it is inconceivable to even imagine invisible or voiceless black women. Wherever one looks in the black world, one finds in black women a living, working, struggling presence—the primary source of life itself. And their voices—their prodding, probing, commanding, caressing, captivating, caring, melodic, melancholy voices are omnipresent in black families and communities everywhere.

—Howard Dodson, in Schwarz-Bart,
In Praise of Black Women, Volume 1, foreword

CHAPTER 2

Reclaiming History: Ancient African Economic Traditions

We have a history....

—Sharon

The book is beautiful, a work of art in and of itself. It is a heavy tome, replete with wonderful color plates of ancient African women, artifacts, maps, symbols, myths, and legends. It was, published initially in French, the first volume in a series called *In Praise of Black Women: Ancient African Queens*.[1] Written and translated by two French women of the African diaspora, the volume documents and displays the activities of Black women as queens, Amazons, warriors, leaders, economists, and business owners, beginning ten thousand years ago. The place of Black women on the world stage since the dawn of time can be seen in this artistic and literary monument to them; it is long overdue. "Of course black women have been central to the development of mankind since its inception."[2]

The Earliest Women

The *Praise* book illustrates the effect these ancient women had on their kingdoms, their clans, their families, and their history. The initial plate is a rendering of Black Eve, the first woman. "Lucy," so named by the Leakey anthropological team, who found her in the Olduvai Gorge in Africa in 1974 is a fossil some 3.5 million years old. Her Ethiopian descendants named her

Dinknesh, meaning "You are lovely."[3] This little woman, three feet, six inches tall, is

> the grandmother of us all, blacks, whites, yellows, reds, people of the sea and dwellers of the steppes, those who live in the sun or with the polar cold. She is the one who from which all of humanity came.[4]

The next plates in the *Praise* book are photos of cave paintings or frescos created by ancient inhabitants of the Sahara in the Tassili caves some ten thousand years ago that portray daily life. The frescoes depict African women in family settings, caring for children, grooming animals, planting and harvesting, and using bows and arrows. The silhouettes of these Black women have profiles, clothing, hairstyles, and ornaments that can be seen in many parts of Africa and in the world today "from the shores

Queen Hatshepsut, Pharaoh of Egypt, fifteenth century BC.
Courtesy of Aziza Bey for Patterns by Design, © 2004.
Great Women Leaders Doll Collection.

of Senegal to the edges of the Zambezi River, from the hills of the Caribbean and the streets of Harlem to the favellas dotting Rio's skyline."[5] The
images portray not only people but also activities that are reflective of those
that continue to be the purview of women the world over, and especially of
women in the Black diaspora, grounding us firmly in our ancient history.

The other images and stories continue in a chronological sequence, recording the activities of these ancient women who dazzled the world. Their
stories are full of the stuff of human drama: love, hate, betrayal, passion,
compassion, war, peace, money, and power. A few representative women of
note whose work and lives are particularly relevant to women entrepreneurs are
profiled below. Some commonalities are readily apparent. Many women were
warriors and fighters, taking to the field as combat soldiers and as heads of
armies. They often wore men's clothing and symbolic "beards" and loincloths
as they established their leadership positions but then shed those clothes as they
became wives and mothers, while retaining and wielding their power. As
mothers, they founded dynasties—giving birth to and ruling through their sons,
who became kings, or their daughters, who became queens. As queens, ngolas,
and rulers, these women directed not only the political, religious, and social lives
of their kingdoms but also the economic systems. They fought fiercely to protect
their people, ruled with compassion, and managed with skill.

The Nubian Egyptians

Ahmose-Nofretatari: The woman who became divine. Known as the
"liberator of the kingdom" alongside her brother Ahmose, Ahmose-Nofretatari
was the first queen to share the bed of the god Amon. Born in Egypt at the end of
a second-century occupation by the Hyksos, Ahmose-Nofretatari married her
brother Ahmose after accompanying him in battles against them, becoming a
"sister-wife" in a royal tradition that lasted for generations. In her forties when
her husband-brother died, legend has it she became the spouse of the god Amon.
She ruled alongside her son Amenopolis I, controlling the material and spiritual
life of the kingdom. She was the only woman in Egypt's long history considered
to be divine and was the object of a cult that lasted for over five hundred years.
Seen in her funerary temple in the "million-year castle" in wood, stone, and
frescos, she is described as having "black skin, beautiful face, elegant, her hair
crowned with feathers." She was Egypt's first recorded goddess, ruler, and
priestess, setting the stage for many who followed.[6]

Queen Hatshepsut is the direct descendant of Ahmose-Nofretatari
through royal incest. She is notable because, as the daughter of a god, she chose
not to rule as a regent but declared herself pharaoh. When she did so, she shed
her feminine exterior, appearing with a symbolic beard and loincloth. Her
achievements included a rule of peace that was an oasis between wars. She
focused on the prosperity of the kingdom, managing its wealth skillfully and
exercising her strength and desire for peace such that no war occurred during

her reign. Trade was established with people of the East and with the Greeks. Turquoise mines were opened in the Sinai, and rather than use slaves, Hatshepsut requested and obtained Egyptian volunteers and Bedouins to harvest the stones. The Bedouins were desert dwellers in the Sinai who were called upon to harvest the turquoise. They were workers as opposed to Egyptian volunteers who came down from Egypt to work the mines. She also sent caravans deep into Asia and the land of Punt around 1495 BCE.[7]

The land of Punt, or Nubia, was seen as the country of the ancestors and the cradle of the Egyptian race or civilization. The reason for Hatshepsut's excursion to Punt was both economic and scientific: to obtain resins and spices used for incense for the temples which were in great demand, and to enable her engineers to understand the origin of the Nile and its ebbs and flows that controlled Egyptian life. Hatshepsut had Nubian origins and was reportedly fascinated with this country that had special meaning to her. She also took a Nubian Black man, Senenmut, as her secret lover, because as a widow of the pharaoh she was not able to chose her own mate. Senenmut was also the prime minister, official architect of the kingdom, artist, scientist, counselor, and most important, protector of the crown.

Queen Hatshepsut behaved in such a way that her kingdom prospered without cruelty or war. She was a leader who used cooperation rather than competition and coercion to rule and manage, providing a tradition that was to endure after her reign.[8]

The Candaces were the rulers of the Kingdom of Kush. "The Kingdom of Kush was renowned in antiquity, and its reputation stretched beyond the seas: its queens were called the Candaces."[9] The Black Kingdom of Kush was born some three thousand years ago and lasted a millennium until its fall in 350 CE. In 750 BCE, the kingdom expanded north along the Nile and conquered Egypt, establishing the splendid twenty-fifth dynasty of the Black Pharaohs. The kingdom disappeared when the Assyrians, armed with iron weapons, conquered the kingdom. All the queens of the kingdom were called Candace, and they were known as warrior-queens. One, called Amanirenas, was queen of Kush when the Romans came to the Nile after Cleopatra's defeat. Amanirenas was described as being "a very masculine woman who lost an eye in battle"— masculine in this case meaning courageous—and she fought and beat the Romans. The dressing of African women in men's clothing for battle and for leadership (as with the pharaohs) seems to be an ongoing strategy used to establish dominance. Another noted Candace, the queen of Ethiopia, was noted in the Old Testament of the Bible as being the first to embrace the Christian faith, influenced by her own minister, who was converted by Philip.[9]

The Later Queens

Perhaps the most well-known African queen is Makeda, the queen of Sheba. The ruler of Ethiopia, Makeda went to Jerusalem to test King Solomon's wisdom. The two rulers exchanged many gifts and spent many hours in conversation. He was struck by her miraculous beauty; after her six-month visit, she gave birth to their child, called the "Son of Wisdom." Her last descendant was the Negus Haile Selassie.[10]

Yennenga was the Mother of the Mossi Kingdom. The Mossi Kingdom is one of the most ancient in Africa and traces its beginnings to Yennenga the Svelte, an Amazon warrior-queen. The kingdom is best known for its resistance to colonialism. Around 1100 BC, north of the Kingdom of Ghana, lived a king named Madega, who had a beloved daughter named Yennenga. She accompanied her father into battle from the age of fourteen years and was so fearless she was often compared to a lioness "with stubborn chin and flowing mane." A formidable warrior, Yennenga had her own battalion and was put in charge of the king's granaries, which she filled to overflow from loot from battle.[11]

However, she soon realized she wanted marriage and children, and when her father would not approve of her suitors, she "dressed up like a man and rode on horseback from the paternal domain." On her journey, she met a solitary elephant hunter—the exiled son of Mali, who was a mighty warrior in his own right. Yennenga continued her disguise for three weeks, until the helmet covering her hair slipped and she was discovered. "The game was up!"[12] The first child of Yennenga and the son of Mali, Riale, was Ouedraogo, who, with the blessing of his grandfather and parents, founded his own kingdom, the Mossi. This warrior queen founded a dynasty whose hereditary chain remains unbroken from its beginnings in the early twelfth century to the present day.[12]

Amina of Zaria "was the best rider and finest archer in Hausaland, and she would charge advancing enemy troops." In the fifteenth century, Africans who were Muslim converts invaded the land of the Hausa. "That's when the pink-heeled young woman showed her colors to the world, the ancestors and the gods." In her thirty-four years of reign, Amina reconquered all her lost territory in Hausaland and expanded her domain beyond her own borders to the sources of the Niger and the banks of the Benue.[13]

Heleni, Empress of Ethiopia, was "An enigmatic woman, who managed to pull Ethiopia out of its traditional isolation at the very moment when this old Christian kingdom of Africa was in distress."[14] In their quest for gold, ivory, and slaves, fifteenth-century Portuguese explorers and sailors looked for the imaginary Christian Kingdom of John Prester, the mistaken name of Ethiopia and its ruler. The real ruler of the Kingdom of Ethiopia was the Empress Heleni, wife of the Emperor Vayda Maryam. A pious woman, a warrior, and a scholar who had written two books, Heleni (or Helena) was also a great politician who realized the value of forging a treaty with Portugal to help the Ethiopians in their fight against the Muslims. A charming, enigmatic woman, Heleni ruled Ethiopia for fifty years, maintaining alliances that enabled her to protect her country.

In contrast, Ana de Sousa Nzinga was the queen who resisted Portuguese conquest. Nzinga was born in 1581 in Kabasa, the capital of the Kingdom of

Ndongo (now Angola), which was ruled by people called ngolas. The Portuguese had converted the Kongo and were after "Black ivory," or slaves. Nzinga's father, Ngola Karensi, distrusted the European expansion and banned the missionaries from his kingdom. This action resulted in a war of resistance that lasted forty years. Nzinga, Amazon and warrior, dressed in man's clothing, and was considered to be the best politician in the country. Her strategies angered her brother, Mani a Ngola, however, who became ruler after their father's death. In his anger, Nzinga's brother sterilized her and killed her only son; however, after suffering many defeats, he begged for help, and while not forgetting her son or her sterilization, Nzinga agreed to aid him to keep her people from being enslaved. Because she spoke Portuguese, she was sent to negotiate a treaty, which was signed but, as suspected, was not honored. Nzinga then returned home, jailed her brother, declared herself ngola, and issued her first orders. She fought for thirty years without being able to rebuild her homeland, but she was never defeated. "In Angola, every living, breathing thing, down to the least blade of grass in your path, still remembers our great queen, Ana Sousa Nzinga."[15]

The Warriors, Traders, and Leaders

There were many more African queens—warriors and leaders who continued to rule either directly, as regents for their children, or as co-rulers with their husbands. From the late fifteenth to the early nineteenth century, African women continued to affect their worlds. Some, like Nzinga and Nandi, the mother of the fearsome Shaka Zulu in southern Africa, fought against the Europeans, the slave trade, and colonialization. Some were warriors—the Amazons of Dahomey, who protected the king, were organized as an army corps, including the Gulonento, or the "riflemen"; Gohonto, the "archers"; the Nyekplonento, or "reapers"; and the Gbeto, or "hunters."[16] Tata Ajache, who was herself a trophy of war, was, as custom dictated, trained as an Amazon. She became the queen of Dahomey by marrying King Glege, and in spite of her crown, she continued to fight as an Amazon and died a royal widow.[17] Other women, such as Modjadji I and her descendants, were rainmakers who saved their empire from drought for more than two centuries. Trade was also the purview of many women, including the women of the powerful empire of Timbuktu, a place where women did not wear veils, where they were free to come and go as they pleased, and where they prospered because they were clever and industrious in trade.[18]

As can be seen by the histories offered here, women were not only an integral part of the African social, political, and economic systems but in fact were central to these systems. Entrepreneurship, a central facet of the economic system in West Africa, had its beginnings well before the Three Great Empires of the Western Sudan. These empires operated from the seventh century BC to the sixteenth century AD, and the best known were the

Kingdoms of Ghana, Mali, and the Songhay Empire.[19] Before and leading up to the growth of those massive trading empires, trading market centers became trading empires as they established cities and then governments, and women traders were key in those market economies.

Trade primarily consisted of caravans that spanned three major regions of Africa—West Africa, the Nile region, and North Africa. The trans-Saharan trade routes were used to trade gold, ivory, and salt from West Africa or ancient Ghana for copper, silks, and metalware from North Africa and the Berbers. Between 1000 and 1500 BC, these empires became a valuable part of a wider international network of trade that also included southern Europe and Asia.[20] As mentioned previously, many of the warrior-queens often initiated and controlled the trading caravans. In addition, non-royal women controlled the production and distribution of agricultural and crafts products as well as the profits that accrued from these products on a local level. These early Market Women, working in their own families, clans, and villages, were just as important in African social structures and systems as were their queens.

Chancellor Williams conducted a massive study of Black civilization and found a uniformity in basic social structural outlines throughout Africa and across history. These included an economic system based on communal ownership of land, a value system based on the right of individuals to obtain an education and learn a living, and a social system in which kinship groups were paramount. The educational system was structured around age-set roles and gender-specific education, in which apprenticeship provided both intellectual and operational skill learning.[21] The gender-specific education and age-set roles provided the basis for much of the division of labor and specialization that accounted for the economic and entrepreneurial activities of women in African society.

Williams, Herskovits, and Meier and Rudwick all describe the West African economic system as being sophisticated, tightly structured, successful, and far reaching.[22] This recognition is important in the light of the need to "correct the record" of Black economic activity, as until recently, "African" business was thought to be primitive, unsophisticated, or non-existent. Additionally, little was also known or reported in America of the historical role of women in the African economy.

Herskovits, in his 1941 groundbreaking work *The Myth of the Negro Past*, discusses the role of African women in an economic system which included production of both agricultural and craft products that surpassed the needs of subsistence and personal use, with the surplus being used for trading in the markets and beyond. Emphasizing the importance, discipline and genius of these women, Herskovits found that

> In the field of production, this discipline takes the form of cooperative labor under responsible direction and such mutual self-help is found not only in agricultural work but in the craft guilds, characteristically organized on the basis of kinship. This genius for organization also

manifests itself in the distributive processes. Here the women play an important part. Women, who are for the most part sellers in the market, retain their gains often becoming independently wealthy. With their high economic status, they have likewise perfected disciplined organizations to protect their interests in the markets. These organizations comprise one of the primary price-fixing agencies, prices being set on the basis of supply and demand, with due consideration for the transportation of goods to market.[23]

These women were also instrumental in maintaining craft guilds and mutual aid societies that were organized on the basis of kinship, which are felt to be the predecessors of the formal and informal support networks that have always existed within the Black community. Women ran those networks and founded those organizations. Historians Walker, Herskovits, and Williams make a case for the adaptation and acculturation that shaped the forms and structures of enterprises developed by African-American women, "having as their base the commercial activities of women in Central and West Central Africa."[24]

The ancient African queens who were described briefly above epitomized qualities of leadership, commitment to family and community, cooperative economics, and a warriors' will. They took to the field as Amazon soldiers and heads of armies. They established dynasties and ruled their kingdoms for decades with honor, grace, and compassion. They protected their people and their kingdoms. These women are role models, unknown mentors, and sources of inspiration. Their behavior, skills, and values laid the groundwork for the economic and leadership activities of women of the African diaspora throughout time and across place. Their stories set the stage for the retention of the Africanisms that enabled women, some of whom were of royal blood, who were ripped from their homelands and enslaved to survive, protect, and prevail.

The qualities, ideals, and strengths of these ancient African ancestors were passed to their descendants, both in Africa and the "New World." Leadership, money management, connection to community, and love and protection of family were all present in the African American culture that evolved in the United States as well as in other cultures in the African diaspora, such as the Caribbean and Latin America. Those values, skills, and abilities provided survival strategies necessary for these women to organize their lives and those of their families in the early days of the development of the United States. As we will see in the next chapter, those Africanisms that were retained and adapted contributed to the economic and business activities of Black women from the early colonial era to the present.

African culture, instead of being weak under contact, is strong but resilient, with a resiliency that itself has sanction in aboriginal tradition.

—Melville Jean Herskovits, *The Myth of the Negro Past*, p. 19

CHAPTER 3

The Continuum: Early African American Women's Business History from the Colonial Period to the Twentieth Century

The economic position of women in West Africa is high. It is based on the fact that women are traders quite as much as agricultural workers and on recognition that what they earn is their own....They unquestionably contribute their share to the support of the household and the community.

—Melville Jean Herskovits, *The Myth of the Negro Past*, p. 58

The Early Days: The Colonial and Antebellum Eras, the Seventeenth through the Early Nineteenth Centuries

In 1619, the first group of Africans arrived in what was strangely called the "New World." There were seven of them, both men and women. They were part of a group of people, including White indentured servants, brought from Europe to provide cheap labor. They had been stolen from Africa, survived the Middle Passage, and brought to a place that was not even a country. For the Africans, this new world was the antithesis of their way of life, their culture, their values, and their worldview. They were stripped of their families, customs, languages, and religion but still held on to their core cultural values of kinship, community, and spirituality, and to each other.

In what is called the colonial era of U.S. history, the seventeenth and eighteenth centuries, Africans made adjustments to an increasingly restrictive, discriminatory, and ultimately horrific system of oppression based on race and

racism. Women were additionally subjected to sexism, sexual abuse, and exploitation from both White men and White women. The Black women had to
dig deep, drawing on their cultural traditions, individual strengths, value
systems, and skills to survive. They not only survived but also shaped the face
of the developing country that would become known as America, building the
nation, bearing its children, fighting its wars, and contributing to its economy.

Black Women Entrepreneurs in the Colonial Era

Black women brought their entrepreneurial skills from Africa to the new
world. Unlike most European women, African women were used to participating in the economic and political life of their nations, cities, and villages. As
queens, they often planned and managed the economy of their kingdoms;
as traders, they dominated the local economy. African women were able
to control their own money, buy and sell property, participate in political
decision-making that affected daily life, and enjoyed a financial independence
that put them on an egalitarian footing with their husbands. They

were accustomed to being resourceful, determined and somewhat
independent economically ... and ... [were] expected to participate in
[the] economic life of the community outside their home ... to own

*Oyster and Fish Women, Charles Town, South Carolina, 1870. Stereograph.
Courtesy of Robert N. Dennis Collection of Stereoscopic Views, Miriam and
Ira D. Wallach Division of Art, Prints, and Photographs, The New York
Public Library, Astor, Lenox, and Tilden Foundations.*

and control some of her own property after marriage without the permission of her husband....[1]

The women brought those skills, abilities, and most importantly, attitudes with them. Those retained Africanisms could not be and were not stripped away even as legal and societal structures increasingly restricted their rights. In fact, women of African descent had a cultural advantage that enabled them to negotiate the colonial systems and, later, chattel slavery in the South, as well as the de facto slavery in the North. To survive and feed their families, the women used those entrepreneurial abilities and attitudes to craft businesses, using creative methods to add value to ordinary goods and services to make money and profit—a definition of entrepreneurship.[2]

Present-day historians generally concur that many of the Africans brought to the new world were

> highly intelligent and talented people...[M]any were not only profi-cient in their own languages and culture but could write in Arabic and speak it fluently...and many were from the upper levels of African societies: kings (and queens) priests, chiefs, military experts, artists.[3]

Many of the entrepreneurial skills, strategies, and values used by African Americans in the colonies were in part brought from Africa and were retained and adapted in the Black community in such a way as to enable them to survive and, in some cases, prosper under oppressive conditions. Economic self-sufficiency was critical to the survival of the African community in the United States. The values and strategies of Black women were especially apparent in their day-to-day commercial activities. Their challenges were great, as their lives were markedly different from any other Americans because of gender bias as well as racial oppression.

Numerous scholars have found evidence that many of the Africans were highly intelligent people who brought with them skills they had already acquired in Africa, and who quickly began to learn new skills to manage their new roles in America. Many became multilingual, learning and retaining European languages to which they were exposed on plantations in the South and in the colonies in the North. In fact, Walker points out that "'human capital' factors were those which made Africans the most desired laborers in the plantation colonies of the Americas."[4] African women in particular retained "traits brought from Africa that ranged from resourcefulness to the ability to weave baskets using the patterns of [their] grandmother[s]."[5]

As in Africa, gender-specific apprenticeship seems to have been the primary method of training, ranging from the casual to the intentional. Women's areas of expertise paralleled their activities in their homelands. In addition to having trading, farming, and gardening skills, they had specific work areas they used to their advantage. These areas included all kinds of textile work, including spinning, weaving, sewing, and dying; health care work including nursing, midwifery, and herbal healing arts; child and elder care; candle and soap making; and basket weaving. Domestic service was the venue in which most of the enslaved house servants and free Blacks labored and included cleaning, laundering, and cooking. All those domains were later easily transferred to self-employment and small business ownership, although for the most part those activities have not usually been identified as such in history.[6]

Juliet E. K. Walker states that,

> reviewing the economic activities of African women in America from the Colonial period to the development of the new nation provides a basis on which to establish the foundation of business activities of African-American women.[7]

The very earliest Black entrepreneurs were enslaved women who used their knowledge, expertise, and talents to hire themselves out to earn money to buy their freedom. Some bondwomen were bought out of slavery by their husbands or inherited homes in which they had had worked from White women. When freed, Black women used those homes for a variety of businesses: boarding houses, inns, restaurants, laundries, and the like. Others, once free, used their profits to hire others, both enslaved and free—enabling a degree of economic control for themselves, for community-based services, including benevolent societies that provided care for the sick, poor, and indigent; schools; religious organizations and churches; and organizations that supported political and antislavery activities. The motivations for starting businesses and the use of profits from those businesses distinguish these early entrepreneurs from their contemporaries, especially White male landowners, whose primary goal in business was individual asset accumulation—a European tradition.

There are several examples of successful Black women entrepreneurs who operated businesses during the colonial and antebellum eras of American history—periods when most Africans arrived in America and when chattel slavery, an extraordinarily brutal system of oppression, existed and became entrenched in the economic, political, and social systems of the country. Whether in the slave South or racist North, women still owned, operated, and grew businesses, building on their traditions, knowledge, skills, and abilities. Some of the businesses were owned jointly with their husbands or other family members, but others were solely created, owned, and operated by women in need of financial security. The nature of the businesses in part was determined by the places in which they developed.

Hine and Thompson tell a "Tale of Three Cities" in their discussion of Black women in colonial and antebellum history, emphasizing the differences in settings that contributed to a difference in response to oppression, while celebrating the steadfastness of the values of family and community and strategies for survival across place. The three cities were Philadelphia, which was the free Black capital in the North; Charleston, South Carolina, which was predominantly Black and enslaved; and New Orleans, a city of Creoles, or mixed people, in a place that was not yet part of the United States and that was more French than "American."[8] Recognizing the "polyrhythmic realities" of the lives and experiences of Black women is essential to understanding the matrix of factors, including place and space, that shaped their unique experiences in and effect on the development of the U.S. economy.[9]

The types of businesses owned and operated by these early African Americans clustered in the service and retail sectors of the economy, much as they do today. However, some of the women owned manufacturing businesses, ran farms and plantations, and bought and sold real estate. Stories of these women and their businesses rarely make it to light in the wider U.S. history because much of the activity was undocumented, ignored, or trivialized. Even in fairly good business histories of women, such as that written by Kwolek-Folland, their accomplishments, although mentioned, are for the most part marginalized in a "by the way, some black women were also ... petty traders"[10] manner. To be fair, the author does tell some of the history of women of color, including that of individuals who are generally well-known, such as CoinCoin or Marie Therese, a former bondwoman who became the owner of a large plantation and who herself bought enslaved people; Elizabeth Keckley, a skilled seamstress who bought her own freedom, owned her own business, and became the dressmaker and confidant of Mary Todd Lincoln and the Walkers—Madame C. J. Walker, the first self-made Black woman millionaire, and Maggie Lena Walker, the first woman to open and operate a bank in the United States.[10]

Much of the information about Black business activity is based on oral history; of necessity, much was hidden from White society. However, there are several sources of information about the business activities of Black women in the colonial and antebellum eras—information later meticulously gathered by Black and White women historians—in publications of the times, including city directories, traveler's guides, and advertisements in Black-owned newspapers. In addition, because vendors were obliged to pay for city fees and licenses, the market activities of Black women were recorded. Laws proscribed or prohibited the participation of Black entrepreneurs, thus making the tracking of their businesses possible. Fortunately, an increasing number of scholars and historians, especially Black women, are making the invisible visible through their telling. Here are a few of their stories.

The Stories

There were two prominent free families in Philadelphia during and after the Revolutionary War whose women made an impact on the economic, social, and political life of the city: the Fortens and the Bustills. James Forten was born to free parents in 1776, fought in The Revolutionary War and returned to Philadelphia, later making a fortune in the sail-making business. His wife, Charlotte, and three daughters, Margareta, Harriet, and Sarah, were charter members of the first biracial antislavery group in America, the Philadelphia Female Anti-Slavery Society. Also members of that group were Grace Bustill Douglass, who owned a Quaker millinery store, and her daughter, Sarah Mapps Douglass. Sarah, who was tutored at home, became a teacher and in the 1830s opened her own high school for Black girls and taught them science, which was unheard of at that time.[11] Douglass's school was the first such establishment in the nation and was an illustration of how the provision of education was a business, begun and used for womanist purposes, that is, a concern with the survival of an entire people, over the next two centuries. The women from these free Black families and their activism are examples of women using their economic capital, knowledge, and skills to address the conditions of Black people's survival as a whole—a "womanist" following of their African traditions.

There was also a great deal of entrepreneurial activity in the New England colonies, known for its "female economies" of the eighteenth and nineteenth centuries. According to Kwolek-Folland, 10 to 25 percent of the female population in pre-industrial America was engaged in entrepreneurship, primarily in retail trade in urban areas. Kwolek-Folland also recognized that the largest portion of gross colonial production (GNP) came from plantation agriculture. Although she talked about the White women involved in retail trade in the Charleston, South Carolina, market, however, Kwolek-Folland did not acknowledge or discuss that dominance of both those produce markets and agricultural production by Black women. Although she talked about the business activity of New England women in those "female economies" that included cheese making, textile work, and shoe making, she did not mention Elleanor Eldridge, a public figure whose activities are well documented in New England history.[12]

Eldridge (1784–1845) was from Rhode Island and was an entrepreneur and amateur lawyer who started a series of businesses in her lifetime that were based on the skills she developed as an apprentice in several places where she was employed. She was born free on March 27, 1784, in Warwick, Rhode Island, to Hannah Prophet and Robin Eldridge. Robin, an African, had been captured with his entire family and brought to the colonies on a slave ship. Her mother, Hannah Prophet, was a Native American. The reason Eldridge was born free was because a bill enacted in 1784 in Rhode Island emancipated slaves gradually by freeing the offspring of enslaved people. At age fourteen years, she was a full-fledged master weaver, skilled in "double and ornamental" weaving, and made carpets, tapestries, and the like. After leaving the weaving business at age sixteen years, Eldridge worked at a dairy owned by Captain Benjamin Greene, soon becoming a cheese maker and was said to have been the best "premium quality" cheese maker in Warwick.

After the death of her father and Greene, she and her sister Lettise went into business together, weaving, making soap, and providing nursing services. With the money earned from that business, Eldridge began to buy real estate, buying a lot and building a house that she rented out for $40 a year.

On the request of another sister, Eldridge moved to Providence, Rhode Island, where she opened other businesses, including a wallpapering and painting business that were so successful she was able to expand her real estate holdings. She continued making significant profits in all her areas of endeavor and continued buying and building houses. Having accumulated $600, she bought a lot that cost $100, which she paid for "all in silver dollars."[13] She then built a house for $1700, which she lived in, adding an addition on several years later; she rented the addition out at a rate of $150 a year.[13] In 1831, while she was recovering from typhoid fever, her White male neighbor tried to swindle her out of her property. The sheriff was in collusion with him and covered up the illegal activity. However, Eldridge fought the case in the courts, only regaining her own property by being able to pay $2,700 for it—a vast sum of money in those days—a testimony of her financial success in business. A White woman friend and admirer, Frances Hipple Macdougal, who helped document Eldridge's work life, was so outraged by this injustice she wrote:

No MAN would ever have been treated so; and if a WHITE WOMAN had been the subject of such wrongs, the whole town—nay, the whole country, would have been indignant: and the actors would have been held up to the contempt they deserve![14]

We know Eldridge's story because it was documented in a legal proceeding in the Court of Common Pleas in January 1837, and a fellow citizen was moved to write about it. More significantly, we know her story because she wrote and published her own memoir, *The Memoirs of Elleanor Eldridge*, in 1838, one of the few narratives published by a free Black woman. The story is also important because it is illustrative of the multiple challenges and obstacles faced by Black women entrepreneurs in colonial times, resulting from the institutionalized racism and sexism that prevailed in that era, as well as of Black women's strategies and responses to dealing with these difficulties successfully.

Another remarkable story is that the Remond family, beginning with that of Nancy Lenox Remond, who owned a successful cake-baking business, owned an exclusive restaurant, and dominated the catering trade in Salem, Massachusetts. She was an ardent abolitionist who used her profits to further that movement. Her daughters were equally remarkable businesswomen who also were politically active. The three Remond sisters, Cecilia, Maritcha, and Caroline, owned and operated an upscale hair salon for Black women in Salem, Massachusetts. They also owned the biggest wig factory in the state and created and manufactured a popular hair-loss product, "Mrs. Putnam's Medicated Hair Tonic," which they sold retail and wholesale, locally and nationally, through a mail-order distribution system.[15] They were the forerunners of Madame C. J. Walker and others like her, who made their marks in the beauty industry.

The Remond sisters' story illuminates the effect of Black women on the beauty business and culture. Early African American women, both free and enslaved, used berries, herbs, and other natural substances to heal, soften, and color skin and hair, using ancient remedies and formulas from the healing and beauty traditions of their ancestors. In addition, many Black women were hairdressers to White as well as Black women, using those same skills to make their own pomades and potions.[16] The Remond's activities reflect the marketing, distribution, and manufacturing traditions of ancient African Market Women, as well as the connections to family and community and the use of profits as a source of financing for political activism—here aimed at eradicating slavery.

Free Black women in the North were often located in urban areas and were able to operate businesses out of their own homes and, in many cases, to dominate areas in trade: personal services and beauty care and domestic services such as cooking, catering, laundry, and cleaning. Expertise in cooking and baking led to the establishment of businesses such as restaurants, catering houses, and bakeries. For example, Charity "Duchess" Quamino had a catering business in Newport, Rhode Island, that was the most successful in town. In fact, according to Birmingham, "Free blacks virtually invented the catering business in America,"[17] and Black women led the way. In 1736, Mary Bernoon and her husband owned and operated an oyster and ale house in Providence, Rhode Island. The "seed money" to start the business was earned by Mary, selling illegal liquor.[17]

Enslaved and free women in the South had businesses that ran the gamut from brokering agricultural products to the operation and management of agricultural plantations and farms. The Market Women of Charles Town (Charleston), South Carolina, and other southern cities dominated the sale of fruits, vegetables, and produce during slavery:

> The Charles Town Market was a place of tremendous activity.... [A]t the heart of it all were the expert traders, who always got the best goods, knew how to corner the market on a highly desirable commodity, and could set the prices that the public would have to pay for virtually everything in the market. These traders were black women and they were slaves.[18]

Regardless of attempts by Whites (from creating a law in 1686 that forbid the purchase of goods from slaves to the establishment of a White-owned official marketplace in 1739) to break their hold on that sector of the economy, nothing could stop this "black market" trading, and the African American Market Women soon controlled almost all of the city's food supply.[19] The dominance of the traders and their abilities and skills in business management, pricing, brokering, and trading is eerily reminiscent of the description by Herskovits of West African market women of the fifteenth and sixteenth centuries. The route to economic success employed by the Market Women is also remarkably similar to that followed by microentrepreneurs in the retail sector today: starting out as vendors or hucksters in a market, opening a stall in the market, and once having achieved a level of profitability, renting or purchasing property for the operations of their businesses regardless of the obstacles placed in their way by the White establishment and economic community.

Madame CeCee McCarty, who lived and worked in the 1800s, was a former slave who became a prominent merchandiser, herself owning more then thirty slaves. She owned a depot in Plaquemines Parish that served as a base for warehousing and distributing her goods outside of New Orleans. After purchasing goods from importers, McCarty used her slaves as her sales force, giving them regional territories in rural parishes outside of Louisiana. In 1848, her net worth was more than $155,000.[20] The paradoxical state of affairs of ex-bondwomen owning and working other Black people was also the case with Marie Therese of Louisiana (1747–1816). Mentioned earlier, Therese was otherwise known as CoinCoin—an African name given her by her mother. A slave until age forty-six years, she used her business skills to establish a 12,000-acre cotton plantation, worked two hundred slaves, and used her profits to purchase her children and grandchildren from slavery.[21]

In the agricultural South, characterized by large plantations, several families became free and prosperous via the route of Lucy McWorter (1747–1870) and her husband, Free Frank. McWorter, an ex-slave entrepreneur who purchased her freedom with the profits of Free Frank's businesses, lived on the frontier in Kentucky and Illinois; she engaged in commercial farm activities that included the raising and sale of poultry, making processed food products such as cheese, canned fruits, and vegetables, and collecting and selling bee honey and wax. Lucy's earnings, combined with Frank's, who founded a town on the Illinois frontier, enabled them to purchase the freedom of sixteen family members.[22] This story illustrates the strength of the societal and economic forces that motivated Black women and men, both enslaved and free, to succeed in business.

Other vignettes illustrate the breadth of types of businesses owned and operated by women in seventeenth and eighteenth centuries, based for the most part on gender-based roles and activities as well as areas of expertise in traditional African enterprises and adjustments to the restrictions placed on Black women's work in the United States. An enslaved woman named Sally (1790–1849), living in Nashville, hired out her own time as a cleaning woman and earned enough money to establish her own laundry and cleaning business while manufacturing soap for sale.[23] Another bondwoman, Lucy Tucker, was sold away from her mother in Virginia and sent to live on a plantation in Alabama. A letter to her mother, probably written by an amanuensis or scribe, told of her life over the intervening decade, including her self-supporting, hiring-out activities:

> I have been very sick for the las two or three years But now am doing well. Have a good husband & give the white people 25cts. a day. I follow washing and ironing.... This is from your daughter.[24]

According to Sterling, Tucker supported herself by doing laundry and paid her White owners for the privilege.

In the field of health care, Janet Minor of Petersburg, Virginia, who was skilled in nursing, midwifery, and the pharmacopeia of folk medicine, ran a home-health-care business before she was manumitted or freed in 1825. Similar to other successful entrepreneurs of the time, Minor used her profits to free sixteen women from bondage. One of those freed, Phebe Jackson, became her apprentice, becoming a cupper and a leecher specialist who also had accounting skills and kept the books for the business.[25]

The prevailing social, political, and economic conditions in the nineteenth century provided strong motivation for Black women to choose entrepreneurship as a vehicle for freedom, economic survival, and empowerment. One such woman was Elizabeth Keckley (1818-1907), who was enslaved in Virginia. After buying her own freedom with the money she made using her expertise in dressmaking, she moved to Washington, DC, where she became dressmaker to Mary Todd Lincoln. The business was quite successful, as it catered to the needs of Washington's elite political wives; Keckley employed twenty seamstresses in the enterprise. She was one of a handful of Black women entrepreneurs who became nationally known because of her connection to Mary Todd Lincoln and was, according to Lincoln, "my best living friend."[26]

Keckley wrote her own autobiography, *Behind the Scenes: Thirty Years a Slave and 4 Years in the White House*, in 1898, in which she documented her life as a slave and her years in the White House. Mary Todd Lincoln was not pleased with the book and its revelations about Lincoln family life and from then on had nothing more to do with Keckley. Although recognized as an important resource on the Lincoln years by scholars, the book was not a commercial success because it was written by a "colored historian" who was also a woman. Keckley, as was the case for many economically and socially successful Black women of the antebellum era, contributed her earnings and her time to the abolitionist movement. Economic success to her, as to many like her, was not just for individual and family financial self-sufficiency but was a means to a larger end—the abolition of slavery and the betterment of the race.[26]

Black Women in the Old West

The presence of Black women in the Old West is virtually nonexistent in typical history textbooks, including those that document Black history, or in

Hollywood films and television because, as stated by William Katz, an historian who has filled some of that gap in his quarter of a century studies of African Americans in the West, reports that "It has been argued that since African-American women were a tiny minority within a western minority, omitting them was hardly an act of discrimination."[27] However, according to Katz, African Americans were present almost everywhere on the frontier, both before the Civil War and after, when they made an impact on their families and new communities as they fled the slave South and racist North, seeking opportunities and better lives for themselves and their families:

> One drove a stagecoach and delivered the US mail in Cascade, Montana (Stagecoach Mary Fields)....Another, in early Seattle, helped her husband run a newspaper (Susan Cayton)....In early Texas, another started an impassioned crusade to elevate women and liberate the workers of the world (Lucy Parsons)....An African-American owned huge parcels of Los Angeles real estate (Biddy Mason); one founded a black town in Oklahoma (Abigail Barnett); another ran a large carting business in Nevada (Sarah Miner).[28]

A newly discovered book, *What Mrs. Fisher Knows about Old Southern Cooking, Soups, Pickles and Sauces*, was published in 1881 in San Francisco. It is believed to be the first cookbook written by an African American woman and has been purchased by the Schlesinger Library on the History of Women, situated in the Radcliffe Institute of Advanced Study at Harvard University. A significant contribution to culinary history, this book also highlights the entrepreneurial nature of Abby Fisher's work—she was a successful businesswoman who owned and operated a factory that manufactured pickles and preserves. The influence of Black women on the cuisine and culture of the United States is clear to most food historians.

> Transfigured by the genius, indeed the very presence, of the African women cooks in the kitchen of wealthy slaveholders....[W]hile there are certainly many other influences in southern cookery, it was defined by the African Presence.[29]

One of the most fascinating figures in history is Mary Ellen "Mammy" Pleasant (1814–1904), a Black female entrepreneur and activist in San Francisco whose life spanned the late eighteenth and early nineteenth centuries. Her life history provides a window into several watershed events in U.S. history: slavery, the Civil War, John Brown's raid, Reconstruction, the gold rush, and the settlement of the West. Given that Pleasant was a free Black woman, her experiences provide a race, gender, and class lens that illuminates the historical context of American history not often known. Her life, her perspectives, and her business skills, attitudes, and behaviors challenged the prevailing and stubborn negative views of Black women, both past and present. In contrast, her connection to the Black community, her activism, and her use of profits connect her to the traditions and values of the women of the African Diaspora, although her methods were not those usually attributed to "good race women." For those reasons, her life and times are discussed in some detail below.

According to Pleasant's biographer, Lynn M. Hudson, everything about her life was contested. Called a madam, a voodoo priestess, an ex-slave, a mammy, Pleasant manipulated the press and the media so that she told her own story, rather than having her identity and personhood defined by others. Possibly born and definitely raised in New England, including on Nantucket Island in Massachusetts, Pleasant learned her business skills from being employed by Quaker women business owners on Petticoat Row, where a "semiautonomous female economy" of whaling wives dominated the local retail and craft trade. She also learned about "entrepreneurship and institution building: public spaces and institutions that black people controlled" from the Black business community in New Guinea, the Black neighborhood on Nantucket. Leaving Nantucket, she went to Boston, becoming involved in that city's "female economy," comprised mostly dressmaking and millinery business owners, further honing her skills and accumulating the capital, both financial and social, that would enable her to go west during the gold rush.[30]

Like many other Black people, Pleasant went west somewhere between 1849 and 1852. It was felt that in the West, the climate for business and living was more hospitable for Black people than any other area in the country. Using her domestic skills and taking advantage of the prevailing stereotypes about Black women and mammies, Pleasant worked as a cook, picking up investment tips from her wealthy clients, buying laundries, purchasing real estate, and trading commodities and stocks. She chose her businesses well, watching and analyzing the needs of the mostly male population in gold rush California; for example, purchasing and running an exclusive brothel, in which she picked up even more investment tips.

> Pleasant's business activities in San Francisco ran the gamut from operating boardinghouses, traditionally women's work, to investing mines and real estate, considered men's work. She financed enterprises that shaped the Western economy in the second half of the nineteenth century. And she practiced the financial strategies of robber barons common to this era: stock speculation, insider trading, and monopoly. Pleasant also used tactics that fell outside of the realm of traditional business—those most often practiced by entrepreneurs on the margins of the economy. The secrets she knew—about real estate, stocks, miscegenation, and adultery—translated into social as well as economic power.[31]

As Pleasant's wealth grew, so did her activism; she was highly visible in the abolitionist movement as a speaker at political events and a participant in the abolitionist and later civil rights movements of the time. She used her considerable wealth to support John Brown's unsuccessful raid in Harper's Ferry in 1859, which is said to be the event that triggered the Civil War.

Given the tenor of the times, the rampant discrimination that mitigated Black people's business activities, the control of every aspect of enslaved people's lives, and for women, the loss of control of reproductive rights, their sexual exploitation, and the commodification of their bodies, it is not surprising that a few women turned to illegal activities to become economically "free" and gain some modicum of control over their lives. Some of those activities included the operation of grog shops or taverns and acting as madams of houses of prostitution or luxury boarding houses. Kwolek-Folland wrote that many women in the early days of American history—White, Asian, and Black—turned to prostitution and other sex industries including pornography as a defense of themselves and a way to control their economic and, thus, daily lives. For example, Kwolek-Folland says prostitution and laundering were the most profitable businesses in the Old West during the gold rush era. By taking control of their bodies and the use of them, women transformed themselves from victims to survivors.[32] Although not pretty, and while contributing to an entrenched stereotype of Black women, sex workers in the past and in the present continue to have a place on the economic landscape. Viewed differently, their behavior can be seen as a survival strategy for when all else has been taken from them by the prevailing social, sexual, and economic systems of their time.

The Later Years: The Late Nineteenth and Twentieth Centuries: The Civil War, Reconstruction, Jim Crow, The "Movement," and Integration

The late nineteenth and early twentieth centuries in the United States was a time of war fostered by economic changes including rapid expansion, life-changing inventions, and a market economy that changed the nature of the country and, in doing so, changed the conditions of people of African descent in all parts of the country—and not for the better. Across the spectrum of American history, Black women continued to dominate certain sectors of the economy, engaging in entrepreneurial activities and training within settings that, at times, were informal and often clandestine, as well as within formal settings. Survival and success were strategies of resistance. Those "habits of survival" were retained informally, as "people teach these habits to each other, often by example."[33] As pointed out by Hine and Thompson, of necessity, little of the learning during slavery days involved "textbooks or slates" because it was dangerous and often fatal for slaves to learn to read or write. In a like manner, visible success in business, especially for women—enslaved or free, North or South—resulted in increasingly restrictive laws meant to control Black people on every level in order to maintain the economic dominance of Whites, as was done in Charles Town. Violence was also one of the main responses to the success of Black people or any people of color. Some of the worst riots on American soil were perpetuated by Whites who were jealous of the economic achievements of people of color. In the 1830s, Whites burned, vandalized, and destroyed Black businesses, neighborhoods, and homes in the South; those riots were followed by the artisan's riots of the post–Civil War era, the burning of Black Wall Street in the early part of the twentieth century, and the forcible removable of Cherokee from their homes, land, and businesses in the Carolinas and onto the Trail of Tears. The tradition of violent reactions by jealous Whites against successful businesspeople of color contributed to a reactionary tradition of informal or hidden economic activity in the Black community. Methods of surviving and resisting of necessity had to include a kind of invisibility. This need to be invisible contributed to the resulting beliefs about the lack of business tradition, experience, and skills by people of color—and especially Black women.

Institutionalized chattel slavery, created and maintained by Southern plantation owners, was a unique system of servitude unprecedented in the world because of its cruelty, dehumanization, and unending nature. Its presence and its destruction was a critical and crucial battle that drove the social, political, and economic lives of the entire country. By following the money, one can achieve a clearer understanding of the Civil War, which was not about slavery but was about the effect of this practice on the South's economy and the competing economic interests of the North. Enslaved people and abolitionists, for differing reasons, committed their lives to its demise. Enslaved women and free women played a central role in this war, as entrepreneurs who freed themselves and others through the use of their profits, as clubwomen who boycotted slave-produced goods, as soldiers and warriors in battle, and as guides, camp cooks, and nurses. Most of the women's activities and contributions remain unidentified, however, and are thus unappreciated.

The story of a few good women entrepreneurs will illustrate their value in the development and preservation of the Black community as well as their contributions to the larger society as it changed from a slave-based agricultural economic system to one in which industrialization, the rise of the market economy, and the prevalence of wage work prevailed. Equally as important were the collective efforts of Black women, both enslaved and free, as they sought to provide economic support, education, and social services to people in need. A few of those stories follow.

The Stories

Maggie Lena Walker (1867–1934) was a Black woman who established the first bank in America owned by a woman, the St. Luke's Penny

Savings Bank. Born free to free parents in Richmond, Virginia, Walker lived as comfortable a life as possible for a Black woman in the post–Civil War South. As the daughter of a widow who became a laundress after her husband was murdered—probably lynched—Walker grew up helping her mother in the laundry business, delivering and picking up clothes, and learning the business and the value of hard work along the way. After graduating from the newly established public school system, Walker became a teacher until she married and withdrew from the workforce, as was expected of middle-class Black women of the era.

Following the same expectations, she became active in a service organization, the Independent Order of St. Luke's Order—a mutual benefit society that sprang up, as did many others, after the Civil War. Its mission, to provide financial benefits to its members in times of illness and death, was both practical and spiritual, again in keeping with the tradition of such organizations in the Black community.[34]

Walker started as a volunteer and quickly moved up the ranks, becoming its Grand Madame Secretary in 1899. In her twenty-five years of leadership, she left a lasting legacy that prevails to this day: "She "collected more than $3.4 million dollars, expanded the membership to more than one hundred thousand members in twenty-four states and built up a $70,000 cash reserve."[35] More than just using her management skills, however, Walker understood the importance of economic self-sufficiency for the community of Black people and had a vision for how that could be achieved, especially for Black women. Soon after assuming her leadership in St. Luke's she established a newspaper, the *St. Luke Herald*, which had multiple purposes: to serve as a vehicle to promote the organization and build its printing business, and to provide a forum for people to speak out against continued injustices such as lynching and to document the status of Black women and the issues of the day. Next, Walker saw the need for a bank to meet the commercial needs of a growing Black working class in Richmond, and she established it as a part of the Order of St. Luke's.

Intuitively understanding the principles of cooperative economics, community economic development, and the need to keep money made in a community circulating in that community as long as possible, she established the St. Luke's Penny Savings Bank in 1903, becoming the first woman bank president, Black or White, in the United States. Calling on Black people to patronize the bank, she said to them, "Let us put our money out as usury among ourselves, and realize the benefit ourselves. Let us have a bank that will take the nickels and turn them into dollars."[36] The St. Luke's Penny Savings Bank was a forerunner of the community and Black-owned banks that have long served the Black community. The Bank is still in existence after several mergers and is called the Consolidated Bank and Trust Company of Richmond.

Once the bank was established, Maggie turned to another project intended to empower more Black women by providing employment as well as and goods: the Luke's Emporium, a department store located on Broad

Street (the main commercial thoroughfare in Richmond). The Emporium
lasted for only a few years, from 1905 to 1911, before being forced to close
because of the pressures of White merchants on Broad Street and of Black
customers who preferred to "shop the labels" in White-owned stores.[37]
These factors are similar to those reported by Butler in his discussion of
Black business and self-sufficiency and their difficulties over time, most of
which are still operating today.[38]

Maggie Lena Walker is not only notable in business history for her position as the first woman bank president but, more important, for her vision of
true community economic development and the recognition of Black women
as economically empowered individuals and contributors. The washerwom-
en and domestics of Richmond heeded her call both by depositing their pen-
nies and nickels in the bank and by remaining connected to and involved in
the community and activist issues, in part made possible by their improved
financial stability and her own modeling of activism and commitment.

Perhaps the best known and possibly the only Black woman entrepreneur
known in mainstream America is another Walker (not related). Madame C. J.
(Sarah Breedlove) Walker (1867–1919) was a contemporary of Maggie Lena
Walker. Madame Walker is recognized as the first self-made Black woman
millionaire in the United States. Her hair care empire consisted of products and
services and education and distribution systems that were reminiscent of the
African ancestors' ancient trade enterprises. Similar to her closer predecessor
mentioned above—Madame CeCee McCarty—Madame Walker's use of a
traveling sales force of Black women trained in the "Walker method" and her
use of vertical manufacturing systems, advertising campaigns, and intimate
connection to Black communities, especially Black women, contributed to her
enormous success. She was a millionaire when the majority of Black women
were engaged in low-end agricultural or domestic service jobs.

Like Maggie Lena Walker, Madame Walker provided salaries for
thousands of Black women that paid far more than the barely livable wages
of domestics and laundry workers in the North and the South. Madame
Walker also provided a sisterhood, a network of support, and a venue for
Black women to interact, instruct, and empower each other. Madame
Walker used her fortune to join the fight for social justice and equality of
Black people, joining and helping to run the fledgling National Association
for the Advancement of Colored People. The movement, dominated by men
yet run by women, had to listen to Madame C. J. Walker.[39]

She was a voice for Black women not only in the economic arena but
also in the political and social systems of the day. Cognizant of the gender
politics of the times that affected the visibility of Black women, Madame
Walker used her wealth, her influence, and herself as a role model for others
to follow. Her great great-granddaughter, A'Lelia Bundles, has written
Madame Walker's definitive biography. It is scholarly and rich in detail,
primary source material, and photographs. Yet, in a continuing backlash of
racism and sexism, Bundles's meticulously researched and well-written

book has received less attention, less marketing, and fewer awards than have more recent works by White authors with less credibility and scholarship than Bundles has exhibited. The battle continues.

Cooperative Economics

As stated previously, one of the most interesting occurrences in response to slavery and the entrenched racism, sexism, and discrimination against Black women, especially in the economic sphere, was their cooperative economic strategies, based on ancient traditions, that fulfilled several functions: enabling a collectivism that supported the community by providing goods and employment, providing an outlet for products, and offering quality goods in the community at fair prices. There are three outstanding examples of that collectivism: The Colored Females Free Produce Society of Philadelphia, the Female Trading Association of New York City, and the Detroit Housewives Union. The Colored Females Free Produce Society, which functioned separately from White groups because integration was either dangerous or denied, had as its purpose the provision of goods, flour, sugar, rice, and the like that had not been produced by slave labor. In addition, the societies promoted boycotting of slave-produced good from southern plantations. The result was the purchase of more goods from free agricultural laborers and traders, many of whom were Black women. These actions, although not entrepreneurship activities in the purest sense, had an economic impact on lives in the Black community and acted as testimony to the growing economic power of Black women both as producers and consumers.

The Female Trading Association was a cooperative grocery store with one hundred members. An editor of a local Black-owned newspaper at the time called attention to the Association's ad, because of his admiration (writing):

THE FEMALE TRADING ASSOCIATION

Continue their establishment, consisting of *Dry Groceries* of every description, at 157 Orchard st (near Grand st) where they dispose of articles, cheap for cash. They solicit the patronage of their friends and the public. No pains will be spared to accommodate the public. Families will do well to call and examine for themselves.

Flour, Indian meal, grits, hominy, rice, beans, peas, coffee, cocoa, Teas, chocolate, hams, pork, beef, fish, shoulders, butter, lard, soap, starch, candles, cheese, oil, raisins, citron, spices of all descriptions, sugars, white and brown, brooms and brushes.[40]

Similar to the Emporium of Richmond, though, this store did not last long, and probably for the same reasons. However, other advertisements in local Black-owned newspapers promoted the businesses of Black women during the nineteenth century. Although the papers, used primarily to inform the Black community of the events and issues of the day in the Pre–Civil War, Civil War, and Reconstruction times, had more male than female advertisers, the existence of the latter inform us of their presence and business activities and their competition and provide a window into to the social roles and activities of women:

MISS VIRGINIA WILLIAMS
FASHIONABLE DRESSMAKER
1 King Street, New York

MISS A.E. FREEMAN
TEACHER OF VOCAL AND
INSTRUMENTAL MUSIC
148 JAY STREET,
Brooklyn
Terms reasonable 13-tf

EMBROIDERY AND BRAIDING
Done to order, by Miss Addie M. Hamiltion,
No. 22 Tallman st., Brooklyn 15-tf

FAMILY BOARDING HOUSE
MRS. S. BABCOCK
541 Broome street, near Sullivan,
New York 10-tf

THE PROVINCIAL FREEMAN
And
SEMI-MONTLY ADVERTISER
is published by A.D. Shadd & CO.,
CHATAM ,C.W.
Terms — One Dollar per year, invariably in advance[41]

LEGHORN BONNETS
MRS. SARAH JOHNSON
No 551 PEARL-STREET, respectfully informes her Friends and the Public, that she has commenced Bleaching, Pressing, and refitting Leghorn and Straw hats, in the best manner. Ladies dresses made, and Plain Sewing done on most reasonable terms.
Mrs. J. begs to leave assure her friends and the public, that those who patronize her may depend upon having their Work done faithful
Ly and with punctuality and dispatch
New York May 29, 1829.[42]

BOARDING HOUSE
TH takes great pleasure in announcing to the traveling public that she
has a meticulous Boarding House at No. ..Providence, RI. This
pleasant, healthy and recreative city. No pains will be spared to all
who may favor her with their business
1855[43]

The classified sections in the Black papers provide us with a glimpse into the
world of Black women entrepreneurs of the time and of the prevailing social
mores that shaped their activities and businesses. Ads for businesses run by
men and women were placed side-by-side with funeral announcements,
notices of social events, establishment of new schools, and meeting announcements. The *Anglo-American* of New York ran ads for the *Provincial
Freeman*, a paper we will learn more about in the next chapter, as it was
cofounded and edited by a Black woman, Mary Shadd Cary. In the *Douglass Papers*, excerpts of Frederick Douglass's speeches and those of others
were placed in the paper, usually on the front page, as well. "Acceptable"
social behavior was indicated by the ads as well. For example, although all
the women operated "women's businesses," single women did not run
boarding houses, while married women or widows—indicted by the title
"Mrs."—did.

Another fascinating episode in Black women's economic history that
illustrates those values and strategies that are foundational to their lives is
the Detroit Housewives League actions. On June 30, 1930, during the
height of the Depression that of course impacted Black people and Black
women the most, a group of fifty women gathered together at the request of
Fannie B. Peck, the wife of William Peck, pastor of the two thousand–
member Bethel African Episcopal Methodist Church and president of the
Booker T. Washington Trade Association. Modeled on the success of
housewives in Harlem, New York, Peck sought to consolidate the spending
power of women in Detroit for the economic well-being of the community.
Heeding the call and following the examples of Maggie Lena Walker,
Madame C. J. Walker, Maria Stewart, and Mary Shadd Cary, Peck sought
to "focus the attention of women on the most essential, yet most familiar
factor in the building of homes, the communities, and nations—the
Spending Power of Women."[44]

The league grew from the founding fifty members in 1930 to over ten
thousand in 1934. It had as its mission the economic survival of Black
people, families, and businesses during the Depression. The only require-
ments for membership were a commitment to support Black businesses, buy
Black products, and patronize Black professionals, keeping money earned
in the community circulating in the community. That commitment went
beyond purchasing patterns. Members visited local merchants, urging them
to stock Black products; if they refused, the establishments were boycotted.

The members also visited neighborhoods, urging the housewives to buy in those stores owned and operated by Black merchants or by those White ones employing Black people. Their officers traveled around the country telling their story and presenting data from their research arm that told of their outcomes and needs assessments of communities, pointing to the types of businesses that needed to be created in communities. In short, the Detroit League had a wide-ranging effect reaching well beyond its locality. The women's work resulted in the creation of over seventy-five thousand jobs for Black people—second only to government jobs as a source of new employment.[45]

The league was a source of community pride and vitalization for men, women, and children, and it serves as a model of economic growth, directed "spending tactics," and the establishment of individual and neighborhood self-sufficiency. A model of Black economic nationalism and community economic development at its best, the league used strategies that were attempted in the 1970s and beyond but which dissipated as integration took hold. It is the precursor of more recent Black women's business organizations such as the Coalition of 100 Black Women, the Council of Negro Business and Professional Women, and the organizations of Black Women Entrepreneurs. However, those organizations would do well to look back and learn lessons from the Harlem and Detroit Housewives, who have much to teach about economics as well as the unique culture of the Black community in America.

A Bridge to the Twentieth and Twenty-First Centuries

As the nineteenth century was coming to a close and the twentieth century was unfolding, Black women's activities changed, as did the nation's. In the twentieth century, the challenges for Black women in all areas of the country increased; emancipation did not really occur with Lincoln's proclamation. The Jim Crow laws, a legacy of the Black Codes of the slave-owning South, were intended to return Black people to as close a state of reenslavement as possible. Nowhere was this intention more visible than in the economic sphere. Newly freed and free Black men were prevented from practicing their skilled trades and professions; the majority of Black women—those who were newly free—were prevented from obtaining employment that paid more than subsistence wages. Black lands were stolen as the people who in fact did obtain "forty acres and a mule," as promised under Reconstruction, witnessed their holdings being taken back by force, guile, and law when they became financially successful, continuing the tradition of exploitative economic relations between Whites and people of color.

The documentary *Reconstruction: The Second Civil War*, a public television production, vividly and graphically presents the torments and

cruelty visited on the freed men and women as well as the resiliency and
determination of a newly freed nation of people who were not going back
to slavery. Black women were at the forefront of that battle.[46] Hine and
Thompson identified three ongoing enemies of Black people—law, custom,
and violence—that continued to operate with a vengeance, particularly as
Southern Whites tried to regain their way of life, which had been built on
the backs of Black people.[47] The creation of the Ku Klux Klan as an in-
timidating force and the use of rape, lynching, burning, and the establishment of Jim Crow laws were all in play during the late-nineteenth-century
time frame.

Yet, like the Market Women of Charleston, Black people, and Black
women in particular, withstood the force because there was a great
difference—they were free and they could walk away! There have always
been instances of revolt and resistance in the history of Black people in the
United States, and many of these instances have been initiated by women.
For example, in the 1830s, enslaved women in the South refused to go to
the fields on several occasions. In the latter part of the nineteenth century,
Black freedwomen continued their domestic work in White households
and farms, but with a difference: They now negotiated their pay as self-
employed individuals—and often won increased wages. Although they
needed the little money they could make, a new resistance strategy
emerged—quitting. According to Hunter, in her seminal work on the Black
washerwomen of Atlanta, they could and did quit their jobs in protest.
Because elite White women, especially in the South, rarely did any kind of
domestic labor, they were at a loss as to how to care for their families'
domestic needs such as cooking, cleaning, and laundry. For the first time for
many Black women, they had some semblance of power and control over
their own lives, and they used it. They did not sleep in if possible, spending
their time with their own families and in their own communities rather than
being at the beck and call of Whites—especially women. They came and
went as they pleased if they had other pressing family or community events,
and they refused to work when Whites tried to pay in leftover food, hand-
me-down clothes, or not at all. A standout event occurred in Atlanta when
the washerwomen staged a strike, shutting down the city as other service
workers joined them.[48] This activist event will be discussed in more detail
in the next chapter.

Black women's growing economic power, although woefully less than
that of White women and Black men, resulted in a renegotiation of the
ways in which they worked. These unnamed entrepreneurs, considered
"wage workers" by many historians, were engaged in entrepreneurial activities. The nature of these activities and its grounding in African economic
traditions has been overlooked and has contributed to a misunderstanding
and the continuing dismissal of Black women as entrepreneurs. In modern-
day terms, the women who continued the hiring-out process but kept all
the earnings for themselves were creatively self-employed independent

contractors and owners of home-based businesses—thus, entrepreneurs. The next chapter will highlight these "unexpected entrepreneurs," presenting those activities through a new angle of vision, providing a different view of the nature of their work and of their formidable accomplishments in the economic sphere.

> *The strengths and skills that black women were forced to develop had been transmitted to their descendants...thrown on their own resources....[T]hey learned the art of survival, of acquiring a vitality that made them unique. They were full of sturdiness and singing.*[49]

—Dorothy Sterling, *We Are Your Sisters*, p. xv

CHAPTER 4

Unexpected Entrepreneurs: A Different View of Business

Mary Edmonia "Wildfire" Lewis (born ca. 1843) was a sculptor who lived and worked in the mid-nineteenth century. Of African American and Chippewa heritage, Lewis's marble sculptures made her the first female sculptress of color. She lived most of her adult life in Rome, as did many African American and female artists of her time, because of its welcoming atmosphere. Lewis made her living selling her pieces, both by commission and retail sales. She was an artist/entrepreneur and an example of the commercial ethos and economic rationality practiced by Black women.[1]

Black women have always been actors on the economic stage of their countries and communities, but they have not always been seen as such because of racism, sexism, classism, and ignorance. The invisibility of Black women as human beings, their silences—either because of choice or by force, and the systematic dehumanization of their very being created obstacles to their survival, but it did not break them. Their full lives as complex, thinking and feeling human beings were ignored, as were the strengths, attitudes, and strategies they used to preserve and protect an entire population. Their hopes and dreams for themselves, their families, and their people have not often come to light.

It has been heartening to see a growing body of literature and history by, for, and about Black women, but equally disheartening to note that their accomplishments and excellence in the sphere of economics have not been fully recognized, even by noted Black women scholars and historians. The best definitions of entrepreneurship and its activity come from women: Juliet Walker defines an entrepreneur as "an individual with the ability to make unusual amounts of money using commonly available resources."[2]

Suzanne Lesbock, in her study of free Black women of Petersburg, Virginia, from 1784 to 1860 described Black women's entrepreneurial and survival abilities as follows: "[They] assumed enormous burdens with pitifully slim resources...and developed a routine of female responsibility different from that prevailing among whites."[3] Because entrepreneurship is the creative management of available resources and the sale of goods and services for profit, Black women are especially good at it because:

> We are the folk who took rotten peaches and made cobbler; we took leftover pieces of cloths and made quilts; we took the entrails of pigs and cleaned them and rinsed them in cold water until the water ran

Edmonia Lewis, Sculptor. Courtesy of Photographs and Prints Division, Schomburg Center for Research in Black Culture, The New York Public Library, Astor, Lenox, and Tilden Foundations.

clear then chopped up onions, shredded some red peppers, dropped a few fresh bay leafs and one large peeled potato in to pot to let it simmer over the open fire until we returned from the fields so that our families could have a hot meal at the end of the day. Every time something was taken away we took something else and made it work.[4]

Black women as social and political activists, educators, lawyers, artists and performers, writers and journalists, domestic workers, and "wage workers" are well documented by Black women historians and scholars, who place them at the center of their research. However, given that their work has multiple purposes and effects, the entrepreneurial nature of their work is not seen for what is truly is in my view: an outcome and continuation of the legacy of entrepreneurship and community economic development formed by our African traditions and shaped in a new cultural reality in the diasporic tradition of Black women. I believe this thread is woven through all our activities, and a different presentation of our accomplishments in those areas will provide patches to be woven into our economic story quilt.

This chapter will make a case for unexpected entrepreneurship in many areas of endeavor by Black women. The women were entrepreneurs in that they sold their products, their work, and their services for profit and for the betterment of the lives of Black women and Black people in general.

Literature as Business

The thoughts and feelings of these women, including those about their economic activities, are often best captured in literature or fiction, so we will start with Black women as writers whose work was created for both economic and literary reasons and that reflects economic activities and intentions. One of the earliest works of fiction written and published by a Black woman in the United States was *Our Nig; or Sketches from the Life of a Free Black, in a Two-story White House, North SHOWING THAT SLAVERY'S SHADOWS FALL EVEN THERE*, by "Our Nig" Harriet Wilson. Wilson's novel received a copyright on August 8, 1859, and first appeared on September 5, 1859. Her preface lays out the purpose of the book:

> In offering to the public the following pages, the writer confesses her inability to minister to the refined and cultivated, the pleasure supplied by abler pens. It is not for such these crude narrations appear. Deserted by kindred, disabled by failing health, I am forced to some experiment which shall aid me in maintaining myself and child without extinguishing this feeble life.[5]

The main reason Wilson wrote the book was to try and earn enough money to save her sick child; she did not, and the child died. The second reason was to indict White racism, wherever it was found. According to Henry Louis Gates, who found and republished Wilson's book, this early novel was a third-person autobiographical work that blended the slave narrative and the sentimental novel of the era. The book was ignored for over one hundred years or more because, according to Gates's speculation, it was not used as a forum for antislavery activity, presented a happy interracial marriage between a White woman and Black man, and most important, identified the prime oppressors of indentured Black women in the North as being White women.[6]

Wilson's main character Frado, a thinly disguised version of herself, suffers under the yoke of her tormentor, Mrs. Bellmont: "Mrs. Bellmont felt that [Frado's] name and person belonged solely to her...she was under her in every sense of the word." Wilson's novel was probably also unread because it highlights the paradoxical and troubled relationships that characterize the interactions between Black and White women—then as now. Just as she tried to make a living for herself to supplement the income of her husband and save her child, her main character, Frado, a mulatto, tries to survive economically by practicing the same needle trades as White women of the day "girls make straw bonnets, easy and profitable. But how could she, black, feeble and poor, find anyone to teach her."[7] The economic opportunities and outcomes were not the same for poor Black women as for poor Whites.

Another Harriet, Harriet Jacobs, also wrote an autobiography in the mid-1800s to make money to buy her own freedom and that of her children. Her work, *Incidents in the Life of a Slave Girl Written by Herself*, was published in 1861. Presented initially as a work by a White author, the book, later revealed as a slave narrative written by a former enslaved Black woman but published by Whites, was more well-known and better received and thus was more financially successful.[8] Slave narratives, including that written by Elizabeth Keckley, not only provided sources of income for the authors but also presented the daily lives of enslaved women and, in some instances, their interior lives, including their thoughts and feelings, hopes and dreams. Other early authors included Frances E. W. Harper, abolitionist and worker in the Underground Railroad, who published the first short story written by a Black woman, "Two Offers." Probably the best known early writer is Phillis Wheatley, recognized as the first Black woman poet and the second woman to publish a book (in 1773) in the United States. Her first poem was published when she was fourteen years old, in 1767. Her work, published while she was still enslaved, provides a window into the interior and exterior worlds of bondwomen in the early days of the country, including her political views.[9]

These women were the predecessors of the novelists, playwrights, poets, and essayists who followed in their footsteps, making a living from the work while telling the stories of Black women in all the aspects of their lives, including economic. Many of these writers used their writing to supplement their incomes or used their incomes from employment to support their writing. Others have made a comfortable living from their written words. Recognizable twentieth-century names include Nora Zeale Hurston, Dorothy West, Nikki Giovanni, Gwendolyn Brooks, Tina McElroy Ansa, J. California Cooper, and Alice Walker; there are many more too numerous to mention here.

Two novels that provide excellent examples of works written primarily to tell the stories of Black women but that have significant entrepreneurial events in the protagonists' lives that mirror the tenor of their times are *Family* by J. California Cooper and *The Color Purple* by Alice Walker. *Family* is a lyrical, mystical novel by a successful and prolific Black woman author. This novel brings us into world of an enslaved woman in the plantation South throught the thoughts of. the main character. Always was a woman who decided the best way to freedom and economic self-sufficiency was through the use of her own skills for her own benefit and that of her family. The story is told from the perspective of the spirit of her mother, who killed herself and tried to kill her children to release them from the unbearable cruelty of chattel slavery. After her death, the mother, who was in despair because she did not free her children, who were then left motherless by her own death, watches over those who survived for generations and recounts the stories of their lives.

The oldest daughter was named Always by her mother so that she would know that her mother would always be with her, no matter what happened, as her mother was aware of the fragile home and family lives of enslaved people. When Always wanted to learn how to become a midwife and a gardener to make enough to buy herself out of slavery, she used various learning strategies to do so:

> She had walked to the closest farms, asking questions about babies...bout things growing and plantin...bout seeds and catalogues...she tried to learn about everything. She was equally clear about her motives "I want silver money to come out my garden. I wants silver and gold from what I grow."[10]

Always and her family, as recounted in the novel, prospered and survived slavery and Reconstruction because of her financial expertise.

Another more widely known and more financially successful author is Alice Walker, whose breakthrough cross-over novel, *The Color Purple*, was made into a feature film. Although the book has been discussed and analyzed from the perspectives of women's relationships, sexual politics and orientation, spousal abuse and incest, family, and connections to Africa, very little has been said about the entrepreneurial success of Celie, the main character. As she struggled to survive, Celie conducted business in farming, real estate, and the retail trade. When she moved from her abusive husband's farm to Memphis, Tennessee, with her lover, Shug Avery, Celie unexpectedly created a very successful business making loose, unisex pants; the business was even given a name in the novel, Folkspants Unlimited. Her business development process is as classic as her ability to manage and grow it. In Celie's own words, her survival as a poor Black woman in the South was a success measured and enhanced by her will and perseverance, characteristics of successful entrepreneurs: "I'm pore, I'm black, I may be ugly and can't cook, a voice say to everything listening. But I'm here."[11] We see from these examples that writing fiction was a way to make money as well as a way to describe the activities of women that made money. Journalism, a different form of writing, also had multiple purposes including making money.

Journalism as Business

Journalism is a writing genre that has been a part of Black women's activities from the early nineteenth century. Newspapers and magazines were used as mirrors of the issues that faced Black people, vehicles for activism, and business ventures. Black women always were visible in the world of the Black press. Some of the best-known Black-owned and Black-operated newspapers of the early nineteenth century across the country and in the territories were *The Freeman's Journal* (1827–1829) and *The Colored American*, first known as the *Anglo-African* (1837–1841), published in New York City; *The National Reformer* (1838–1839), Philadelphia; the *Mirror of the Times* and the *Elevator* (1855) of San Francisco; and those published by Frederick Douglass in Rochester—the *North Star*, the *Douglass Monthly*, and the *Frederick Douglass Papers* (1847–1860).[12] The relationship between Black women and the editors was often strained and at times antithetical, as the male journalists were middle- and upper-class Blacks whose values unfortunately reflected those of White patriarchal society. They needed to keep women in their place—in the home and out of the workplace: "Middle class black males who edited and published newspapers 'preached the gospel of gender oppression even as they lobbied for social freedom for the race.'"[13] Yet, a mutually beneficial compromise was reached as the press presented the truth about Black women, mitigating the negative stereotypes perpetuated in the White press and providing a forum for the publication of their own work, as the women "were not stymied by black editors but were impatient and outspoken about the progress of their people" in a true womanist tradition.[13] The women's financial acumen and management skills were reflected in their ability to raise funds that provided much needed support necessary to run the papers.

The papers also provided a place in which Black women entrepreneurs could place their ads for their "creative self-employment" activities (i.e., their small businesses as "dressmakers, music and voice teachers and [owners] of boarding establishments."[14]). Black women also used the papers to make announcements about their social and political meetings and events. In turn, these hardworking, responsible, and efficient women assisted with the day-to-day operation of the papers as editors, writers, and columnists, especially of women's pages.[15]

Black women were also founders and editors of periodicals and newspapers across the country, and as such were businesswomen. Two periodicals were founded by Black women in the early twentieth century, *Women's World* in Fort Worth and *Colored Women's Magazine* in Topeka, Kansas, in 1907. The latter was edited by two women, C. M. Hughes and Minnie Thomas; women maintained editorial control until 1920, while the magazine lasted.[16] Earlier, Mary Shadd Cary, one of the first Black female lawyers in America, also cofounded and edited the *Provincial Freeman* in Canada as a vehicle for abolitionist work, promoting emigration to Canada for free Blacks and social justice and equality for freed Blacks. Cary established the first integrated school in Canada. The newspaper placed ads in other prominent U.S. papers such as the *Anglo-African Weekly* with wider circulations. One of the ads seen was placed in the *Weekly*. The ad reads: "The Provincial Freeman will be devoted to Anti-slavery, Emigration, Temperance and General Literature."[17] Another reads:

THE PROVINCIAL FREEMAN
And
MONTLY ADVERTISER
is published by A.D. Shadd & CO.,
"CHATAM, C.W."
Terms — One Dollar per year, invariably in advance[18]

Cary was known for her aggressive and feisty manner, felt to be "unseemly" in a woman. As is the case today, these characteristics are applauded in "successful" businessmen but disparaged in women. She traveled extensively to raise money for her school and newspaper and in doing so became a "businesswoman whose lifestyle was not typical of an antebellum woman." Staying true to her view of self-sufficiency as the best route to emancipation and equality, Cary used the newspaper to take to task the people who "begged" for money to help runaway slaves. Her paper's motto was "Self-reliance is the Fine Road to Independence" This stance and manner did not sit well with the ministers and organizers of such drives, yet she was described as a "superior woman" in the February 1, 1856, issue of the *Douglass Papers*.[19]

Charlotte Spears Bass was also a leading Black woman journalist in the early part of the century in California, taking over and running the *California Eagle* and marrying its new editor, Joseph Bass. Like other members of the Black press, the Bass's used their paper to promote social and political activism. As a business woman who understood the importance of money, Charlotte also founded the Industrial Business Council, which promoted entrepreneurship among Black people and fought discrimination in employment and hiring practices.[20]

Journalism was a means of making money and of using those profits to fund their social activism for many women. We have seen how Maggie Lena Walker established her own paper, the *St. Luke's Herald*, which provided employment for local community people, especially women, and made profits from its ancillary printing business. The paper also provided information on events that affected Black people, fostered economic co-operation, and provided a forum for social justice work. Ida Wells-Barnett is most well known for her editorship of two Memphis, Tennessee, newspapers, *The Evening Star* and the *Living Way*. She was also an entrepreneur, a co-owner of another weekly newspaper, *The Memphis Free Speech and Headlight*, which became a forum for her antilynching campaign, shedding an unwavering light on the incidence and pervasiveness of lynching that was commonplace in the early days of the twentieth century. Wells-Barnett was also active in the "Movement," cooperating with Mary Church Terrell to found the first truly national Black women's organization, the National Association of Colored Women, becoming founding members of the National Association for the Advancement of Colored People in 1909.[21] Activism as business was part of the fabric of African American women's lives, both personally and professionally.

Activism as Business and Business as Activism

Black women have been in the forefront of the call for economic independence, self-reliance, and economic self-determinism as a route to full equality. They understand that political activism and social progress could not take place unless there was simultaneous economic advancement and achievement. Activism was used to make money, and money was made to support activism and social service and advance the cause of full citizenship for all Black people. For example, both Walkers mentioned previously used the profits from their business enterprises to finance their activist activities, starting from different points. Madame C. J. Walker began as an entrepreneur and used the profits for the business in the cause of racial and gender equality for Black people. Maggie Lena Walker used her benevolent society's organization as a base for entrepreneurship that led to economic development and self-sufficiency in her community.

Maria Stewart, an orator and essayist from Boston, was the first Black woman to give a speech to both Black and White women and men. Her first speech in Boston in 1832 called for Black people in general and Black women in particular to arise and unite and become economically independent and self-reliant and to become active in business, politics, and education.

O, ye daughters of Africa, Awake!!...What have ye done to immortalize your names beyond the grave? What examples have ye set for the rising generation? What foundations have ye set for the generations unborn?[22]

Mary Shadd Cary, whom was previously discussed, was also an essayist and political activist whose platform of black self-determination was considered to be a forerunner of the Black Nationalist movement. Her first published work as was the political pamphlet *Hints to Colored People of North America*, which called for economic self-reliance. It was published in 1849, when Cary was just twenty-six years old. Three years later, she published *Notes on Canada West*, in which she exhorted Black people to move to Canada, as she herself did following the passage of the Fugitive Act, stating that Canada was a more civilized and hospitable place for African Americans.[23] As we have seen, Cary put her ideas into action by becoming a lawyer, founding a school, and establishing a newspaper, all of which enabled her to use the profits for the advancement of her ideals. She put into practice what she preached.

Economic activism was critical to the well-being of newly freed bondwomen in the South after the Civil War. The work that had been done for no pay under slavery was now paid work, and the terms were negotiable in a way they had not been before. Political activism, trade unionism, and economic justice were intricately entwined in the days immediately after the war and during Reconstruction. Women who had washed the clothes, cooked and served the food, and cleaned the houses of Whites now were paid for their work and their time. Whites, who could not accept the new order, made every attempt to relegate workers to a status as close to slavery as they could, but the times and the laws had changed. In a broader context, the industrialization of the economy and the rising number of poor Whites and immigrants involved in factory work meant they too were also exploited by mill and factory owners. Revolt and resistance was in the air.

Washerwomen and domestic workers, especially in the South, began to organize and manage wide-scale strikes in Jackson, Mississippi, in 1866 and Galveston, Texas, in 1877, striking for better pay and working conditions. The laundry workers of Jackson, independent contractors of their own labor, resolved to "join in charging a uniform rate for our labor," (Hunter, 1997) one that was not exorbitant but was fair enough to live on and to support their families. Their strategy for collective price-fixing is reminiscent of the Market Women of Ancient Africa and the vendors in the Charles Town Market of South Carolina. However, the washerwomen of Atlanta and their strike in 1881 epitomized the collective bargaining power, organizing strategies, and resistance to exploitation of post–Civil War Black women. Called the "Washing Amazons," a group of twenty women and a few men formed a "Washing Society" with officers, established local neighborhood or ward subgroups, and established a uniform rate of dollars per dozen pounds of wash. On July 19, 1881, they called a strike for a higher rate those of uniform charges. Their timing was well thought out, as they aimed to strike when Atlanta, the model city of the "New South" had planned to hold its International Cotton Exposition. The city needed its washerwomen, maids, cooks, waiters, and other service workers to make the exposition happen. The owners of the hotels, boarding houses, and private homes gave in, although they tried imposing taxes, changing laws, raising rents, and increasing intimidation to break the strikers down. Those actions only outraged the Amazons, who inspired other domestic and personal service workers to demand higher wages and better working conditions.[24]

> Through the use of formal and informal community networks in which they shared work routines, work sites, living space and social activity, the strikers organized thousands of women and men.... The areas of everyday survival, on the one hand, and resistance and large-scale political protests, on the other, were mutually reinforcing: both were necessary parts of a collective cultural whole of working-class self-activity.[25]

Throughout history in the United States Black women's activism has been critical to the survival and progress of the nation. Activism is usually reported as political activism, but all of the work in the major movements—the Abolitionist, Suffrage, and Civil Rights movements—of the nineteenth and twentieth centuries, and now the ongoing battle of the twenty-first century, for full social, political, and economic equity have profited from women's work. Their wage work and their self-employment, their community organizing and service work have at their base their leadership and managerial skills. Those skills include attention to detail, the ability to make "a way out of no way," and to use common resources—in short, their entrepreneurial skills—have been used to make uncommon progress in an inequitable world. Cooperative economics, "giving back" to the community, and service as leadership are all elements of activism that is, at its core, entrepreneurial. Nowhere is this pattern more noteworthy than in the area of education and community service as business.

Education and Service as Business

Education has long been considered the "salvation of the race" for African Americans, whose own African traditions of teaching and learning were assaulted by Whites who obtained indentured servants in the early colonial days, by slave owners in the South, and by racist Whites in the North. Literacy was considered a way to freedom. In spite of the best efforts of Whites to stop Black people from learning and reading, education has always taken place in Black communities, and much of the teaching has been carried out by Black women. In colonial days, before chattel slavery became entrenched, Black indentured servants were taught to read so they could read the Bible, which was felt to be a "civilizing" force for the Africans. For example, Phillis Wheatley was taught to read by her Dutch owners in New York so she could read the Bible. Some enslaved women learned to read in the White plantation homes from their owners or their owners' children, who were their playmates—either directly or by eavesdropping on their lessons, or from religions groups such as the Quakers in the North.

Both free and enslaved women risked beatings and death teaching others to learn. They taught by candlelight in slave cabins and in secret schools on and around plantations, in "moonlight schools" in post–Civil War settings, and the Freeman's Bureau schools in the Reconstruction era. Black women opened and managed schools around the country throughout the nineteenth and twentieth centuries. The success of the school as a functioning entity was in part dependent on their ability to raise money to manage their resources—financial and human—efficiently, so that learning could take place; thus, all school founders were entrepreneurs. Whether the school was begun as church or mission schools or as an arm of mutual benefit societies, good management was critical. The motivation for teaching for middle-class Black women was not just employment, as it was for their White counterparts, but also "an almost holy calling, an opportunity for service to the race."[26]

The ability to make and maintain strategic alliances was also important in the success of the schools; many such alliances were forged with White women who taught in Black schools in the post–Civil War era and beyond. Some were good and included White women who were anti-abolitionists and educators. Yet some were bad, mere purveyors of the domesticating function of education for Black people, especially women. Kwolek-Folland, in her history of women and business in America, found that White women who were slave owners and responsible for managing thousands of slaves used those managerial skills to found schools and colleges. They often began their financial activities with dowries that included other women they owned as property—Black women.[27] Nowhere does she acknowledge the oppressive effects of that heritage on the Black girls and women they taught and the effect of those attitudes on the tension that still remains between Black and White women. In addition, the use of the schools as purveyors of the racist values and social mores of the culture for their White students was not mentioned.

Some outstanding yet usually unheralded examples of education as businesses founded, owned, and operated by Black women are presented here. One early example was Milla Granson, a bondwoman born in Kentucky in 1800. Granson persuaded her owner's children to teach her to read, and her teaching of other slaves was allowed. However, when that owner died, Granson was sold to a planter in Mississippi. She continued to teach group after group of enslaved people who came to her after working in the fields and stayed awake until 2 AM in her secret school, believing the knowledge was freedom.[28] Although she didn't take money, she provided a service in an organized not-for-profit way.

Because of political and social customs of the time, many Black schools and Black schoolteachers were hidden from the White community and went underground; therefore, many details of how they survived financially are not known. We can surmise that those who went it alone without the financial help of churches or organizations survived in part from their own earnings elsewhere, supplemented in part by payment in goods from their pupils, such as eggs, butter, chickens, and the like. Julian Froumountaine opened a free school in Savannah and had to go underground in 1830 when stricter laws were passed diminishing Black people's movements and restricting any activities thought to be threatening to the White status quo. Catherine Deveaux also maintained a secret school in her living room in Savannah, Georgia, for twenty-seven years, from 1834 until the Civil War. Mary Smith Kelsey, a member of the Black elite of Hampton, Virginia, taught behind closed doors until she was sanctioned by the Union Army to teach at the beginning of the Civil War.[29]

It is almost impossible to separate the role of religious organizations from education, as many church and missionary groups had as their mission the education of the community, and the educational community in turn had as its purpose not just teaching but the provision of a spiritual community and social, health care, and support services to those in need. There were many social service needs during the nineteenth and early twentieth centuries in Black communities, such as child and elder care, health care, provisions for widows and orphans, and housing. Life was tenuous in those days, as families were separated by slave owners; people were beaten and killed by being lynched and by White rioters; schools, orphanages and churches were burned to the ground for being too visible, politically active, and successful. Nonetheless, schools continued to be opened and operated.

For example, the Oblate Sisters of Providence were Black nuns who ran a school for Black immigrants in Baltimore in the 1840s. To support themselves and the school, many of the nuns took in laundry, a method of "income patching" used by many organizations to supplement their church support. Anne Marie Bancroft founded a day school for Black girls in Georgetown when she was only fifteen years old. She found church support when a priest asked her to open a day and boarding school, which she ran until 1831, when she joined the Oblate Order.[30] Catherine (Katy) Ferguson (c. 1774–1854) was born on a schooner to a slave mother on the way to their new owner in New York City. Free at age eighteen years, having earned her cost of $200, Ferguson became a renowned baker and caterer who was described as "charitable, folksy and 'simple-hearted.'"[31] It was said that she probably didn't need to advertise her talent as a cake baker and caterer in the Black newspapers because she was so well known and thought of. In 1793, Ferguson began a Sunday or Sabbath school for orphans and impoverished children in her neighborhood, both Black and White. Reverend John M. Mason, the pastor of her church, the Murray Street Church, invited her to move the school from her living room to the basement of his new building, providing her with assistants to teach secular courses in addition to her scripture lessons. Ferguson ran the school, New York City's first integrated one, for forty years, supporting it with her own funds. Her contributions were recognized when a home for unwed Black mothers, established in 1920—the first of its kind in the country—was named after her.[32]

Perhaps the best known entrepreneur/educator/activist is Mary McLeod Bethune, who founded the Daytona Normal and Industrial School for Negro Girls in a rented house with "five little girls, a dollar and a half and faith in God."[33] Responding to a need to educate the children of railroad workers, Bethune, who had been educated and taught in girl's schools, was determined to use education to effect change in the lives of Black women and girls. The school grew and became successful as Bethune used tried and true strategies of working the farm for food and profit; making strategic alliances with other community, social, and political organizations; and managing masterfully. She also used the school as a forum for community discussions, activism, and agitation, becoming well-known throughout Florida and the nation.

Using the school as her base, Bethune became visible and effective in national and international forums, including women's clubs such as the National Association of Colored Women, founding member of the National Council of Negro Women and the National Association for the Advancement of Colored People, member of Franklin Roosevelt's "Black Cabinet," colleague and confidante of Eleanor Roosevelt, and advisor to the United Nations, ensuring that the voices of Black people would be heard in circles of power and policy making in the United States and abroad. In 1923, the school was merged with the co-educational Cookman Institute in Jacksonville, Florida. Bethune-Cookman College in Daytona remains the only historically Black college founded by a Black woman, and it continues the legacy of Bethune to this day.[34]

Religion as Business

Mary Mcleod Bethune's last will and testament is a classic example of the connection between the ethical and activist orientation of Black women's spirituality and education. She espoused "a legacy of faith, hope and love" alongside practical strategies such as "education, dignity, harmonious living, and devotion to youth."[35] Black people are spiritual people, having brought an Afrocentric humanism from Africa that recognizes the importance of the human spirit, faith, and belief, grounded in community and family. African women were priestesses, cult leaders, and prophets and continued the tradition of spirituality as a source of support, resistance to oppression, and achievement throughout centuries of racism and discrimination. Jarena Lee, Amanda Berry Smith, Julia Foote, and Zilpha Elaw were nineteenth-century preachers, often self-employed, operating outside the purview of organized churches. Smith, a formerly enslaved, self-taught woman, was known as the "singing pilgrim" and "God's image carved in ebony."[36] A successful evangelist and singer, she became well known through her revivals, conducted with many White audiences, and her missionary work in Europe, India, and Africa. On her return to the United States in 1890, Smith began conducting revivals again, wrote her own autobiography, and with her own money, earned from her career and fundraising activities, opened an orphan home and industrial school for Black orphans in Harvey, Illinois, in 1899. Once the school was opened, she continued to invest in real estate, buying eighteen additional lots. Drawing on her strong network of other activists and supporters, such as Ida B. Wells, her husband, and local realtors, philanthropists, and church leaders, Smith continued building her empire.[36]

The Black church, like the Black press, is a pillar of the Black community and was "masculinized" as the Black community became more assimilated into the White mainstream and took on its values. The organized Christian churches have always been supported and operated by women while being "run" by men. In a particularly Afro-Christian tradition, Black women have had four basic areas of influence and leadership: preaching, prayer, music, and testimony. The role of women has been especially prominent in the area of music, epitomized by their presence in gospel choirs and bands such as the Excelsior Temple Band of Brooklyn, New York, in 1929. Black female preachers and ministers have always been prominent within the church, but they have had difficulty in breaking the "glass ceiling" until fairly recently. Many have made strides in opening their own churches and are taking their place as recognized leaders within the larger denominations in more recent years such as Barbara Harris, the first female Episcopal bishop. Spiritual Black women are not a monolithic group, embracing many organized religions such as Islam, Baha'i, Buddhism, and traditional African religions such as Santeria. Many Black women are also deeply spiritual without embracing any organized religion. Regardless of their religious expression, women have continued to take leadership positions and use that power to exercise their service to self, children, family, and community, continuing the tradition of spirituality as an integral part of their lives and work.[37]

Service as Business

Just as education and spirituality has long been the purview of Black women, social and community service have also been central to the survival and prosperity of the Black community. It is also hard to separate the interdependent nature of service from education, religion, and activism. The mutual benefit societies, the Black women's club movement, sororities, and the not-for-profit service organizations such as the National Council of Negro Business and Professional Women, founded by women in the early twentieth century, are linear descendants of the mutual aid associations and craft and kinship guilds of the women of West and Central Africa.

In the early days of the nation, women's organizations sprang up with the names that acknowledged the connection to Africa: the Daughters of Africa (1812) in Philadelphia, The Abyssinian Benevolent Daughters of Esther and the African Dorcas Society (1827) in New York City, and the Daughters of Zion (1899) in Petersburg, Virginia. Others had names that reflected their purposes: the American Female Bond Benevolent Society; the Female Anti-Slavery Societies of Boston and Salem, Massachusetts, and Philadelphia; the Colored Females Free Produce Societies of Philadelphia and New York; and later organizations such as Maggie Lena Walker's Order of St. Luke's Benevolent Society and the Penny Savings Bank.[38] These societies were all founded by Black women in response to the sexism and racism encountered in larger groups, in which Black women were relegated to supportive rather than leadership roles or were not admitted at all. Although having as their main objectives the abolition of slavery, the promotion of education, and the provision of services, these eighteenth- and nineteenth-century organizations had at their base an economic agenda. For example, the antislavery societies had as their main function raising funds for the abolitionist cause; gender issues still prevailed, however, as Black men continued to be chosen to present the voice of the Black community to White society.

Many of those women who founded and ran not-for-profit organizations also provided support and protection by Black women for Black women. The mutual aid and support networks, based on the notion of sisterhood, recognized the dangers Black women faced from the White community and, sometimes, from Black men. After emancipation, women were still not free from sexual abuse, rape, and exploitation, wherever they were. Young single women were especially vulnerable, and as opportunities opened to them in the North that enabled them to distance themselves from daily contact with Whites in their homes, where they were virtually powerless, many Black women took part in the Great Migration North. Northern free middle- and upper-class Black women took it on themselves to offer protection for these young women both during the journey and when they arrived in the "big cities. The White Rose Mission of New York City was one such group. Opened on February 11, 1897, on East 97th Street, the mission's stated purpose was to "protect self-supporting Colored girls, to direct them amid the dangers and temptations of New York City."[39] The mission was nondenominational and operated as a settlement house, providing shelter for women and children and providing co-educational vocational classes in addition to protection for women coming from the South. It was also the first site of travelers' aid services in 1898, placing their agents at major bus and train terminals to meet the travelers from the South.[39]

This section is focused on service as business. The examples offered are in fact connected in that they all illustrate, in different ways, the themes that reflect theoretical and philosophical positions of Black women entrepreneurs: sisterhood, community connections, cooperative economics, economic empowerment of Black women and in the womanist tradition defined earlier, of the entire community. "Service" business and not-for-profit organizations are not often thought of as being business enterprises and they are; they provide examples of theory and philosophy in practice. Strategies that are evident in the stories are entrepreneurial attitudes and actions, collectivism and care of each other and those less fortunate. This section is a particularly cogent one that has a goal of illuminating this "different view of business."

Another example that illustrates the elements of sisterhood, cooperative economics, and financial acumen was the Working Girls Home Association, founded in 1911 in Cleveland, Ohio, by Jane Edna Hunter. Hunter had trained as a nurse, and when she went to Cleveland to try and find work, she found she could neither find work or shelter. She took work that was typically available to Black women—domestic and laundry work, as well as some private duty nursing. In 1911, she gathered together a group of friends in similar situations, and with contributions of five cents from each member, each week; by 1913 they collected enough to open a twenty-three-room residence for Black working women in 1913. The business grew, and by 1917 they had replaced the first house with a seventy-two-room building. In 1928, the association expanded to 135 rooms, four parlors, six clubrooms, a cafeteria, a beauty salon, and an employment agency. They named it the Phillis Wheatley Association.[40] There are many other such stories and example of cooperative associations, formed for the protection and prosperity of sisters—their "fictive kin." Investment strategies, financial management and leadership skills, and a womanist connection to family and community were necessary for their growth and success, and Black women had all these qualities.

There was also a group of similar organizations that formed nationwide—the Associations for the Protection of Negro Women. The scope of the need was documented by a book, *Out of Work* (1904) written by social worker Frances A. Kellor, which exposed the viciousness and prevalence of exploitation of Black migrant women from the South. The organizations made advances providing housing, employment, training, and other social services for women in the cities.[41] Community service organizations and organizational development efforts are the antecedents of the not-for-profits now run by, for, and about Black women, ensuring that the traditions continue.

Several organizations in the antebellum and Reconstruction eras were experiments in community economic development that depended on the practice of the cooperative economics that were a long-standing tradition among Black women. Some of the most fascinating organizations include the Free Produce Society, the cooperative grocery store, and the Detroit Housewives Union discussed in Chapter 3. The Port Royal Experiment of 1862 in the South Carolina Sea Islands is another example of the intersection of education, service, religion, and economics as a means to financial self-sufficiency and independence.

The Port Royal Experiment tested the prevailing wisdom about the inability and unwillingness of Black people to work on their own after slavery. The Union government needed to save a large cotton crop left behind by southern plantation owners who fled during the war, leaving the crop and thousands of former people who had been in bondage. Conceived of as an experiment by a young abolitionist cotton planter named Edward Philbrick, cotton was grown in the Sea Islands by free, formerly enslaved, workers who were paid by the bale and given a plot of garden space to use as they liked. These freedmen and women used the land to grow produce they used for their own consumption, selling the excess in the marketplace and achieving a higher level of economic autonomy.

The second part of the experiment consisted of sending teachers to Port Royal to teach both children and adults. Several White teachers were sent and many Black as well. One of the first Black teachers was Charlotte Forten, descended from the prominent family of entrepreneurs and activists in Philadelphia. Her grandmother, aunts, and mother, mentioned earlier, had all been founding members of the Philadelphia Anti-Slavery Society. Working with two other Black teachers from Philadelphia in a school at Central Baptist Church on St. Helena's island, Forten educated hundreds. Her account of this experience, "Life on the Sea Islands," told of a people ready for freedom and education; it was published in *Atlantic Monthly* in May and June of 1864.

The Port Royal Experiment was also notable for the changes that occurred in the Black laborers' behavior. Although the venture was extremely profitable financially for Philbrick, who made a net profit of $80,000 in the second year, the profits did not "trickle down" enough to the workers, many of whom were women. In protest, a woman named Old Grace and her delegation of women confronted Philbrick:

> I'se been working for the owner three years, and made with my children two bales last year, two more this year. I'se a flat-footed person and don't know much but I knows those two bales cotton fetch enough money, and I don't see what I'se got from them. When I take my little bit of money and go to the store, buy cloth, find it so dear, dear Jesus—the money all gone and leave children naked.[42]

The confrontation, although not successful, served notice that Black people, especially Black women, would negotiate and protest if they were exploited and their children and families placed at risk. A sea-change had come to the

Sea Islands and elsewhere in the country, reflected in many aspects of life, including cultural expression.

Culture as Business

The African American community is an amalgamation of people and places that is a "masala" or "gumbo" mixture that is different from either Africa or White America. A unique culture arose from those Africans who made their first stop in the colonies, spiced by those who came later from other parts of the diaspora—the Caribbean and Latin and South America. The "gumbo ya ya" resulting mix is a rich cultural heritage that also has economic roots in the expression of this distinctive culture. Literature as business was discussed earlier; art, both fine and performing; music, both popular and classical; and theater all provided entrepreneurial opportunities for Black women, either out of necessity or desire. Those activities enriched the lives of many through time and place and continue to do so as the cultural contributions of Black women maintain and sustain the vibrancy of the traditions. Some of those stories follow.

Quilting

Quilting is being used as a metaphor to shape and frame this book. Quilting is traditional "woman's work" and has its place in many cultures. It is a quintessential woman's art form, a method of connecting women with each other and connecting the past with the present. Quilting as an art form has particular meaning in Black women's history because, as said by Nikki Giovanni, quilts were a way for Black women to make something out of nothing, adding value to their parts by creating something more than the sum of their parts—a cultural tradition and survival skill. Making quilts was also a way for many Black women to express their creativity, their talents, their feelings, their vision of everyday life, and possibly most important, their support of one another. Quilts were also part of a process—that of binding Black women to one another in a shared activity, as sisters in the black sense of the word and as mothers to daughters, as a way to connect past to the present, using symbols that tell the stories of our origins and experiences. Quilts were tools for resistance and revolt, as they were used to warn enslaved people of the presence of slave catchers, to point the direction to the North, and to let them know when it was safe to meet Harriet Tubman, a conductor on the Underground Railroad. Yet another Harriet, Harriet Powers, epitomizes the value of quilts as an art form and as an economic tool.

Harriet Powers was born a slave and became "free" after the Emancipation Proclamation. She and her husband owned and operated a prosperous farm in Athens, Georgia. Harriet was also a quilter, and as mentioned earlier, her work was seen by a White woman, Jennie Smith, in the Athens Cotton Fair and tracked her down. Smith offered Harriet $10 for the quilt, a great deal of money in that day. Harriet refused, as she and her husband were doing well and she did not want to part with her work. However, Harriet and her husband fell on hard times, forcing her to return to Smith with an offer to sell the quilt. Since Smith did not have the $10 but only $5 she offered it to Harriet who reluctantly agreed to sell "the darling offspring of her brain" for half the price, at the behest of her husband. The Black community of Atlanta had raised $10,000 in 1895 for an exhibition of Black art, and Smith intended to exhibit the Powers quilt she bought there. Her quilt was passed on to a friend, who then gave it to the Smithsonian Institute, where it hangs today.

The quilt is one of two made by Harriet Powers that have survived to this day. The second is on permanent display at the Boston Museum of Fine Arts, having been commissioned by the faculty of Atlanta University in 1898 to be presented as a gift to Reverend Cuthbert Hall, the then-president of Union Theological Seminary. Harriet's quilts are story quilts, made in the appliqué method used by men in Africa—a style that originated in Dahomey, the ancient capital of the Fon people of the kingdom of Ahomey in ancient Africa. In the United States, African American women such as Harriet perfected the style and craft. The quilts use scenes from Africa, with symbols of animals, suns, and stars, as seen in African story quilts; it is said that Harriet remembered these symbols from stories from her African grandmother. The scenes were also integrated with Judeo-Christian symbols that were part of African-American religious traditions. Harriet's story and quilts epitomize several aspects of African American women's quilting cultural tradition—use as products for sale when needed, creative expression, and preservation of the past and present.[43]

In the present day, Faith Ringgold is an artist who is world renowned for her appliqué and collage quilts. Her work, which began at the height of the Civil Rights movement, is known and shown throughout the world. She has both made money for her quilts, dolls, and soft sculptures and employed Black people, mostly apprentice Black women artists, and mentored and taught them. Her "Family of Women" masks were expressions of Black women's sensibilities and issues. She has also used her talents in the preservation of a multicultural history of Crown Heights of Brooklyn, New York, in a quilt which hangs in an elementary school there. Ringgold was commissioned to create the quilt to tell stories, continuing the tradition of Harriet Powers and their African ancestors. She says of her work, "I don't want the story of my life about racism, though it has played a major role. I want my story to be about attainment, love of family, art, helping others courage, values, dreams coming through."[44]

Powers has many other artistic descendants in the quilters who followed her, including Ringgold and the Women of Gee Bend, a group of women quilters in an all-Black town, whose work has been created to tell the tale of the Black experience in the United States. A show of the work of the Women of Gee Bend is traveling and, as such, is making money for the quilters, enabling an expression of the visions and experiences while creating capital for themselves and their families. Their quilts became business, and the process is the subject of a PBS documentary.

Fine Art

Other fine artists and sculptors, both past and present, also created art that served multiple purposes as creative expressions of their talents and as a source of income. Selling their products and their services, including teaching, made the these artists entrepreneurs.

Black women, whether in Africa or the United States, have always expressed themselves and their culture through artistic creations. Whatever the medium—quilts, baskets, sculpture, or painting—these women's creations, reflections of daily life, of connection to others and to spirituality, served to present their experiences and perceptions of the world around them. In the United States in the early days of the nation, artists such as Harriet Powers created works that were not considered to be "art." By the mid-nineteenth century, racism and sexism made it all but impossible for Black women artists to either enter art schools or be recognized in the mainstream art worlds. By the 1880s, some Black men and White women were allowed into schools, but Black women were often not. If they were allowed in, they were the most severely restricted in what they could do. A case in point is Annie E. Anderson Walker, the wife of a prosperous attorney in Washington, DC, who had taken private drawing lessons and applied to the Corcoran Gallery of Art School. When she showed up to start school, she was denied entrance because of her color; she was told that if the committee had known she was Black, her portfolio would not have been reviewed. Despite the efforts of Frederick Douglass, the committee would not back down, and Walker had to go to Cooper Union in New York City for her art education and to Europe for her work to be shown. Walker's experience was typical of African American fine and performance artists, who often had to leave the United States to accomplish their goals

Sculpture was the most common African artistic tradition; therefore, many of the early artists, both men and women, were sculptors. Edmonia Lewis, a sculptor whose story opened this chapter, was the first African American/Native American woman to be recognized in the artistic mainstream, shortly after the Civil War. Others would not emerge until the next century. Two such women were Elizabeth Prophet and Augusta Savage, whose backgrounds and life experiences were totally different, although their talent was not.

Prophet came from a Northern middle-class background and studied at Ivy League Schools, including Brown and the Rhode Island School of

Design, and studied and exhibited in France. On her return to the States, she found that racism and discrimination affected her ability to exhibit or sell. She ended up teaching at historically Black colleges, unrecognized by the White art world and distancing herself from the Black community. She had a nervous breakdown and died alone and poor after having to work as a domestic to merely survive. Savage, however, came from a modest background in the South and exhibited and sold her first creations at country fairs. On the recommendation of the superintendent at one of those fairs, Savage went to New York City and also studied at Cooper Union, a tuition-free art school. With the help of scholarships, she was supposed to travel to France to study, but the offer was withdrawn when several White women from Alabama refused to travel with her. Instead, Savage was invited to study with an individual mentor, Herman McNeil. After her return from Europe, Savage reconnected with her own community and gave back by opening a studio, the Savage Studio of Arts and Crafts in New York City—a place to teach other young Black artists.[45]

Elizabeth Catlett, a modern-day sculptor and artist, also had to leave the country to practice her craft. Having entered the University of Iowa in 1938, she became the first person of any gender or color to receive a Master's degree in Art from that institution. However, she continued to experience discrimination because of her color and gender. Her powerful sculpture portrays images of Black women in all their aspects, and her paintings do the same. However, Catlett had to move to Mexico, where she still lives with her Mexican husband, to be fully able to practice her craft and to be recognized on a wider stage. Her work has sold all over the world, and her teaching in historically Black colleges and universities continues to influence the lives of many after her. Her art is business and service.[46]

Music and Dance

Music and dance have always been integral to the Black experience in America and, in fact, have been an element that has sustained the community during its worst times and lifted it up in its best. From the early days of slavery, when music was used in the fields to move the work along and to send messages of resistance and revolt, musical artists steeped in the tradition developed troupes, clubs, "juke joints," and nightclubs where Black people could go to entertain and be entertained. Of necessity, Black people created and maintained their own entertainment industry, comprised of clubs, traveling troupes of actors and musicians, and the boarding houses and restaurants that sheltered and fed them. Women were at the forefront of all those endeavors, especially as singers, particularly those who sang the "blues" that came out of the pain of being a Black woman in America. Similar to some artists and quilters who had to sell their wares on the street to survive, in the 1800s, singers sang on the corners. Blueswomen such as

"Ma" Rainey, who first wrote blues songs and performed them in public in the early 1900s, and those who came after them, such as Bessie Smith and Billie Holiday, made their living as independent musical contractors, writing and performing both independently as well as with big bands run by men. They were, however, often exploited by men, especially the Whites who owned and controlled the record companies. However, there were those women who obtained more control over their environments by creating their own businesses.

There were groups of women performers in the later part of the nineteenth century who had their own musical groups and companies. One was the Ladies Orchestra, formed and owned by Black women in 1884 Chelsea, Massachusetts, and the Colored Female Brass band, which toured in the Midwest in the 1880s. Women as instrumentalists were not frowned on at this time, as they would be later in the century. One entertainer who owned her own business was Ada "Bricktop" Smith, who opened and operated nightclubs in Paris as well as in New York—all called "Bricktops." These clubs provided a place for her to perform as well as to hire others—she had control.[47]

The world of classical music, considered to be the sole purview of White Euro-Americans, was also breached by Black women, albeit unsuccessfully in the early days and not without major battles in the twentieth century. Black opera singers, such as Black Patti, Marian Anderson, and Leontyne Price were few and far between, spanning a century. Black women composers were scarcely noted but were present from the 1800s on. Their compositions were an eclectic mix, including solo songs and choral works such as gospels, symphonies, and operas. One early composer was Amanda Aldridge (1866–1956), the daughter of an established actor. Other early composers included Florence Price, the first Black woman to receive international recognition as a classical composer, and Eva Jessye (1895–1992), who worked with George Gershwin as an arranger and conductor. One well-known modern composer was Shirley Graham Du Bois (1896–1977), the second wife of W. E. B. Du Bois, who was a musician as well as a writer. The youngest Black woman composer to find commercial success, Micki Grant (1941–), is a composer of musical stage works including *Don't Bother Me, I Can't Cope*, which was a commercial success on Broadway.[48] For over a century, Black women trained in the Western musical tradition have been composing music, much of which reflects and celebrates the Black experience while providing sources of income for its authors.

Musical theater was not far behind, as was dramatic theater. The face of theater in America, especially in Black America, was changed by women. Two notable groups typify the impact women, as independent business owners, have had on the genre and the culture. Nineteenth-century musical theater was dominated by the minstrel shows, which originally denigrated Blacks but were taken over by them so they could make a living in the theater; however, no women were involved in the organization and production of these minstral shows. Yet, two women, sisters Anna and Emma

Hyer, are credited with the founding of Black theater in America. They created a musical traveling troupe in 1875 whose mission was to produce plays that told the story of the Black experience through music and drama. The group was called the Coloured Operatic and Dramatic Company and operated for many years, producing plays with story lines and serious music that were works of "education and refinement."[49] A little later, in the early 1900s, the Anita Bush Players, a troupe created in New York City by its founder, Anita Bush, produced Black dramas in the Lincoln Theater in Harlem. As the company prospered, they moved to larger quarters in the Lafayette theater and became known as the Lafayette Players. For seventeen years after its founding, the Bush Players put on quality drama with all-Black casts. The troupe became well respected in the larger community, and the Black community, in a show of cooperative economic development, formed the Quality Amusement Corporation. The corporation enabled the Lafayette Players to tour the country and provided open community theaters meant to provide entertainment as well as training grounds for Black actors to learn their craft and hone their skills.[50] These ventures were the predecessors of many other groups across the country, such as the Barbara Ann Teer's National Black Theater in Harlem, that provide both entertainment and education that is in their control.

Black women in the arts who owned and operated their own companies were also visible in dance, such as Katherine Dunham's Negro Dance Troupe of Chicago. Dunham, a dancer and choreographer, earned enough money by starring in "Cabin in the Sky"—an all-Black theater production—to start the troupe. It was so successful that White theater producers continued to support it by making sure the members, including Dunham, continued to perform in numerous Broadway musicals. With the money earned from those performances, Dunham then founded the Katherine Dunham School of Arts and Research in New York, another training ground that enabled the preservation of the culture and the passing on of the skills of artists, actors, and dancers in the performing arts.

These entrepreneurial ventures, begun and managed by women, both built on old traditions and created new ones, in which Black women would be in control of many aspects of their interior and exterior lives. Playwrights and poets such as Ntozake Shange and Maya Angelou and filmmakers such as Julie Dash continue all the traditions of using art and media created by and for Black women that celebrate their lives, present their own visions of themselves, and use entrepreneurship as service. There were many other groups formed by Black women during different eras, building on the history and strengths of those who came before them and continuing today. Of course, the ultimate entertainer, media mogul, and entrepreneur is Oprah Winfrey, a self-made Black woman billionaire. As has been shown, the Black women's tradition of using individual success, both monetary and personal, for the education and the "uplift" of the race has continued. Entrepreneurship—the creation, ownership, and management of companies, troupes, and schools—was a vehicle that enabled that success. These professions, not usually thought of as entrepreneurial ventures, also provided "nontraditional" routes to economic success.

The Professions as Business: Not Just Women's Work

Law and medicine were professions closed to Black people and White women in the continental United States, especially after the establishment of the colonies as the United States of America. However, medicine and healing were practiced by Black women in the early days of the country, as women brought many of the nursing, midwifery, and pharmacopoeia skills with them from Africa. Enslaved women were often the only source of health care on plantations; free women often bought their freedom by "hiring out" those skills. As the country evolved and Black people moved increasingly out of slavery and into institutions, especially in the North, Black women availed themselves of the scant opportunities open to them, usually on the fringes of those offered to Black men and White women.

In the area of health-care services, Black women who did earn nursing and medical degrees often had to open their own schools, hospitals, and clinics to be able to practice their professions. For example, the story of Susie Baker King Taylor, who was a nurse in the Civil War, is interesting in that it illustrates many of the intersecting factors that affected Black women's lives and endeavors. She first learned to read in a "secret school," conducted in a Black teacher's living room in Savannah, Georgia. Taylor was in Savannah and not on the plantation where she was born because her grandmother had been "hired out" to work in a house in Savannah, and Taylor went with her. After Taylor had learned all she could from this teacher, her White playmate, who had entered a convent school, was permitted by her playmate's mother to teach Taylor more; this teaching and learning was hidden from the playmate's father. On learning that Taylor could read and write, army officials sent her to a Civil War unit in the Union lines as a teacher at age fourteen years. She then became Company E's laundress and later their nurse, learning nursing, as had most Black nurses, from observing and doing. As a result of the Civil War, nursing became a trained profession with formal schools—first independent and then attached to hospitals.

However, as nursing became more of a route out of domestic service for poor White and European immigrant women, Black women were excluded from nursing schools and the profession. Once those routes were taken away, Black women did as they had done for centuries—they formed their own organizations, networks, and schools. By 1920, there were thirty-six Black nursing schools, many of which had been founded by women, such as Alice Bacon, the founder of the Hampton Nurse Training School of

Dixie Hospital. Because Black nurses were barred from working in White hospitals and from membership in the American Nurses Association, Martha Franklin, a Black graduate nurse, founded the National Association of Colored Graduate Nurses in 1908 for support and distribution of information; by 1920, the organization numbered five hundred members.[51] Nonetheless, discrimination in this field continued until relatively recently. Black nurses, who had such a tradition of service in peace and war, were barred from the U.S. Army Corps of Nurses as recently as World War II.

Black female physicians faced similar challenges of racial and gender discrimination. The number of women physicians fluctuated with the political, social, and economic contexts of the times. In 1860, there were two hundred female physicians in the United States; by 1900 there were seven thousand. Between 1860 and 1900, eleven of the nineteen medical schools for women were disbanded. In the Reconstruction Era and shortly thereafter, only 115 female physicians were Black, and in the 1920s, after the Black Codes and Jim Crow laws were enacted to roll back Black people's progress, there were only sixty-five Black female physicians. However, there were 3,885 Black male physicians. The double yoke of racism and sexism continued to take its toll on those women who wanted to practice medicine.[52] However, as usual, Black women found a way not only to achieve their personal dreams of becoming physicians but to provide health care to their community.

During Reconstruction, several Black medical schools were founded, but only two remain to this day, Howard and Meharry. As White schools, these institutes began to admit Black men but not women. Women did graduate from Howard, Meharry, and the Women's College of Medicine in the early part of the twentieth century, but even those few hundred who did manage to obtain their degrees were not able to establish practices easily, as neither Black men nor White people of any gender patronized Black female doctors. They had to open their own institutions. Matilda Evans, the first woman to practice medicine in South Carolina, had to treat her patients, mostly women and children—the poorest of the poor—in her home. Nonetheless, she was able to earn enough money to open her own hospital with a nursing school attached. In all, she founded three hospitals between 1896 and 1916, created a free clinic for women and children, and organized the Negro Health Association of South Carolina in 1930.[53]

White women physicians, facing gender discrimination, founded the New York Infirmary for Women and Children in New York. The first Black woman doctor to work there was Rebecca Lee Crumpler, who graduated the New England Female Medical College in Boston in 1864. Rebecca Cole, an 1893 Black graduate of the Women's Medical College of Philadelphia, became a resident at the infirmary that was one of the few institutions open to female physicians. In 1873, she returned to Philadelphia to found the Women's Directory Center with a fellow female physician; the center provided medical services to destitute women and children.

Black female physicians, facing continuous obstacles over time, continued to be entrepreneurial in their approach to practicing their chosen profession. They continued to open private practices, group practices, schools, community health centers, and organizations. In more recent years, as their numbers have increased, so has their acceptance, visibility, and leadership in the profession, as they continue to break gender and racial barriers that continue.[54] For example, in 1991, Vivian Pinn-Wiggins became the first permanent director of the National Institutes of Health Office of Women's Health Research and was the first Black woman appointed Surgeon General in the United States. Patricia Bath founded the American Institute for the Prevention of Blindness, and in 1988 she was the first African American woman to obtain a patent. She received the patent for her laser probe, which removes cataracts from eyes.[55]

Women in law did not fare as well—neither Black nor White. Although some Black women, such as Charlotte Ray, graduated from law school, they were not admitted to the Bar. Ray did not make enough money from private practice to make a living. Mary Shadd Cary, whom we met earlier, completed Howard Law School in 1883 but was not graduated because of her sex. Undismayed, she went on to open a private practice and found her own school, her own newspaper, and her own activist organizations. Since that time, law has become a way in which many Black women have advanced personally through the establishment of their own practices which are business enterprises. They have also advanced professionally through employment in traditional law firms and faculty in law schools and politically through the practice of public law and advocacy and as stepping stones to political office. People such as Barbara Jordan, Constance Baker Motley, Lani Guinier, and Maxine Waters are testament to the outcome and continuation of the battle.

Other professions that are often practiced as entrepreneurship, and certainly not associated usually associated with Black women, are aviation and architecture. The best known African American aviator was Bessie Coleman. Born in 1896 in Atlanta, Texas, Coleman became interested in flying while she worked as a manicurist, overhearing men's tales of this new, growing field. Because she was both Black and a woman, Coleman was not allowed into any of the flight training schools in the United States and had to go to France, where she obtained her aviator's license in 1921. She then returned to the United States and made her living as a barnstormer and parachutist; in other words, as an entrepreneur and entertainer. Coleman was also an activist in that she refused to perform in shows that had segregated audiences and lectured extensively about flying and the field of aviation in African American schools, churches, and recreation facilities. She also intended to use her earnings to start her own school of aviation for African Americans; she unfortunately was not successful in that endeavor, refusing to compromise her values by performing to all-White audiences. She died an untimely death in a freak accident while rehearsing for an air show. However, her life and deeds continue to influence many other Black women and people of color who are interested in the field of aviation. Among her direct "descendants" are Janet Harmon Watertown Bragg, a nurse and aviator who attempted to enter the field in Chicago but who was turned down because of her sex and race. Bragg then became the first and only woman in the Aeronautical University—a segregated flight school founded by two Black male graduates of the Chicago-based Curtis Wright School of Aviation, Cornelius Coffey and John Robinson. With Charles Johnson, Bragg became a co-founder of a co-educational, interracial school connected with Coffey's at the Harlem Airport for people who could not enter Coffey's school. She went on to obtain her commercial license and founded the Challenger Air Pilots Association in 1931 for Black aviators— inspired by Bessie Coleman. She, with Willa Brown, a graduate of the same school, which also trained pilots, Cornelius Coffey, and Dale White, began the annual memorial flight over Bessie Coleman's grave in 1935, which continues today.[56]

Architecture is a profession that lends itself easily to entrepreneurship. While few in numbers in this traditionally male profession, a growing number of women have entered the field, many of whom start their own practices after working for established firms. Norma Sklarek is one such woman who paved the way for others. Norma Sklarek was the first Black woman architect to be licensed in the states of New York and California, in 1954 and 1962, respectively. She was hired by firms in New York and later in California, eventually becoming a managing partner. The firms she was associated with were Gruen and Associates and Welton Becket and Associates. However, in 1985, she left to form her own partnership with two other women, Margot Siegel and Katherine Diamond, forming Siegel, Sklarek, and Diamond, the largest totally woman-owned architectural firm in the United States.[57]

Law, medicine, aviation, and architecture, professions considered to be non-traditional for women, especially Black women, are those in which they have also excelled. Those professions, practiced as businesses that provide self-employment and the employment of others, maintain Black women's connections to education, social justice, community service, and activism as well as personal accomplishment, continuing age-old cultural traditions.

Use of profits for the greater good is an example of social entrepreneurism, using self-employment earnings for social services and political activism and a cultural tradition. The Market Women of today have opened businesses in many fields in traditional and nontraditional areas. The Market Women profiled in the next chapters practice everyday economics that reflect the culture, strategies, and values that are their historical and cultural tradition. Their businesses have acted as "patches" for family incomes; provided sole sources of income; and offered sites of educational, religious, and community services, as well as art, literature, and entertainment. These women, ordinary individuals who have shown "the ability to make unusual amounts of money using commonly available resources,"[2] are unsung heroines whose stories need to be told. Those stories provide a significant patch in the story quilt—one I am sure is reflected many times over among the community of present-day Black women entrepreneurs. Their stories follow.

The history of black women from slavery to freedom, however, has been distinguished by an entrepreneurial tradition of establishing enterprises that parallel American business activities.

—J. K. Walker, 1999, p. 612

PART II

The Present:
The Lived Experiences
of Black Women
Entrepreneurs

This section presents, in their own words, the stories of present-day Black women entrepreneurs, whose experiences as businesswomen provide inspiration, lessons, role models, and mentors. Each chapter highlights outstanding themes that document their experiences and illuminate their connections to their ancestral traditions.

These stories were gathered through qualitative research conducted for my doctoral dissertation. I came to this research because I had searched for information about the history of Black women entrepreneurs in the United States and found few resources that focused primarily on their activities in the economic sphere. I knew there were stories in both academic and popular literature, but I had to search across disciplines to find them. I also determined that it would be useful to interview Black women entrepreneurs of African descent to learn about their experiences and perspectives in their own words as well as to provide a way to honor them by sharing their stories with a wide audience. I conducted the research with graduates of an entrepreneurship training and technical assistance program in New York State, the Entrepreneurial Assistance Program (EAP). I directed one of the programs and taught in it, so I not only had knowledge of its mission and outcomes but also had full access to the participants.

I interviewed nineteen women business owners. Prior to the in-depth interviews, I conducted focus groups with clients of agencies and organizations that had populations different from and the same as the study group: The American Women's Economic Development Corporation (AWED), Black Women Enterprises of New York State, and the York College Small Business Development Center. The purpose of the groups was to get a baseline sense of how the entrepreneurs in those organizations defined success. The study population consisted of graduates of the EAP of the (New York) Empire State Development Corporation's Division of Minority and Women's Business Services participated in the program between 1993/1994 and 1997/1998. The women had also been nominated by their EAP Center directors as being successful and had completed the training and technical assistance program classes between 1993 and 1998. Thirty-eight women from fourteen centers who self-identified as Black were nominated; nineteen women from eleven centers participated in the study. There were no participants from thirteen centers because most of them were in upstate New York, where there were few if any people of color.

The women were from a variety of ethnic groups including but not limited to African Americans, Caribbean Americans, and Africans. In addition, those individuals identifying themselves as both Hispanic and Black were included as part of the population pool. The defining characteristic for inclusion, therefore, was self-identification of individuals who classified themselves as being Black. For the purposes of this study, "Black" was assumed to mean being of African descent, understanding the fact that race, a social construction, is different from ethnicity. Although recognizing the fact that this group is far from monolithic, I also assumed that the experiences of these individuals as Black women in American society have more commonalties than differences, especially as they conduct business within the larger society.

To situate the study population within the context of the larger EAP program, an overview of the total number of program participants, their racial/ethnic and gender breakdowns, and the number of total success stories reported to the EAP director were compared and contrasted with the study group. The statistics on the EAP were obtained from the 1998 overview report on the EAP program. The EAP total population served from 1990–1997 was 7001 participants.

The specific demographics of the women in the group tell us something about who they were along a number of parameters that are generally considered in entrepreneurship research. Level of education, place of birth, age, marital status, and number of children were the characteristics gathered about the study population. All have been found to be factors that affect business development. The intersection of those factors has been especially important in the business success of female entrepreneurs.

Pamela Thomas-Graham, president and chief executive officer of CNBC. Courtesy of CNBC.

CHAPTER 5

The Present-Day Context: Business, Balance, and Time

The girls and women of our race must not be afraid to take hold of business endeavor and, by patient industry, close economy, determined effort, and close application to business, wring success out of a number of business opportunities that lie at their very doors.

—Madame C. J. Walker, 1913, in A'Leila Bundles,
On Her Own Ground, p. 153

Devya was the first of nineteen women interviewed for this research. She is a mediation mentor, guiding people to a calmer, better space for themselves though meditation, "gong" ceremonies, and retreats. She is sixty-something years old, and when I first met her, she had been running her business, selling mediation services and products, for over ten years. She came to my entrepreneurship class to learn how to take her business to another level, feeling it had reached a plateau and needed to change to grow. Her husband, Robert, also took the class, wanting to expand the small business he had started in retirement. Devya had never taken a business course in her life but had a wide range of work and business experience she brought to her own enterprise:

I trained as a teacher.... I've been in the publishing industry for quite some time...I was in, would you believe?...computer entry data stuff....I was an administrative assistant and then each job that I took, when I left I went to a higher position.

Member's Badge, National Convention of Madame C. J. Walker's Agents.
Courtesy of A'Lelia Bundles/Walker Family Collection, Washington, DC,
madamecjwalker.com.

However, working wasn't enough. She had an epiphany, a life-changing experience, when she went to a meditation session herself. She reports that shortly after the event, she had a "calling" from outside of herself, a message that disclosed that her true life's work was to become a mediation mentor and to work for others. She trained for this vocation and integrated it with her previous education and experience and began her business.

> I also realized that everything I've ever done in my entire life was training me or developing me or moving me to this life...building me up...and I think that's what moved me into the life's purpose....People have told me that I have a mission...and I do have a mission...I had a vision.

She had a vision—a calling she turned into a viable, successful business that continues to change and grow.

Devya's story is not unusual. She is a member of one of the fastest-growing groups of new entrepreneurs in the country. This chapter sets the background and context for the story of these Black women entrepreneurs, doing business in the United States at the end of the twentieth century. Their experiences are illustrative of issues that are important to Black women's business development, including business motivations and goals, the search for balance, and time. As Devya notes, "I had no goals for business but I had goals for individuals. This is my life's work!"

Business: Motivations and Goals

Black women were opening new businesses at a rate faster than almost any other group in the nation in 1998, and in 2002, only Hispanic and Native American women were opening businesses at a faster rate. However, Black women are still well represented among the ranks of Black entrepreneurs and women entrepreneurs. Demographic and statistical evidence points to the fact that women and minorities accounted for the largest segment of new business owners in the closing decade of the last century and beginning of the new one. The trend continues among women and minorities but is most striking for minority women. The U.S. Census Bureau releases economic survey reports every five years, including special reports on minority-owned firms and women-owned firms.[1] The highlights of this report indicate certain trends, some of which have changed, some of which have continuity. For example, regardless of race or ethnicity, male-owned firms were the largest in terms of number of firms, sales receipts, and number of employees.

In contrast, women-owned firms, regardless of ethnicity, exhibited the fastest growth rate in number of businesses owned and receipts, although the receipts remained consistently lower than those of either firms owned

Table 5.1   Percentage of Minority-Owned Firms by Gender

Minority-Owned Firms by Gender	Firms (Number)	Sales and Receipts (Millions of Dollars)	Percentage of Total by Gender	
			Firms	Sales and Receipts
All minority-owned firms	3,039,000	591,300	X	X
Black	823,500	71,200	X	X
Men	443,600	51,100	53.9	71.6
Women	312,900	13,600	38.0	19.1
Equal	67,000	6,600	8.1	9.3
Hispanic	1,199,900	186,300	X	X
Men	666,500	133,200	55.6	71.5
Women	337,700	27,300	28.1	14.7
Equal	195,700	25,800	16.3	13.8
American Indian and Alaska Native	197,300	34,300	X	X
Men	106,900	20,600	54.2	60.1
Women	53,600	6,800	27.2	19.8
Equal	36,800	7,000	18.7	20.4
Asian and Pacific Islander	913,000	306,900	X	X
Men	497,500	217,400	54.5	70.8
Women	248,000	38,100	27.2	12.4
Equal	167,500	51,500	18.9	16.8

X = not applicable.
Source: 1997 Economic Census Survey of Minority-Owned Business Enterprises. http://www.census.gov/csd/mwb/

equally by women and men or those solely owned by men. However, the number of women-owned firms with revenues of more than $1 million has grown rapidly in the early twenty-first century.

The Center for Women's Business Research, formerly the National Foundation of Women Business Owners (NFWBO), has extracted the data from the Census Bureau and issued reports specific to women-owned businesses by race/ethnicity. Their findings document the fact that women in general are continuing to make a significant impact on the growth and health of the U.S. economy. The most recent numbers are clear. In 2002, there were 6.2 million privately held women-owned businesses. Those businesses employed 9.2 million workers and produced $1.15 trillion in sales.[2] However, all recent statistics regarding the rate of growth of new entrepreneurs between 1980 and the present indicate that growth is the

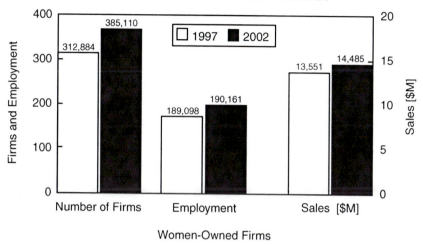

Figure 5.1 African American Women-Owned Businesses. Courtesy of Bureau of the Census and Center for Women's Business Research, © 2001 Center for Women's Business Research.

fastest among women of color. As can be seen by the 1997 economic report of the Census Bureau (see Table 5.1), that trend has continued, as growth rates for all minority-owned businesses were 30 percent, and 16 percent for all women, as opposed to 6 percent for all U.S. firms. Sales receipts increased 60 percent for minority-owned firms and 33 percent for women-owned firms. However, the rate of sales growth and employment was slower for Black women enterprises than for those firms owned by Hispanic and Asian women. That fact was true in 1997 and remains true in 2002.

As shown in Figure 5.1, the Center for Women's Business Research 2002 report does offer good news about the continued growth trends of African American women businesses owners based on the most recent census data available:

- As of 2002, there were an estimated 365,110 firms owned by African American women, employing 200,000 people and generating almost $14.5 billion in sales
- Nearly 30 percent of all minority-/women-owned firms are owned by Black women and represent 6 percent of all privately held majority women-owned firms in the United States

- Between 1997 and 2002, the number of firms owned increased by 17 percent; employment has grown at the same rate, yet sales have only increased by 7 percent
- More than 35 percent of all Black-owned businesses are owned by women, who employ 25 percent of the workers and generate 15 percent of the sales of those businesses.[3]

The most disturbing finding is that although the number of businesses opening with a parallel increase in employees is increasing, sales have only increased by 7 percent. These figures are not surprising, as Black women's greatest business growth was in the service sector of the economy, 29 percent, and 75 percent of the Black women total were in the service industry, and 7 percent in retail.[4] Those industry sectors traditionally generate the smallest revenues but are easier for women to build and manage, as they are labor, rather than capital, intensive; that is, they can be started and operated with more work and less money. In addition, service businesses are in areas historically considered to be "women's businesses"— food and beverage businesses, personal services, health care, child care, and educational services. In general, the biggest firms with the largest bottom lines are those in manufacturing, construction, and more recently, technology. Although more and more women are entering those fields and succeeding, they are still largely "men's" businesses, predominantly owned and controlled by non-minority males, who are still loath to let women "in."

While business ownership is highest among Black workers of women business owners, statistics also indicate that Black women still only account for 3.8 percent of the total population of small business owners. The rate of export activity, a traditional indicator of growth, is minimal for this particular population segment. It has been reported that 83–93 percent of businesses owned by women of color do not export any goods or services.[5] The 1996 National Foundation of Women Business Owners survey cited earlier also found that although access to capital was not a major concern of non-minority women, it remains of greater than average importance to minority-owned firms. The survey also showed that Black women were more likely to have started their businesses on a part-time basis while holding another job, less likely to start with a partner, and more likely to have sought training and advice.[6] Those facts have a definitive influence on business success measured solely by profits. Clearly, gender alone does not account for universal business concerns, outcomes, and issues among women business owners. The experiences of the women in my research on Black women entrepreneurs will demonstrate experiences in their lives and businesses that are both similar to and different from those of entrepreneurs in general.

The businesses owned and operated by the women in my study of Black women entrepreneurs ran the gamut from janitorial and cleaning services to a shoe-repair business. Most clustered in the retail/service sectors, with a few branching out into manufacturing of their products. As we will see, the words of the participants highlight the issues, experiences, and perspectives of these Black women and also serve to illustrate the similarities and differences among entrepreneurs. "Their words best describe their strategies for life."[7]

Some aspects of Devya's route to entrepreneurship are not unusual for many entrepreneurs; for example, the choice to change careers, to work for themselves, and to make life changes. However, there are some things that may be distinctive to Black women entrepreneurs. One of the factors that might be different for Black women entrepreneurs is, like Devya, feeling this work is a calling, a call to service. As seen earlier, the cultural traditions of Black women include work with a higher purpose, almost "a holy calling." In addition, Devya's business strategies were sound, and her view of business seems to have heeded the call of Madame C. J. Walker to take advantage of business opportunities, to manage well, and to "wring success" out of her efforts.

Human Capital: Developing Expertise through Formal and Informal Education

When asked to describe the personal characteristics they felt most influenced their business success, all participants in the research described the business skills they had accumulated as well as personality traits—in other words, what they knew and what they could do—their "human capital." The skills reported included marketing, pricing, purchasing, negotiating, strategic planning, budgeting, cash flow management, human resource management, and time management, all of which are core skills involved in operating a small business successfully. How they learned is also part of who they are.

Outstanding findings about educational experiences of this group were related to their levels of education, their use of both formal and informal learning strategies, and their continual learning for the purposes of improving and expanding their businesses. They are a group of lifelong learners. A conspicuous difference between the entire Entrepreneurial Assistance Program (EAP) population and the participants is the fact that 100 percent of the study group had some college education, mostly undergraduate and graduate degrees, compared to 61 percent of the EAP population as a whole. Two participants had doctorates; two had master's degrees, including one master's of social work; two had bachelor of fine arts degrees; six had bachelor's degrees; and the rest had two to three years of college. They also had years of work experience and both business and communication skills, and thus had a high degree of human capital accumulations that they brought to bear on their businesses.

This information provides support for one generally accepted theory that business owners with higher levels of formal education and "human capital" accumulations are more likely to be successful in business.[8]

However, the fact that the participants reported learning from a variety of people in a variety of ways makes a case for the informal learning that so often takes place outside of the classroom and that contributes to success. These women also engaged in more business and entrepreneurship education and training experiences than the general population, as noted earlier. This highly educated group of women had degrees in a wide variety of disciplines yet chose to further their learning by engaging in training and technical assistance programs that were targeted toward business skill development, as well as those programs in areas relating to specific products or services they were offering. In their own words, the women talked about their experiences with and views of education, especially how their lifelong learning was helpful to them in their businesses and why they enrolled in the entrepreneurship classes.

Formal learning is defined as classroom-based learning, including classes, seminars, workshops in which there is a formal "teacher," and a course or area of study.[9] All study group members were graduates of the EAP program, and they had all engaged in formal, classroom-based learning aimed at acquiring the particular skills related to opening and operating a small business. Their own words best describe their experiences with and perspectives on learning as a business development tool.

The Stories

Frankie is an accountant who was in the process of expanding her catering business by opening a sit-down restaurant with a take-out service, and a site from which she could continue and expand her catering business. She talked about why she enrolled in the EAP classes:

> And information I did not have I found to be vital...that was the preparation of the business plan. That's the key. You have to put it down, you're giving yourself a guide to accomplish certain things, at certain points.

Ava is the owner of a health-food/herbal product retail store. She, like Devya, had owned and operated her businesses for a long time—over ten years. They both marveled at that fact that they were running their businesses without knowing "anything" about business. The talked about why they had decided to take the EAP classes.

> *Ava*: I say, oh fool (laughter), you know nobody but God that saw you through this business. What basically happened, by the time I finished the course (EAP) I had found I did the complete opposite of what traditional business operations are. Nobody would believe I was in the store for ten years and didn't know

anything (laughter). You know?...I was really shocked....I took the course ...I got the whole blueprint for operating a business...to get the blueprint for establishing the business.

Devya: I decided to take the course...you have to have the knowledge. You get the training you need in order to do the work that you want to do. They let me know that my business from the financial end needs to look more like a business. I'm still running it the way I ran it when I first started.

Half the women talked about the formal degrees they had obtained or courses they took they felt affected the management of their businesses. Deborah, the owner of a flower arrangement/gift basket business said

I took merchandising and management in college. I went to Pratt. I got my bachelor's in Fine Art at Pratt....So, I went to school. And took courses in flower-making. I went to the Botanical Gardens and I also took classes at Parsons and FIT.

Jackie L., a designer and manufacturer of high-end hats, also went to Pratt Institute and then went on to the Fashion Institute of Technology for advanced millinery design training: "I went to Pratt Institute studying architecture first....I went back to FIT." She is still studying and sharpening her skills.

Other women talked about the degrees they had earned, some that related to directly to their businesses, and others that did not. Helen is particularly interesting because she is very different from the other women business owners: She is a Tibetan nun whose business is a not-for-profit retail and community services store. Her degrees relate directly to doing business and to her vocation:

My associate degree is in marketing. My (bachelor's) degree is in buying and merchandising. And I did my internship at Hong Kong, in China. In import and export.

Cheryl O., an artist and sculptor, has degrees in English and social work and has transferred that seemingly non-business knowledge to her successful business:

I have two and a half degrees. I was an English major in undergraduate school. I can make a lot of things sound good.

She illustrated how myriad skills are transferred. Yet, not all participants felt that their formal degrees in some academic disciplines helped with their businesses. For example, Ava, the health store owner, has a bachelor's degree in professional studies that she felt did not help her at all with her business. Other women had degrees that helped them decide what types of business they wanted to open. Patricia, the owner of a day care/after school educational center did her graduate work in reading. She also took additional specialized training that provided certificates, which enabled her to expand the scope of her business:

> I went to...because they were offering a course in child care, uh how to run a day care center or something...And when I did I was told I'd have to have some training, so I got my certificate there.

Nancy, the owner of a music production company, took many business courses in college, including marketing, economics, and business law, but decided she needed additional training. Another woman, Jackie K., the owner of an Afrocentric marketing and mail order catalogue business, announced somewhat diffidently: "I just want to sort of mention that, uh, last year I finished my Ph.D." The breadth and depth of human capital accumulations are illustrated by the kinds of formal postsecondary education reported by the participants. Many had also taken skill-based courses, seminars, and classes related to the type of business they were operating, which they felt necessary to acquire or upgrade their skills. For example, craftspeople and artists took additional courses related to "how to do" the craft as well as those in which they learned skills that could be translated into new products. Owners of service businesses also took courses related to the specific services they were offering. For example, Efua, who has a cleaning and janitorial service business, told me,

> I went back and took the class again. I took it for the second time....I took it for the cleaning service. That's when I originally started to go and do research and find out information about cleaning services and maid services and things like that.

Approximately half the others reported they took courses or attended seminars related to business management and skill development, such as accounting, computers, marketing, contract procurement, and the like, both before and after the EAP training. They were very clear about the effect of their learning on their businesses. Patricia said it well:

> I probably wouldn't be here if I hadn't taken that course. I probably would not be in business. And...there is no problem with my teaching but I didn't know business.

Informal learning is defined as any learning that occurs outside of institutional formal settings; it is non-routine in nature and occurs in noninstitutional settings.[10] It is a common yet often unacknowledged method of accumulating human capital, including cognitive knowledge and concrete skills. Given the history of Black people and education, including the need to hide their educational activities and doing so by using a variety of informal learning strategies, it is not surprising that many of the skills learned by this group occurred in informal and nonformal learning situations as well as those formal settings mentioned above. This type of learning is unfortunately not recognized or acknowledged for its worth. The learning experiences most often reported, whether in formal or informal settings, were experiential and self-directed learning.

In its simplest form, experiential learning is defined as "learning from experience or learning from doing."[11] Many women discussed the ways in which they learned to do business outside of the classroom. Devya said

> I discovered that advertising didn't work...that led me to know that this was not the way to do it. Everything that happens I view it...as a learning experience.

Efua was clear about the role of learning by doing:

> I think the everyday running of the business is the best learning experience. You don't know until you do it. I mean anybody can tell you what they want to tell you but it's nothing like that actual every day dealing with payroll, dealing with taxes, dealing with the bank...

Paulette, who owns an accessory business she started by selling in flea markets, says

> I was in business before. From experience...so you learn...that this consistency and there is like a routine that business must, you must be predictable in business.

Cheryl O.'s words tell us something a little different about the role of experience; that is, that it can teach you what you don't want to do, which can be a very important lesson.

> It was...experience in...what it's like to have a store and to know that I never want to do that again...but again it was a way of acquiring experience.

Many of the women talked about self-directed learning—learning that they decided was necessary and that they planned in informal settings and nonformal ways. They also measured the outcomes of the learning, particularly how they were able to transfer new knowledge and skills to their businesses. Those activities included researching the environment, finding resources for information, seeking advisors, asking questions, and learning from the books they found. Cheryl H., a young, thirty-something single mother, started out as a baker and creator of custom cakes for birthdays, weddings, and other special events. She decided she had the creativity to become a balloon designer and decorator, having come into the business by decorating when requested and without any formal training. She recalls how she learned this very specialized skill and connected with its trade association:

> I started. At first I taught myself. But then I started seeing um... something in Macy's and I was like I really want to know how to do that and I searched the library. I couldn't find it. I was like how am I going to learn? I called different companies and no one would tell me anything. Yeah, ... I found one book and I decided to xerox the whole book. . . . I called the number in the back and the lady was "oh I'll send you the brochure, we have a whole library and videos you can learn from." And that's how I got started.

Patricia started her educational business as a day care center but then,

> When I started this business, something told me, nobody but something told me, ... that I should look into something about after school. So when I started making calls I found I was nowhere near qualified for this. So, I buy a lot of books. I love reading those books and as I read I teach myself.

Sandy worked as a manager in a city government office and decided she wanted something more and better and started her own family-run business. She wanted something more out of her business than money but wanted to experience inner growth as well. Part of that growth was in the acquisition of her skills and expansion of her knowledge:

> I learned a lot on my own. After I got out of college and then I decided I wanted to do this (her business) it was more self-taught... um, ...following my instinct. There was so much I had to learn on my own.

I have discussed the learning experiences and educational levels of these entrepreneurs in some depth for a number of reasons. First, the findings belie prevailing myths about Black women and their knowledge, skills, and abilities, especially when it comes to business. The prevailing notions about Black women as consumers, as "welfare queens," and as employees imply that Black women do not have viable business skills and do not own "real" businesses, Oprah notwithstanding, contribute to the myth. Second, images of highly educated and highly skilled Black women are all but unseen in the media, which shapes perceptions and perpetuates myths in the wider society. The documentation of their educational accomplishments corrects some of the record. People need to know that we are educated and how we use that education. Third, stories of the transferability of formal educational achievements to the business arena in nontraditional ways may be helpful to all would-be entrepreneurs who are thinking about starting businesses in their areas of expertise or avocation. Yet, levels of educational achievement and learning strategies are but one description of the women. Who they are in terms of population demographics is also important in understanding the standpoint of these Black women entrepreneurs.

Demographic Descriptions

The small number of participants, not unusual in qualitative research, admittedly created a number of limitations of the study but, as discussed, provided windows into the world of a group of women who are fairly typical of women of the African diaspora in the United States. They are ordinary women whose stories provide us with a glimpse into their motivations, hopes, and fears about doing business. The demographic information about the group serves to illustrate their differences as well as their commonalities with women and entrepreneurs in general and is therefore useful.

The age of the participants acquaints us with who they are on a developmental level. Nobody in the study group was under age thirty. A majority of the group was between thirty-one and forty years old; there was one participant (Devya) who was over sixty years old. The study group participants were slightly older than the EAP population as a whole. They started their businesses later in life and continued to run them at a later age. One of the questions this finding raises is: Is maturity relevant to success in business? Or was the pattern just typical for this group of women?

Birthplace and birth language show us that the women, all of whom were doing business in New York State, came from a variety of places of origin, both national and international. The majority of the group was from the Northeast and the South; it is interesting that the two people from the Midwest both came from Detroit, a city with a strong business development history and background for women, as with the Detroit Housewives League activities. Three individuals were from the Caribbean, and the one person born in England is of Caribbean extraction. Caribbean women have a long and deep tradition of entrepreneurship. Two participants were bilingual, one English/Spanish learned from birth and one English/Tibetan. Helen, the Buddhist nun, learned and is studying Tibetan as part of her present work and vocation, which is part of her business. Place of birth may make a difference in the way in which entrepreneurship is seen or valued. Family of origin is also of great consequence in entrepreneurship.

The presence of entrepreneurs in families has been found to be a significant factor in the desire to do business as well as success in business. A few women specifically recalled working or being "apprenticed" in a family business. They told stories about working in their family businesses from a

very young age and learning not only about the value of business ownership
in general but also very specific business skills—accounting, stocking and
doing inventory, purchasing, marketing and selling, customer relations—
from their childhood experiences in the family business. They talked about
how they learned to do business in their families, outside of formal learning
situations, by observation, mentorship, and apprenticeship. Efua, who has
the cleaning business, was born in the South and recalls learning from her
grandmother:

> My grandmother worked for, oh, . . . very rich people and cleaned um
> very large homes. Mansions and things like that. And . . . I used to go
> with her and she used to tell me like this is how you're supposed to
> clean. This is what you're supposed to do. This is how you, people
> look for this and you know people look at that. And you're suppose
> to, you know, clean your baseboards, wipe them down, this and that.
> So I used to, you know I did that and . . . I know about what to do and
> how to clean from early childhood.

Frankie, the restaurateur, remembers learning from her uncle, also in the
South:

> I mean, I have been taught many things over the years because my uncle
> had his own store down south. He had a grocery store. . . . When I first
> started learning to count, I would go in and help him in his little store.
> I've been handling money since that time. I would pay his bills, . . . get
> on my little bicycle and ride into town and pay his bills for the grocery
> store. I had no idea or hadn't even thought I was being groomed for
> entrepreneurship from the time, from the age of about 5 or 6.

Helen, who was born and spent her childhood in Barbados, told a slightly
different but similar story:

> I probably went down there (grandmother's store) from 6 years old
> until I left . . . Because my grandmother ran a boutique. It wasn't even
> really a store. What it was, was it was when the ships came from the
> harbor. It started out as racks. Clothing racks. . . and they would make
> all these dashiki things for the tourists and real cool shirts. So it was in
> my heart . . . (selling) was kind of in my blood.

Family configuration is also noteworthy in entrepreneurship, especially
as motivation for starting a small business, for when the business is started,
for how it is structured and managed, and for whether it is successful. Several
women in the study are single with children. About a quarter of the population are married, the remainder single, which includes never-married,
separated, and divorced or widowed people. Many of the single women

reported having a committed, ongoing relationship with a male partner, most of whom were supportive and helpful in the development and operation of the businesses. A little less than half of the women with children had children who are school-age, for whom they are responsible, and the others had grown children and grandchildren and were thus free from day-to-day parenting responsibilities. Approximately half had no children.

As with their entrepreneurial ancestors, family often provided a strong motivation for doing business. In the early days of the country, self-manumission or freedom from bondage and manumission of family members was a driving force in entrepreneurship, as was economic survival. In the present, family survival, economic self-sufficiency, prosperity, and well-being are related motivators. As mentioned earlier, reports on women business owners indicate that Black women start businesses on their own, without partners, more frequently than other female business owners. Starting and maintaining businesses stretches women in terms of time, energy, responsibilities, and stress. Achieving and maintaining balance for self and family is therefore especially challenging for Black women entrepreneurs.

Balance

Sharon is a forty-something educator whose avocation is business. She is in the process of establishing a tea gallery where women, especially women of color, can gather to drink tea, nibble treats, and talk to each other in a relaxed atmosphere. She had decided on a tea gallery as opposed to a coffee shop, where people load up on caffeine and often work while they talk, because she wanted to provide a different ambiance and feeling. Sharon has researched the calming and healthful effects of tea, tracing its roots to ancient traditions in many cultures. She is also a wife, mother, and educator who is admittedly searching for a holistic balance and calmness in her own life. As an educator, she envisions this tea shop as a place that will also provide a space for discussions, education, and information on a variety of topics, including health, healing, and spirituality.

Sharon is seeking to provide a place where women can step out of their lives for a little while and do something for themselves. The other component of her business is consulting, through which she conducts conferences for, by, and about women that deal with the above-named issues; she provides them a day off not taken up by doctor's visits, parent–teacher conferences, and sick days. Her goal is to provide places and spaces that will contribute to other women achieving balance for themselves, even if only for a little while. In doing so, she feels better able to provide some respite for herself while creating a viable business. She is concerned with "positivity, wellness, wholeness, all the things that women need to support them in their healthy lives."

Balancing family life and business has always been an issue for women around the world and throughout time. In fact, the need to balance work and family is the factor thought to most distinguish female from male entrepreneurs. Because women have always been and remain the primary caregivers of children and managers of households, their entry into business is almost always a "second shift." Coupled with prejudice and discrimination grounded in the patriarchal Euro-American worldview that dominates the market economy, women in general have been left out or barred from the mainstream of business activity. Often faced with the necessity of providing supplemental income for their families or, in many cases, total financial support for the families, women of color and non-elite White women have always had an especially hard struggle with achieving balance in their lives. We know, for instance, that enslaved women had to work in the fields all day long and work for their families' survival at night by gardening, sewing, cooking, and cleaning. The house servants fared little better, being at the beck and call of their owners during the day and throughout the night; many were also forced to clean, weave, sew, and the like at night. Free women worked continuously, as their wages were little better than nothing, and when they needed to produce goods and services for sale as well as caring for family, that work could only be done at night. Achieving balance was elusive, but by connecting with other women and with the community, Black women in earlier times overcame even the most difficult of circumstances to have families, vibrant social and spiritual lives, and even moments of joy and happiness.

In modern times, entrepreneurial women face challenges of work time and personal time. For the women in the study, balance was critical and involved values and relationships. The components of balance for these women not only included valuing and seeking balance between business and life but also seeking a holistic sense of self through the integration of mind, body, and spirit—a connection to the importance of spirituality in their lives. They were also concerned with helping to provide balance for others, especially other women, and valuing money not for itself but its ability to provide an enhanced and balanced lifestyle as well as empowering them to help the lifestyles of others.

Sandy, the owner of the family-run apparel retail and manufacturing business, believed:

> I wanted to do more with my life than having a 9–5 job. I wanted to do something that was family oriented. If you're going to have financial growth then you have to have some kind of inner growth along with that.

Frankie, the cook and accountant, knew what was vital for her:

> So just, you know those being with family, coming together and having dinner, and sitting at the table, food on the table ... and just talking, laughing, that's what is priceless. That's what is meaningful.

So I have dubbed the phrase of "we've been there, we've done that, now we've got to get wealthy for fun!"

Ava, the health-food store owner, was also clear about what she wanted:

But that stuff (conspicuous consumption) doesn't interest me. I just like to have a—what do they call it? An even keel life. It's a business. I'm just doing it. But it's a fulfillment for me. Yeah, I have fun.

Finally, Lani, a relatively young thirty-something woman who is the owner of both a shoe repair and a restaurant with a partner says:

I can honestly say that I'm,...I feel good about what I'm doing because I'm not hurting anyone. When I go to bed at night I can, so for me the business is simply an extension of myself.

Work/life balance or achieving balance among family, business, social, and personal needs and achieving an inner balance, including and having a sense of happiness and fun, was closely related to personal satisfaction—a qualitative measure of success. For these women, achieving balance was a goal and a measure of success. Achieving balance is most often a matter of time.

Time

Deborah is in her forties. Her day job is court stenographer; her business is creating Afrocentric floral arrangements, centerpieces, and baskets for individuals, groups, companies, and organizations. She is the divorced mother of two school-aged children. Her business is successful and growing. She has had several opportunities to take it to a much higher level of business development but cannot because of time constraints resulting from her attempts to balance family, work, and business. Time poverty is a major issue in her life.

It takes time and energy to meet the challenges of entrepreneurship and to make things work well. Burbridge defined "time poverty," as occurring when women who do "double duty" of working and raising families become increasingly "time poor," which directly affects income data used as measures of economic success.[12] This concept can be applied to entrepreneurship, when women, especially Black women, do "triple duty"—starting businesses, working for wages, and raising families while fighting racism and sexism along the way.

For the modern-day Market Women, time poverty sometimes results from being the only person running the business, which of course affects its quantitative success. As reported earlier, Black women, possibly more often than other women, including other groups of women of color, are likely to own and operate business on their own, without partners, and to run them

on a part-time basis while working full-time. These responsibilities constitute a very heavy load. A related matter is the need for financial security
for families, often headed by single women—as was the case with more
than half the participants. The need for absolute security, including a regular salary and health benefits, often precluded their ability to leave their
day jobs to run their businesses full-time. Jill Nelson, in a discussion of her
work as a journalist for a major newspaper, described herself as being in
"Volunteer Slavery" on her job.[13] Nelson's connection to work and
"slavery" calls to mind the discussion of "master's time" versus "slave
time" in Hine and Thompson's exploration of bondwomen's hiring themselves out to make money for manumission.[14]

There seems to be consistent and compelling evidence for the time
poverty experienced by the Black women entrepreneurs in the study, supported by the fact that almost all of the respondents talked about this issue
during the interviews. Some areas of concern were specifically related to the
running of the business:

> *Jackie L.*: I'm one person. One person pretty much runs this busi-
> ness....Me, I'm the only one.
>
> *Wendy*: But if you miss a step, then you'll have a problem with trying
> to do two things as one time. Now with my schedule, I mean...
> that's what happened sometimes.

Some women made reference to the fact that they had too little time to
go to networking events they knew would help them grow their businesses.
Nancy, the owner of a music production company, said:

> It's through no fault of the association (professional trade), I need to
> put more energy, but right now as I said...my time, um,...is
> somewhat limited as I'm sure you know, everyone else's is.

Robin, the ballet school owner, echoed those sentiments:

> I'm still in the stages where I'm standing here and staying...until 11
> o'clock at night. And I may, I may...have to miss a function.

Jackie L., the hat designer, concurs:

> The previous two years, almost three years, I've really just didn't have
> time to go to the activities, the breakfast...They do (networking
> group) a monthly breakfast.

Networking, a way to build social capital and contribute to business
success, presents many opportunities but, as can be seen from the above

statements, is not always accessible because of time. These issues often affect women entrepreneurs of varying ethnicities but do not have the same effect for women of higher economic classes. In addition, as we will see later, networking can also create problems distinctive to Black and minority women business owners.

The most pervasive and powerful reported indicators of time poverty involved family and business balance. They were especially true for those women who were single parents, most of whom were in very labor- and time-intensive businesses:

> *Efua*: I was constantly working....[S]ometimes I'd have to find somebody to watch my son while we go to the building [to work] because my daughter would be with me too [helping in the business].

> *Frankie*: You know I'm a single parent, divorced for almost thirty-some odd years, and being a parent, it...does not allow you to do those things, especially if you care about your children and care about what they're doing, where they are and who they are speaking with.

> *Paulette*: So I'm juggling a lot of things, and um, ...it's scary, and I know that...to make it work is up to me....I had to change my work schedule and start working nights....I needed to do that to go to the trade shows to go out and introduce myself to people...but so...when school starts, I have everything sort of set up because working and with the children...And....I feel good about it, but I feel overwhelmed a lot of the time because it's just me.

> *Cheryl H.*: I kept on saying I can't have a business because I just didn't think I could, you know,....I was just a single parent, how am I going to have a business? But then...I didn't know how to work out the situation with my son like who's going to take care of him...because I'm a real single parent. I've got to do everything with him. So I had to think of all these things.

Concern with the care of children and the involvement of children in the businesses, for pragmatic as well as emotional reasons, brings to light the family issues that make a difference in the business activities and decisions for these women.

Several of the women were in school while beginning their businesses, and three of them talked about not having enough time to go to classes and do well while starting and running their businesses and raising their children:

> *Deborah*: You know to do everything, and I was still running my business, too, so classes might interfere with my time schedule. I was trying to do everything.

Lani: You can't take courses over and over because they figure that you are really, that you need to do it so many times to learn it....And so I was determined to make good grades but at the same time um,...work with the business. And it just seemed to make good grades I've got to take less classes so that I can do the business too.

The concept of time poverty also strikes a chord with many of my adult students in higher education, most of whom are White. They too are trying to balance home, work, and school, and those who are single parents find the effort difficult and draining, and like the women in the study, they do it but pay a price. Those who are married with children experience a similar kind of time pressure as they return to school while maintaining their husbands and families. All understand that time poverty is a problem in many women's lives.

Burbridge's concept of being time poor also involved not having enough leisure time or time for one's self. Several women specifically mentioned lack of time for themselves and the effect on them mentally, physically, and socially. Sharon, who started the tea gallery and consulting business, said she wanted to provide

a time out that women generally don't take for themselves. Somewhere down the line you'll get a chance to do this. But then that's when I started to take care of me a little bit and do a few things for me. Things I had never done.

Other women talked about the personal price they paid in trying to do "everything."

Ava: Because I sleep maybe two hours at a time.

Nancy: I also realize I'm very tired.

Robin: I don't have much of a personal life or ah, you know...a good time or anything like that...[my friends say] "Get a life! (laughter)."

Cheryl O.: I don't do vacations and I don't spend a lot of money, and my house is in shambles (laughter).

Jackie K: I'd say there are certain disadvantages to being a single person—every now and then it would be like...it would be great to call home and say, "look, Hon can you do this? Can you do a load of laundry (laughter)?"

These Market Women are time poor for a variety of reasons. They have all made the choice to do business, delaying immediate and personal gratification. Many hope the financial success of the business will enable them to have a better lifestyle that is more balanced and includes leisure, relaxation, and time for themselves. The irony is that the time poverty they experience also precludes their businesses being seen as successful and interesting. They are judged as being small, inefficient and unsuccessful, resulting in a lack of equitable access to capital and markets and perpetuating the stereotype that Black women are lacking in business skills. The matrix of factors that affect women's business activities is complex and interconnected. Only by truly appreciating their experiences within their unique contexts and using multiple measures of success can statements be accurately made about their business acumen.

Burbridge, who fashioned the theory of time poverty, believes that to challenge the dominant economic paradigm of researchers, scholars, and educators, we need to examine the totality of factors and life challenges of Black women entrepreneurs. As we have heard many times, what doesn't kill you will make you stronger. The challenges, coping strategies, and triumphs of entrepreneurship have enabled women of the African diaspora, past and present, develop a strong sense of self.

[We need to recognize] the importance of kinship networks, time poverty and the valuation of unpaid labor and support received from extended family networks in conducting holistic research on Black women's economic lives.

—L. Burbridge, in *Boston, A Different Vision*, p. 117

CHAPTER 6

A Strong Sense of Self: Who and How They Are

If you only knew.

—Frankie

Throughout history, women of African descent have been warriors, merchants, educators, scholars, and leaders. They have also been wives, mothers, daughters, sisters, and nurturers. As a group, Black women have historically dealt with challenges raised by racism and sexism and view obstacles as "bumps in the road" to achieving their goals. They have negotiated the color line that turned into the color wall and the glass ceiling that, for them, is most often made of bricks. Their cultural traditions include resistance and resilience as well as faith, hope, love, and joy. The polyrhythmic realities of their multiple roles are also factors in their business lives but are rarely acknowledged.[1] This chapter presents narratives that illustrate the numerous roles Black women play in life and business, telling stories most people never hear. Consider these stories as they lend a glimpse into the world of these Black women entrepreneurs.

Frankie is a strong-willed, clear-thinking Black woman who described herself as a no-nonsense person with no failure in her. An accountant who worked in the corporate world and who cooked for others as a hobby for more than thirty years, she decided to start her own business, a take-out and sit-down restaurant specializing in Southern cuisine, when her full-time job was reduced to three days a week with a concomitant pay cut. She discussed the "trigger" that made her decide to start her business:

© Press Ill. Serv.

CHEERFULLY DOING THE WORK REQUIRED.

Transporting tan bark, to be used in connection with tanning leather. No slackers. The colored women did willingly and efficiently their part in helping win the war.

Cheerfully Doing the Work Required: African American women working in connection with leather tanning and in a lumber yard, ca. 1940–1945. Courtesy of the Schlesinger Library, Radcliffe Institute, Harvard University.

That's when I really made up my mind, you know, it's time for me to take charge of my own livelihood, sink or swim.... It's time for me to take charge, so I decided to start putting everything in position, you know. I mean, I have been taught many things over the years because my uncle had his own store.

Her discussions about the efforts she put forth to expand her catering business and to open her restaurant were replete with instances of overcoming obstacles, setting goals, and receiving support from families and "fictive" kin. She applauds the strength of Black women, herself included. When she talked about the things she had to go through, she shook her head and said; "if you only knew," referring to difficulties that were more than most people would have imagined, because "the obstacles are unbelievable." She attributes her approach to obstacles to her mother:

My mom, she identified it. She says these are,...look at obstacles as a learning experience. And that way I don't lose control. I stay focused, Okay?

Frankie gave examples of those obstacles. For example, she talked about the dissuasion she experienced when a counselor at SCORE (Service Corps of Retired Executives) discouraged her from trying to start a business:

About twenty years ago...I had gone to SCORE in New York... because I used to work in the building. I had gone there,...[A]nd they totally turned me around, totally....I understand the whole ramifications of them trying to discourage me, but I never forgot it. I never forgot it. And...[A]t that time I feel that I was not mentally mature enough to assume the responsibility that I'm going to be doing now. I wasn't ready....So by them discouraging me, I said Okay, okay for now....It's just a dream deferred for now.

She talked about the disrespect she encountered from her business counselor, whose job it was to assist her in preparing her loan application:

There's an individual that I deal with, he's supposed to be my counselor at the Small Business Development Center....He's supposed to be my counselor. However, I get the feeling...even though he is supposed to do certain things, or he's supposed to encourage, he'll say certain things to try and discourage you or to see what your reaction will be. He says something to you meaning, he could say well, you need a lot of money. And you can't so this unless — and then he's steadily watching you. And I'm saying to myself wait a minute, this is still America, right? And why —...[I]t's just like...a method that they try and keep you from going into business, all right.

When asked about who "they" were, she replied "White people, yeah, but more men than women." She also discussed the convoluted series of local red tape that put her restaurant opening back by almost a year and the racism she encountered in her mostly White suburban neighborhood.

> Out here, in . . . I find the um, . . . attitudes between the races are maybe twenty-five years behind the City. There's that much of a gap. They don't know how to deal with outspoken Black people. . . . My store's only 750 square feet. But they. . .what they're trying to do and what I have to do is unbelievable. They're trying to. . .[T]hey're doing everything they can to keep, me out of there. And. . .I'm not McDonald's. Or I've said to myself if they're trying so hard, well, then something's got to be happening down the road. There' just got to be. . . . And I've been paying my taxes, being invisible until now.

Frankie refused to be invisible or voiceless. Divorced for thirty years, she raised her children as a single mother. She was able to begin the business only after her children were grown. Frankie is also a grandmother several times over and is quite clear that she is growing the business for her grandchildren. She talked about the importance of family and her nurturing social capital network of family and friends, of her faith and her church, and of the support she received from colleagues, both Black and White.

> They [her family] have been trying to get me to do this for years, especially my sister. I have one sister. . . . I've been putting on parties for maybe what, twenty-five, thirty years already . . . my cousin just told me last week. . .she says "girl, you've been practicing a long time. It's about time you go ahead and make some money at it. All my family's been trying. My immediate family in addition to the extended family. They have been more than supportive.

She continued:

> I didn't realize how many people I told about I'm gonna do this business. My oil man asked "Are you still going to go into business? Then I urge you to take the [EAP] course at the center."
> You think of the PJ's [public housing projects] as a beehive . . . you have other families you grew up with that you live with and that you learn from all. . . . It's like one huge family, one neighborhood. They are the ones that are helping me financially, and morally, and spiritually to get into this thing.

Most of all, she demonstrated her resilience, determination, strength of will, and feisty sense of self:

Things don't come easy as far as I am concerned, right.... I have to pay my dues, all right. It's going to kick me, but I usually get it in the end, all right. And this is kicking me like you wouldn't believe... But I know that it's going to be Ok. So when I open... I think I'll take a deep breath and sigh a little bit... and continue. And not think too much about it. It has taken me a long time to get to this point.

I'm going to sell ribs on Route... whatever. We're going to do this... everybody tells me the same... "you're going to fail. You're going to fail." Outsiders... Studies have been done, da da da, we are not studies.... I got to the point, and I said "Look, don't tell me I'm going to fail. You don't know what's going to happen to me... and why are you telling me I'm going to fail? Well 93 percent [of new restaurants fail]... I could be in the 7 percent." It got to the point where I was getting an attitude. I'd walk inside, and I said "Look, don't even let it pass your lips."

He [a White man at a business event] says "Really? You're making your own business? Can you give me your recipe? I'm looking for a Kentucky Colonel" I said, "Who do you think gave him his recipe?" So... [H]e didn't have anything else to say. I said to him, "Do you have a lot of money...? and for a long time? Now that I have your card, I will make sure to keep your card in a safe place, because when I go on the NASDAQ, that's when I'm calling you." He gave me the strangest look. Couldn't believe it. And I meant it.

I know I can cook and I know I can count... so between the two... I'm not tap dancing or anything. I'm not puffing up feathers. These are just facts.

How They Are: Personal Characteristics that Contribute to Sense of Self

These few vignettes are representative of Frankie's approach to business and life and her multiple realities, many of which are echoed in the stories and words of others. The "self" or personality of the owner of a business is a major factor in business success.[2] When I asked the question "What personal characteristics do you have that make you a successful business owner?" each woman named at least two attributes they felt described or defined themselves as business owners. Many answers were clustered in areas that suggested a theme of sense of who and how they were, especially as they related to the ways in which they dealt with the challenges of doing business. Those characteristics most often reported included will or determination, strength, self-confidence, perseverance, resiliency, independence, and inner-directedness. Those personal attributes helped the women overcome obstacles, both business and personal, both racist and sexist. Many other personal characteristics mentioned are also usually associated with successful entrepreneurs. The women described themselves as hard-working, having a sense of responsibility, energetic, strong, risk-taking, flexible, and smart. Other attributes mentioned that had less to do with meeting challenges and more with the "art" of entrepreneurship included creativity and visioning. This group of women has also found ways to go over or around those "bumps." Their words paint a vivid picture as they describe and define themselves.

Overcoming Obstacles

Many of the women talked about obstacles. Deborah, a forty-something divorced mother of two school-aged children, who also works full-time, declared, "As long as I can stay focused I can get around obstacles. I can go through the obstacle. I can find another way."

As we heard from Frankie, focusing on her goals helped figure out ways to go over, get around, or go through obstacles. Persevering is also a strategy used to overcome obstacles. Many women described themselves as persevering, tenacious, or persistent in the face of obstacles or hurdles.

Devya, our meditation mentor, a retired widow with a grown son, says,

> Something I wanted to happen and that kept me going despite the, ah, intermittent lack of money, mistakes I made, not always knowing the right direction. I do have a vision that keeps me going. . . . [And] I have a good deal of perseverance. Faith and perseverance.

Efua, who owns a janitorial company, is a divorced woman with two grown daughters, two school-aged children, and a supportive partner. She says, "The best thing I have going for me is that I'm not going to quit."

Ava, who is a single woman with a health-food store, says:

> And I think if I had really any less commitment to this idea after some soul searching times, . . . I would have let it go. But even as I started to say it that I would let it go you know, I've had my fill, this is it, um, . . . I came back to it again.

Will and Determination

Closely related to perseverance is will and determination. Scott described Black women as having and needing a "warrior's will" to deal with the behemoth of racism and sexism in the United States.[3] One of the places this will and determination is most needed is in the arena of entrepreneurship. Almost all the women in the study described themselves as being willful, determined, or stubborn—which is common in Black women's self-definitions. Hard work also helped, and their words contradict one of the most pernicious but clearly unfathomable stereotypes about "lazy and shiftless" Black women—women who most often have always done "triple duty" in their lives.

Wendy, a single, engaged woman without children, who owns a bookstore, said:

> I think the determination [is] the key.... I've had my ups and downs but I keep it within myself and ... work it through.... They tell me I'm a workaholic. Constant work ethic, never giving up.

Jackie L., a married woman without children and designer of hats, says:

> Yeah, I'm stubborn. I won't give in. Yes, because I don't want to be another statistic.

Efua adds:

> I get what I want to get and I get it on my own terms. And usually I get what I want from everybody ... this is how I work and this is what you know you see here. This is what I want to do and this is how I'll bring it about.

Nancy, a single woman without children who makes music for and with others, says:

> People tell me, you know you're lucky. And I tell people, no, I've worked damn hard. I'm not lucky. Luck runs out, blessings are forever.

Sandy, a married woman with grown children who work in the family-run business, adds:

> I think my main characteristic is being determined to carry out my desires. I'm basically a nice person. You know, ... [P]eople like me. I have good people skills. I'm a hard worker.

Cheryl O., a married woman with one grown child, says:

> I really do work a lot and I really am tired three-quarters of the time. And my feet hurt, you know, my back hurts. I've got to load and unload by myself and then go to places that are strange ... [B]ut I'm also open to working damn hard.

Arlene, a single woman, owns and operates a full-service beauty salon and continues to work a full-time job as well. She tells us about her day, which illustrates the intersection of hard work, determination, and time poverty:

I'll come in here straight from my night, my night job. I'll come here straight...in the morning and sometimes I don't leave here until seven in the evening. I'll go home and shower, it's nine o'clock— 11:30 I've got to be on my way...It's exclusively mine (laughter). That's why, it's mine...I work really hard, I work really hard to get where I am.

Strength

One of the older cultural stereotypes about Black women is that of the "strong matriarch." That stereotype has its roots in the racist notions used to perpetuate slavery "[one of] two stereotypes of black women...the strong, maternal workhorse 'Mammy'" who could be worked hard without physical or emotional consequences.[4] A newer, modern-day version is that of the "strong Black woman" who can do it all—providing for family, work, and community. That stereotype, although on the surface seems more positive, can be harmful as well, as it does not allow for Black women's humanity, need for comfort, joy, and leisure.

However, strength is a characteristic of Black women, historically and culturally. White reminds us that Black women in chattel slavery drew on their main source of strength—each other—to survive. That strength has been evident in the ways in which the study group women handled struggles they encountered when opening and operating their businesses. Several women described themselves as being emotionally or physically strong, and usually both, as well as being energetic. Jackie L., the hat designer, talked about her ability to deal with crises in the business:

[I]t's made me tougher. Every little thing has made me tougher and stronger. Every little thing that has happened has made me tougher and stronger....And maybe it hasn't made me this screaming loud person on the outside or this ranting, raving lunatic on the outside or anything like that. Or because I think it hasn't really changed my demeanor a lot on the outside...but on the inside it's just made me very much stronger.

Cheryl O., the artist who talked about her feet and back hurting, stressed the idea of recognizing the need to be healthy and strong, in all ways:

I have a thick skin, at least externally. I mean...I may feel bad but you'll never know it. I was lucky enough to have not had a lot of crap happen to me in life. I mean crap can make you stronger if it doesn't kill you...I think I have good health, that's very important and a pretty high energy level. There's that whole physical thing that um,...is going to make a difference.

Robin, a single woman without children who runs the ballet company, has had similar feelings. When several "old-timers" in Black classical ballet said someone needed to start a school for it in Harlem and approached her, she replied:

That is what did it and I just went ahead from there. And that is why I felt the strength that, OK, I'll be the one to do it. You know, I'll be the one to do it because I know, I know I have the strength.

Physical and emotional strength are needed to succeed, and the women connected this kind of strength to their determination and ability to persevere. Interestingly, Herndl, in her discussion of the invisibility that led to the "invalidity" of nineteenth-century African American women's health issues, concluded that narratives written by Black women, such as Harriet Jacobs and Harriet Wilson, both of whom have been discussed earlier, had as one of their purposes a replacement of the racist notions of Black women's physicality with "a new model of womanhood in which physicality and spirituality are linked...that the African-American woman has a 'self.'"[5] Over a century ago, the notion of a holistic approach to life was essential to Black women's sense of self—and it and still is. However, the unrelenting need to keep things inside and the resulting stress has a price. That price is increasingly acknowledged by other Black women, who are writing self-help books for their "sisters" with suggestions for dealing with stress resulting from their polyrhythmic realities. Will and survival are success strategies the women have employed to mitigate that stress, and those efforts have built their confidence in themselves and their abilities.

Self-Confidence

One of the strategies these women use is a strong sense of self-confidence, which also helps overcome obstacles. Self-confidence is part of the development of the sense of self. Most of the women, including Frankie earlier and Deborah, described themselves as being self-confident, especially in their ability to run their businesses well.

Deborah is self-confident in her knowledge and abilities:

I know if I get the work I can do the work. and I can do it to the person's satisfaction and beyond....I know I can handle it....You know I may be small now but you [vendor] don't know what I'm going to be later and if you're not on this bandwagon when it takes off then someone else will be. I'm not nervous anymore.

Cheryl H. is a single woman with a ten-year-old son who talks about the pressure she encountered when she got a big contract to provide the balloon

decorations for a National Basketball Association event at Madison Square
Garden in New York City:

> It was pressure at first but something was driving me just to do it. It
> was pressure but in my mind I knew I could do it.

Jackie K. also knew her strength and skills:

> I guess it never occurred to me that I couldn't do it. And I don't know
> if it occurred to anybody else to suggest it either.

Helen, the Tibetan nun from Barbados, talked about how her grandmother,
who taught her to be an entrepreneur, helped instill a sense of self-confidence:

> I think it has a lot with being confident from a very young age, being
> self-confident. I remember my grandmother used to tell me that...
> how beautiful I was. And.... [T]hat reinforcement of somebody
> telling you, you are okay to begin with. And then you have a certain
> confidence level. You have a certain social level. And you're very at
> ease with yourself.

Sharon, the tea gallery owner with a doctorate, is married with two adolescent children. She is concerned with wellness and energy, and she feels
that hers contributes to her own self-confidence:

> What I've done in my younger years is to give my ideas away. I would
> give them to other people. You have the means, you have the
> resources. I think it will work...but it couldn't work with anyone else
> because they don't have the enthusiasm or sense of nurturance I had
> about this idea to grow this business in my heart first and in my mind.
> So...I don't think anybody could do it better.

Paulette, a divorced woman with two young children, who owns a accessories store, feels

> It's (selling) not a problem for me because I'm confident with what I
> do and the way that my display is. I think that more important.
> And...I believe I can make this into something if I keep, keep, keep,
> keep on.

Cheryl O., who is strong emotionally and physically, although her feet and
back hurt, says:

> I think I'm smart. Um,...I mean I don't want to seem like real...
> egocentric but I think it's just because of how I am. I'm pretty smart.

Inner-Directedness

For women of color, having a strong sense of self-confidence instilled at a very early age is important, especially because the outside world often tells them they are not smart, beautiful, or competent. With a daughter and granddaughters, the mother–daughter bond is often the location of the development of an inner sense of self and inner-directedness. Inner-directedness means people following their own minds, their own voices. Belenky et al., in their discussion of women's way of knowing, talk about the development of voice, mind, and self, but in connection to cognitive development.[6] These women had developed their voices, their minds, and their selves and were self-confident and inner-directed enough to express them and act on them in business:

Devya said: "I was just following what my head was telling me."

Deborah, in discussing her former partner and the differences they had that led to the breakup of the partnership and her operating the business alone, said:

> I learned that you can't tell every little thing. You can't show everybody...[A]lthough I'm not worried about that because if someone wants to make their success off with doing...copying off what I do, they're going to get stuck eventually. I have to just focus on what I have to do and where I have to go. What I'm doing now to get over it is I'm...focusing on what I want to do and where I want to go.

Helen, the Buddhist nun, said:

> You know, you have this other place you're coming from. And your mind is a lot stiller, so it gives you more wisdom. You know?

Lani, a single woman without children who sells health-food and repairs shoes, shared:

> I sort of deliberate on things a lot before I actually do them. I...[I]n that way I can be slow. I say well I do, yes, I do, I will you know....I'm slow about getting things done but I do get them done.

Nancy talks about her inner-directedness:

> I think about everything before I jump in. I tend to have tunnel vision. And don't let what other people say influence me. I can be very focused, intensely so....I'm very resourceful.

There is a cluster of personal characteristics associated with Black women—resiliency, will, determination, and strength and independence. The ability to focus, be proactive, and problem-solve is also evident. Interestingly enough, those characteristics are also associated with successful entrepreneurs. In this group, they are both the same and different from other entrepreneurs because of their context of being Black women in America.

Resiliency

A majority of the group talked about resiliency, making references to having "bounced back" after experiencing difficulties in business and in life. A few representative stories include Jackie L. talking about a major business setback when she placed a non-refundable large order she paid for and found unacceptable:

> Wait to see what happens. Have to get through this...and I had so many little ups and downs that I didn't even want to be here. I can't go on...And to me the fact that it didn't put me under makes me feel that I'm starting to become a business—a real business.

She persevered because, as she said earlier, she refused to become a statistic.

Ava talked about how she bounced back after almost losing her business. She bought the health-food store without knowing anything about the business and trusting her church sister from whom she bought it. When she went to take it over she found the inventory stripped, the books falsified, and the vendor list non-existent. Shortly after building the business back up, she had a major medical problem that required hospitalization, another setback:

> I had to rebuild the business after I got out of the hospital and recovered. And we started a process you know...[b]ecause if anybody knew the amount of problems that I had, when I mean, I can joke and laugh in the store all day long....When I got home, I'm on my knees and putting my keys in the door and crawl in the house (laughter). You know? With the amount of problems that I deal with.

Nancy talked about how she dealt with a series of crises in the three years before the interview:

> I had major surgery...was sued...all in one year. Then, I was involved in a healing process. It's been a trying three years. it's been a trying time for me...Emotionally, financially but when I get depressed um you know...if I get down about something I say look where you came from. Remember your idea was just an idea, look how it's germinating. Look at the germination of your idea, look at the development of it...And that keeps me going forward.

Independence

The desire to be independent is one of the strongest motivators for people to begin their own businesses. Somewhat surprisingly, fewer than half of the participants described themselves as being independent when asked about personal characteristics. Those who acknowledged they were independent personalities said they wanted to own their own businesses for a variety of reasons, including wanting to be their own boss. Their sense of independence also had an effect on the way in which they financed and managed the businesses:

> *Jackie L.*: Well, I wanted to have my own. I thought it was really important not to rely on other people to provide security in your old age and you know you're getting older, just in your life in general.

Patricia, a married woman, mother and grandmother, and educator who had had a long career, started her own learning center because:

> But I knew and I still know I will not go back to work for anybody.... When the decision has been made, I mean ... I'm the only one, I just throw it up in the air.

Jackie K., a single woman who just completed her doctorate while beginning her mail-order small business admits "I'm a pretty independent person."

Wendy, the bookstore owner, is a fiercely independent person who did not want to become too dependent on her mentor or on outside financing for her business:

> I try not to, you know, I don't want to be owing anyone.... I speak to her [mentor] ... you know ... but I try not to be very dependent.... I don't think I've probably ever had to ask for money but once (laughter) and um ... because I have this weird thing of not wanting to owe anybody.

Creativity

In addition to the characteristics mentioned above, a sense of self can also encompass attributes that contribute to the "artistic" nature of entrepreneurship. Creativity, visioning, and flexibility are clusters also associated with Black women, who know how to make a way out of no way, and with entrepreneurs who create new businesses or new ways of doing things. Again, Black women entrepreneurs, as members of both groups, exhibit qualities of both. Various study group entrepreneurs described themselves as being creative. They did so in two ways—first in terms of artistic creativity by those who described themselves as artists or designers, and second by those who see themselves as having the ability to create new ideas, products and services. Artistic creativity is part of the cultural tradition of Black women; art is used as an expression of shared experiences, histories, and vision for the future. As was seen earlier, many artists, craftspeople, and sculptors used Afrocentric designs, materials, and images that reflected themselves and their culture. The creative artists among the group shared those approaches with many of their predecessors discussed earlier. Deborah describes herself as a floral designer and artist; others are Jackie L., a high-fashion hat designer; Cheryl H., an event decorator/cake artist; and Cheryl O., an artist and sculptor who uses wood as her main material. They all talked about their creativity as artists and entrepreneurs:

> *Deborah*: I get satisfaction out of creating and designing, not really multicopying things over and over and over again.
>
> *Jackie L.*: I started making clothes for large women. I started taking their ends [a clothing design firm] and making hats to go with the clothes.
>
> *Cheryl H.*: I love using my hands. I like taking nothing and making something out if it. I would've never said I was creative. Nope...Everybody else says it. It's been very helpful to me to be creative and venture out and do new things. I'm always looking to do something I never did before.
>
> *Cheryl O.*: Mostly, I was using scraps of wood (left over from her husband's business) from the woodworking business...scraps, yeah, scraps of wood and putting them together and making, um, sort of...contemporary kinds of pins and stuff....I also have a real good eye for...and I think for seeing...how materials can be used in unusual ways and I'm open to that and I think that's because I have no art training

New businesses are often started by individuals doing old things in new ways, creating new products, and offering a new way of delivering services. Several participants felt they were able to provide creative solutions to challenges and problems, defining their creativity in that way. Not surprisingly, part of that group was the same as the self-defined creative artists:

> *Devya*: I was always strong and creative. It [the business] created another scenario. I then had to, to do and...create the business in another way. I created jobs too.

Jackie K.: I'm creative ... I'm not the artsy-craftsy type, but ... I can figure out how—I can say I know this is possible and that there's a way to do it. And I will work until I can figure out how to get it done.

Sharon: It's just to point out that we have a different niche, a different way of approaching it. It's not traditional. So I can take the same elements of what I do and shape them into a new day each time.

Flexibility

The ability to be flexible and change directions when necessary to sustain the business is closely related to creativity; this personal characteristic was mentioned by almost 100 percent of the participants. Flexibility is also the hallmark of small businesses and a strategy used when the market changes quickly and businesses have to change rapidly to survive or remain competitive.

Wendy talked about her initial goals for her multiethnic bookstore—opening a retail store right away—and realized

Then the reality set in that at first it would not be possible, it's not feasible, it would not be feasible to get that done ... So I went to Plan B. And Plan B was starting basically mail order, gathering customers that ... so [that] eventually when I do open up I would still have a solid customer base.

Robin discussed how and why she had to change the focus of her ballet school, from a large, eclectic group of teens to a smaller troupe focused on and capable of excellence:

I know this is a transition I have to make. And again, before I never even thought in that direction. We did a Black history tour that was more successful. That was when I dwindled it down to the five best girls.

Vision

Being visionary or having a vision for their businesses and the future was a personal characteristic also reported by all but one of the women. As described by the participants, their vision provided motivation, sustenance, and inspiration that enabled them to persist and prevail in their businesses:

Devya: People have told me that I have a mission and I think that way as opposed to, and I do have a mission. I had a vision.

Deborah: The most important thing is that you need to have a vision. It's the vision that keeps you going.

Lani: Yeah, I have a vision. Because I felt like this...if I make it good.
If I don't make it I'll try something else. I'm not gonna curl up
and just not do nothing any more.

The women also described themselves as being optimistic, efficient,
able to recognize opportunity, committed, concerned for high quality, risk
taking, and proactive. Those characteristics will be illustrated more fully in
the descriptions of how they began and how they manage their businesses.
In addition to personality characteristics, social characteristics such as race,
ethnicity, gender, and class also affect business activity and outcomes.

Race and Gender

Those personality characteristics described above are also identified as
being typical of entrepreneurs in general, but Black women entrepreneurs'
strong sense of self and will have been especially necessary to enable them
to deal effectively with the "behemoths" of racism and sexism in addition
to the challenges of entrepreneurship. Part of the way these women are is
shaped by their experiences with racism and sexism in their personal and
business lives and the ways in which they dealt with these issues. There was
a specific question asked of the study group about their feelings as to
whether and to what extent their race or gender affected their business
success. The answers to this question were organized by identifying factors
felt to affect business activities and success and whether they were perceived
to be positive, negative, or neutral.

Most of the women of the group initially stated that race or gender had
an effect on their business activities and success, both positively and negatively. A few, Wendy, Efua, Ava, and Lani, initially felt that neither race
nor gender had anything to do with what they had achieved or experienced,
either positively or negatively.

Wendy, born and raised in Trinidad:

I think with my personality, the...race or gender really doesn't come
to play much in certain things....Because of what business I'm in
[multicultural books], I'm sort of versed with anything that comes
up. For instance, the majority of people [at book-selling events] were
of other races and we got along fine. I mean basically because I can
talk about other things....I think people have taken me on my own
merit.

Efua, born and raised in the United States:

Um, I can't say I think it has a lot to do with it. But it did have something
to do with it...my first contract had something to do with me.

Both these women rightfully pointed out they felt their own uniqueness and force of personality had more to do with their business success than their race or gender. Individuals have their own distinctive ways of operating—their own characters—and Black women are no less unique in their own distinctive ways than any other individual; individuality is part of their humanness, which is often overlooked in discussions of their lives. For example, bear in mind the differences in the perceptions of Ava and Lani. Ava, born in the United States, said, "I don't really think [race] had anything to do with it." However, Lani, born in Guyana said:

I don't think being Black really, really influenced my success or failure. Would I have failed in any way, I don't think it would have been because of race.

However, as they continued to talk about this issue, without prompting, they recalled incidents and experiences, related to their being either Black or female, that they felt affected their success. For example, Wendy felt that her personality was such that neither race nor gender was a major factor in her business success, but then she said that because her product line is predominantly Afrocentric, most of her customers were of her own race—an admittedly positive effect of race on her business. She also acknowledged that being a woman going into business for herself in the late 1990s was a positive when it came to accessing loans.

I mean a woman, [B]eing a woman will help you in certain situations.... If I was going for any types of loans or stuff like that, then I can say basically... because I was a female certain rules apply for me since certain loans would apply to me.

Efua too talked about how being a Black woman, in addition to her very forceful, confident, hard-working personality, did have an effect on obtaining her first contract at an organization where the director was a woman and the facilities manager was a man of color:

The fact that you are a woman and you're a Black woman in business, they try and help you, you know to get in business... do business with them.... I think the person at the time was the facility manager, a Hispanic guy, and I think he... was impressed with the fact I was a minority and a woman in business.... [A]fter I went and talked with him we had like almost an instant bond... and I think he respects me you know... for being a woman and a minority and took that chance... going out there and trying to start a business of my own.

Similarly, Lani didn't think race affected her business success but, when discussing gender, considered that being a woman might have made her more determined to succeed. She is a small, slight woman whose first of two businesses was repairing shoes.

> Being a woman made me all the more determined. Because I was, prior to doing the bagels, working with organic food, I was doing shoes and people would say don't do shoe repair. And sometimes there were times that you know people came in with, fellows with big jobs to put a whole sole on the bottom of a Timberland boot, and when I took it and looked at it and said I'd do this and that with the shoe, they'd laugh and say you're going to do that (laughter). I don't believe you're going to do that. And there were these big fellows looking down at me and I thought "I'll show him when he's come back to pick up his shoes." (laughter). And perhaps, maybe the fact that I, being a woman, perhaps that did impact me. Maybe it was sort of a driving force to actually accomplish, do, or accomplish....Make it better than, or as good as any man could.

Ava, in contrast, only used her Black femaleness when she needed it: "I only project the black—my being a black woman, when I see something I don't like."

Thus all of the four eventually reported positive effects resulting from being Black or female.

It is interesting to note that two of the four, Wendy and Lani, were not born in the United States but, rather, came from countries in which Black people were in the majority. In contrast, Jackie L. and Helen, born in England of Jamaican descent and in Barbados, respectively, felt their Blackness definitely was a positive in business.

> *Jackie L.:* Yeah, I think even the fact of starting with nothing to me seems, it's probably...a very Black thing, a Black trait. And it's not because we enjoy it or that we're even so great at it, we just...we have no choice, we have to do it, you know....Having to create something out of nothing because it's not fun and it's not a good thing. But I think black people have had to do a lot of that. And um,...[I]t's kind of a terrible thing to say because for me personally I don't consider myself a racist in any shape, form or anything at all, it's just...it's not in me. But I am very, how can I say um,...being Black to me is something to be very proud of. I'm proud of being Black.

She echoes Nikki's Giovanni's thoughts about making something out of nothing from necessity, and she taps into Black women's humanity and the difficulties faced and conquered because "we have to."

Helen, born confident in Barbados and presently practicing a form of religion not usually associated with Black women, thinks:

I think my race has really helped. Because coming from Barbados, from a child...I can interact with all different kinds of people. Because of that boutique, they were all tourists...So absolutely I have an edge, I have very good social skills from young, a lot of cockiness. So, I don't see myself...[A]lthough I am a minority, I don't operate out of being a minority. And I don't keep around people that tell me how bad Black is or how bad you are doing. I'm not saying I haven't experienced, you know...uncomfortable situations because of my color, but that never stopped me in any way. We [the convent business] can get money for me being a woman and for me being a black woman. I have never in my lifetime worried as a negative. I've always made it a positive. Not that I haven't been discriminated against—but it never stays in my mind.

More people felt race was a positive influence on their business; a lesser number reported that gender was positive. Their own words tell us about why they had that belief and perception.

Devya: They were pleased to find out I'm Black. It plays a big part in teaching [meditation] to the African American community.... Gender for sure. In order to help people grow and develop, in order to get past their fears...and everything else that is stopping them, the nurturing, the maternal nurturing I provide. I know when I'm pulling the mother out.

Paulette: I think being Black and a woman right now is a big plus. I think this is a good time for women to go into business for themselves. There are a lot of programs featuring women right now. So I think being a woman right now is great.

Cheryl H.: When we did the NBA [balloon decorations] job, they were so impressed we were Black and could do that type of job.

Jackie K.: I was able to say some things about Black women's experiences (in her dissertation) as a result of making the study comparisons to white women.

Sandy: My race, because they [Black people] are very supportive. And they provided me with my best word-of-mouth advertising.

In contrast, fewer people described negatives: Half reported off-putting incidents around race, and a third described negative effect on their businesses because of gender:

Devya: African Americans have a history of a little bit of abuse here and there in time. And the African American community has a good reason to be paranoid.

Jackie L.: I think the worst thing in the world is to be a poor, old Black woman.... Being a woman in this society, it's already literally

second class...it's just a male society that we live in and like
everything males get privileges. I mean...[W]hen I go to different
places or I go into stores and I talk, the sales people just the way
they treat you...if there's a man "yes sir" and I have to wait.

Ava: Nobody looked at the potential I had in accounting. They
thought all Black women should be phys. ed. [physical educa-
tion] teachers.

Robin: Boys are turned off on ballet. Because they're like oh that's
White stuff....And I had a hundred girls on point and heard
blah, blah, blah....Black girls are not supposed to dance point.

The story of Nancy's encounter in a music supply house and the way
in which she dealt with it are illustrative of positives and negatives, based
on race and gender, and how they can be overcome. She and her business
associate, also a Black woman, were in the market for some high-end studio
equipment:

We proceeded to go downstairs and a guy stopped us and he said "Oh
no. you can't go down there, um...someone has to be with you."
Yeah...[S]o I said "Oh really." And Ah you know...the first thing I
thought was here we go again. So I was annoyed and said "Let's go." I
experienced both sexism and racism.

But then, right as she was ready to leave the store, she turned around, went
back in, and asked why she had to have someone go downstairs with her. The
White male clerk explained it was a store policy for everyone because people
often stole little parts from instruments and equipment, making it impossible for the store to sell them without all their attachments. She explained what
she had thought and the clerk assured her racism was not behind the rule.
He asked her name and business and assured her he would inform the owner
that when she came in she would be accommodated. She continued with the
story:

The next time I had gone into the store, he said "Hi...can I ask your
name?" And I said yes and he said "oh," I mean he fell all over
himself (laughter). So he says "If you ever need any equipment that
you don't want to buy, we'll loan it to you free of charge." So if I had
left that store with some kind of sentiment, of it's a race thing and not
have gone back, number one, I would have been left with a negative
impression of the store. But also I would have missed out on an
opportunity to build a relationship.

A somewhat but not really amusing end to the story was that when the
recording studio was all set up, a young son of a friend came to visit and

The little boy looked around and said "Wow, I didn't know women could own this kind of stuff!"

Race and gender have been and can be impediments, but they have to be tested, as demonstrated by Nancy's story. The last parts of the story show us that stereotypes, both gender and racial, start at a very early age and that building good relationships with vendors and suppliers is critical to good business management. Nancy recognized that fact and acted on it.

That more women reported positive and negative effects resulting from race indicates that they feel race is more important than gender in their business experiences. However, several felt that both race and gender affected them, which gives credence to the need to identify the intersections of race and gender in business and in life. Those who described negative experiences also made it clear that positive personal characteristics—will, determination, stubbornness, creativity, and strength—were the things that enabled them to overcome the negatives. All who discussed negative experiences, either as a result of race or gender, concurred that the encounters only made them more determined to pursue their dreams of owning their own businesses and achieve their own personal goals. Frankie and Cheryl O. remind us that Black women cannot afford to be bifurcated or split into categories of race or gender:

> *Frankie*: These are life experiences. Don't be ashamed of where you come from because that was all part of this that got you where you are.
>
> *Cheryl O. knows*: They provide you with a history. I learned a lot of things because I was Black and grew up in a Black neighborhood and went to a Black church and went to a Black college. And there is a kind of security you develop because of that and if I had not been, I wouldn't be who I am. The other thing I think about is that...gender has been helpful as well as race. Those two things have a lot to do with making you who you are.

Finally, Sharon's words explain the benefits of being a Black woman in life and in business:

On the positive side, it unleashes so much wonderful stuff!

CHAPTER 7

Capital Accumulation: What They Do and How They Do It

I see as my first work to draw around me the women...to put their mites together, put their hands and their brains together and make work and business for themselves.

—Maggie Lena Walker, in Drachman,
Enterprising Women (pp. 131, 133)

Money is sharper than a sword.

—West African Ashanti saying

The "wonderful stuff" from the last chapter is not a term easily associated with business development and the economic theories that underlie entrepreneurship. Economics is considered to be a "rational" discipline, based on numbers and linear equations that profess to measure the economic status of countries and individuals. Those numbers produce macro-, or large-scale, and micro-, or small-scale, economic statistics that permeate our lives and determine the ways in which we are seen and treated. The rationality of Black women's businesses has rarely been addressed; in fact, their presence on the economic scene had all been ignored by mainstream economics, the Academy, and the media. The story of these modern-day Market Women—their efforts at financial capital accumulation via entrepreneurship—are discussed in this chapter, which explores how the women started their businesses, how they accumulated capital, and how they run and value their businesses. The chapter also

Grand Officers Juvenile Department I.O. of St. Luke. Courtesy of National Park Service, Maggie L. Walker National Historic Site.

highlights their logical as well as caring approaches to capitalism that reflect their unique way of doing business as women of color in market-driven America.

Money: Raising, Making, and Keeping It

Paulette is a business owner, a mother, a sister, a friend, a mentor, and a community advocate. A divorced mother of two who enjoys an amicable and supportive relationship with her ex-husband, Paulette is also a devout convert to Islam. She is the owner of a thriving accessories store located in the heart of Harlem, New York, one of the premier Black communities in the United States. The story of why and how she began her business, financed it, expanded it and manages is illustrative of her business skills, management ability, and values. The intersection of human, or learning, and social capital activities with her financial strategies tells a story of how those efforts must be connected. We enter her narrative as she shares a unique, dramatic, and moving moment that provides an illustration of how financing, sisterhood, and group support can be—and are often—interwoven in entrepreneurship development.

I interviewed her in her store, a beautifully appointed, comfortable, and welcoming space glowing with color from the tastefully displayed merchandise. In the interview, she told the story of her move into new permanent retail space. She had been selling as a vendor at fairs, conferences, cultural events, and the like, all in movable venues, and she needed to move her business to a more stable setting.

I came here in April, April 25th was the grand opening. So . . . I had been waiting for the space for quite some time because . . . [the process] is very slow. And so you know, I had to sort of like I didn't know if I'd ever get in there because it takes forever. And then all of a sudden they were ready. You know they said I could move in. And . . . I said to my girlfriend "I should basically be there before Mother's Day comes. I need to be in there and set up." But now we're into April and so I said "Boy, I have to have money." Now I have some stock but I didn't have as much as I wanted, you know in terms of the rent, the two months security, I needed — everything. . . So I was kind of concerned. I said "I'm going in . . . I'm going in with what I have. I'll deal with it."

So what happened is my girlfriend X. told me she needed me to – if I could go with her to . . . to . . . pick up something for her daughter. And then she was rushing me and then I said okay . . . [S]o we went and we came back to my house. And when I walked in, all my girlfriends were there. And they all had $100 bills on the floor. Twelve of them. I had $1200. Because they all said "We knew what was happening. None of us really had any money that we could give you or loan you, but we figured

we could do this together. You know you could do something with it."
So I had $1200 the week...coming in. It was so unexpected...and it
was a gift. I cried like a baby. Because I know that...[T]hey're single
mothers, most of them, and I know that $100 means a lot.

Paulette was able to move into her retail space, and her business is now
thriving. The nurturing social capital bonds of her "sisters" enabled her to
raise the funds she needed to take her business to another level.

The ways the women started their businesses depended in part on why
they started them and what goals they had for the businesses. There were
internal factors, for example, feeling the timing was right in part related to
their age, and external factors, including change in family status and change
in employment. Their goals for the business were also important; some
were clear, others unclear. One or more of the factors were usually inter-
related. We backtrack to see how Paulette's business development journey
demonstrates these factors and this process.

Part of the motivation for Paulette to begin the business was connected
to her need to take care of her family, in this case, her mother. As with other
women in the group, she had been thinking of starting her business for
more than 5 years before she actually began doing anything. She had been
told an early retirement package would be coming up in a few years and

that's when I started thinking about what else I might do...so I was
thinking about doing that (early retirement) and also....I was thinking
in terms of my mother, uh...who was ill at the time. And I needed to
have extra money because I was going back and forth to Virginia every
month. So I was trying to think of what I had done because I always
tend to have an eye for detail...I had helped in a couple of fashion
shows...of buying accessories for them...so I thought I could do
something like that. So I looked into doing shows...some of the shows
like the African Street Festival. I started gathering information, going to
see how they were put together. I went to Virginia and they had a
teacher's conference. And a friend of mine...asked me if I could be in
charge of the fashions, do the fashion show for them. And it was very
successful. And so I decided this is what I'm going to do. I'd like to get
into some kind of retail business or accessories.

Paulette then began to do business on a regular basis, becoming a vendor in
the United African Merchants Society in Harlem, and eventually becoming
the society's chairperson. She sold her products by renting booths in venues
like the Javits Convention Center and the Brooklyn Academy of Music,
as well as at conferences of groups like the Coalition of 100 Black Women
and at various street fairs. Her business grew as she did shows locally and
nationally. She discussed how she financed her initial start-up, or seed,
money—the hardest money new entrepreneurs have to obtain.

[W]hen I started I set a goal and an amount. I said $300. I said this is what I am going to start with...And I bought some scarves. My girlfriend who works for...[a]irways used to travel so I gave her $300 and she brought me back so much stuff. And that's what I started with...I never went outside of that $300 to do shows....I had made a little fund, I kept everything in envelopes. And I had to look into the envelopes to see if I could pay for another show.

As her business grew, those $300 envelopes were not enough to move her business to the next level, so she had to look for additional sources of financing. As with most start-ups, she used a variety of creative financing strategies and "guerilla," or non-traditional, sources to raise capital, starting with using her own money and then leveraging to other more traditional sources as the business grew.

As time went on, I could not support myself because I needed more and more to get into a booth. So what I did was...I took a loan from my 401K,...[a]nd I paid myself back. And then I had some business cards made. I bought some Rubbermaid bins to keep my merchandise in. I made a list of what I needed. I went downtown to all the display stores and started looking around. I'd ask the window dressers different questions. So I knew what I needed.

I have an eye for detail. I watch a lot of things. I'm just figuring out how things are put together. I worked underground. I was into construction for twenty-five years. Cable. Underground, the manhole work. I loved it. And so you always have to come in and do a survey of your job. I'm pretty good at it. I have good organizational skills. I have good people skills. I made lists. I live by my lists. Before I got the space I said "From now on I'm going to have a schedule."

When I finished with [T]he Harlem [EAP] program...They do something with the Trickle Up Fund. Which is $500. And...you get a check for $250 and then later on you get another check for $250. So that's the only money that I got that wasn't my own to start here. Because I had some savings, and...I took some of my savings. And then after I retired, which I retired...three years ago, I turned my 401K, I rolled it over, then...I rolled it over into some investments. One of the women in the Circle of Sisters is an investment broker and she set up a college plan for my two children. And then now she won't even let me...I have to beg for money...I say send me some money and she says no you can't have it. She won't give it to me.

As her business grew and she had a chance to go into permanent retail space, Paulette's "sisters" provided her with the financial capital necessary for her to open her space before Mother's Day. This nurturing network, which provided social capital support, also resulted in the provision of much needed financial capital that enabled Paulette to take advantage of an opportunity necessary to take the next step in business development:

> I know that they all wanted to see me succeed. We represent each other. And...they've been right there from the beginning. They were all here for the grand opening.

Paulette's story, focused here on her efforts to raise money for the business, highlights many themes associated with Black women's entrepreneurship: human, social, and financial accumulation strategies; sisterhood; the mother–daughter bond; the connection to their community, in this case Harlem; and formal and informal learning activities. Other evidence of the themes is found in the reported activities of other women in the study, as seen in the following stories.

Business: Why and When

Jackie L. described why she went into business for herself when she did and what she initially hoped to get out of it:

> When I became unemployed (laughter)...I just started thinking, I should just do my own stuff. Why not just have unemployment coming in, and try and develop something on my own....I thought, "Well, I might as well go onto the design now because that's what I want to do." I figured it was time to leave and just go out 100% on my own...We all want to make some money, you want to make money.

Wendy talked about how long it took her to actually start, even though she had been thinking about business for a while:

> I knew this was what I wanted to do...it took me a year just thinking about it and trying to figure out in my mind, is this what I wanted to do...It was basically a year before I started doing anything...a lot of people just kept telling me they were tired of hearing about it so do something...that was the beginning of the real thing...[was] when I called and decided to take the classes. So that was my commitment in starting the business...and that meant it was something I was serious about. It was not just a dream, it was part being, you know the first step into reality. And into the business world. [My goal] was to survive; we all have to make money.

Efua had wanted to start her business but

I didn't really do too much...during the time that I was expecting. But after [her son] was born and everything, then I really kind of got really rolling into it. I really kind of got with it...I guess when I started I didn't have really have high kind of goals (laughter). I was just concerned with...I just wanted to get one little contract.

Patricia talked about how old she was when she decided to go into business:

I was not fifty at the time, I think I was in my late forties. So at that point, I said you know what, maybe I didn't need it anyway because a $350,000 mortgage and at this age in time...I don't think that's too cool....I think...when I first started, it was just to get started....I wanted to do a day care center, actually...to open up a learning center.

And Sandy talked about the change of employment status that enabled her to begin her business:

I worked with New York State...for twenty-three years...they offered early retirement incentives so I went for it and decided to start my own business to help set a foundation for the next generation of my kids. Well, that's really when I started implementing the plans of going into...thoughts that's been in my mind maybe ten years before then.... [J]ust wanting to make sure that I was secure in my retirement before I made that move...my goal was more oriented around my customer base.

Others had goals that were not very clear, ranging from not having any business goals but having goals for individuals and for avoiding conflicts, accidentally starting without plans, not setting goals for themselves but just wanting to get started. Others, like Jackie L. and Wendy, just needed to make some extra money.

Financing Strategies

Quantitative measures of success are usually numbers that measure financial capital formation and accumulation; in short, how much money is raised, made, and kept. Study participants, when asked how they defined success in business, named three quantitative measures: level of sales and profits; size of the business, measured by the number of employees and locations; and age of the business. Because financial capital accumulation is a standard measure of success in entrepreneurship, I felt it would be useful to establish a baseline record of the financial capital formation activities of the entrepreneurs in the study. To obtain information about their business initial financing, the participants were asked how they financed their business start-up. A preponderance of the group specified they had financed their start-up themselves. Multiple methods were used: eight reported using their own savings; three used credit cards and trade credit; two borrowed against other assets, notably insurance and retirement funds; one obtained money from a prior business product return; and two financed their businesses from their revenues. The latter used their own savings, however, to pay for the initial start-up expenses. The following quotes serve as representative illustrations of the methods employed by the group, some of which were used by Paulette. Most people used more than one method of raising money.

> *Deborah*: Right. I really didn't have any money. I just used that money that I had left over out of my paycheck or I used my credit cards.
>
> *Sharon*: Actually I financed it by the cost of the day's events, per activity. And any deficit was made up in funds that I diverted from my own personal funds.
>
> *Paulette*: I always kept that $300 there. That's what I started with. Because I had done some saving and I took my savings. And then after I retired... I turned my 401K um, I rolled it over.
>
> *Cheryl H.*: I'd been doing temp jobs and buying different things that I need.
>
> *Arlene*: [W]hen I sent all my products back they sent me a check for the products and the check was over $xx,xxx.
>
> *Nancy*: I took out a loan against my life insurance company. I took on a second job to supplement my income so I could afford the equipment, to at least start purchasing the equipment.
>
> *Robin*: I was making really good money and I didn't spend it.... I got a check three four times a week and I just threw them in the bank.

Most of the women had full-time jobs, and the businesses were a patch in their income stream. Those guerilla financing strategies, as identified by Levinson and others, are crucial to business development and business success and, for these women, necessary for start-up.[1] The value of the creative capital formation strategies described above is that they can be useful for other new and would-be entrepreneurs who want to obtain the most difficult financing tool—start-up or seed money.

Some individuals who did not report using their own savings report they obtained money from friends, families, and associates, known as "FFA" financing. Others used a combination of methods, including their own money, as well as raising funds from FFA sources. A number received money in the form of no- or low-interest loans or gifts from a variety of people: one from mother, one from parents, two from friends, and two from pastors and church fellow members—from their support network, as we have seen with Paulette and her sister circle.

Once seed capital is raised, the next step in financing a business is usually to leverage the seed capital into financing from outside sources. Paulette was able to leverage her start-up capital, made up of what she raised herself and what she obtained from her friends, to obtain an expansion loan from a traditional lending source. In a similar manner, other women reported they had obtained or were in the process of obtaining financing from outside sources, which included local loan funds, traditional Small Business Administration bank-based loans, loan funds specifically for women-owned businesses, and in one case, a special grant for businesses started by women living or doing business in low-income areas.

Accessing capital is a traditional measure of success in business, and in fact, according to their nominators, these women were recommended for the study based in part on their receipt of outside financing. Thus, the findings reveal that though a majority of the successful Black women entrepreneurs provided their own initial financing, a smaller group received start-up funds from friends, family, and associates. In addition, close to half of the women were able to access funds from lenders; the remaining half are operating their businesses with capital they raised by themselves and with continued help from family and friends. As reported earlier by the Center for Women's Research, these women's success in obtaining outside financing represents a portion of the 38 percent of African American women who received bank financing. In contrast, 60 percent of White women, 50 percent of Hispanic women, and 42 percent of Native American women had bank credit.[2] Thus, obtaining outside financing is harder for this group than for other women, but they did it.

In-Kind Capital: Non-monetary Support for Business

Non-monetary support for businesses, like unpaid labor in the home, is not usually included in the valuation of capital accumulations available to small businesses, but it is critical to start-up and growth and is therefore detailed below.

Unpaid contributions to the businesses have been included under financial capital accumulation rather than social capital even though they are usually considered to be the latter. The reported goods and services provided to the businesses included in the study have a market value, although that value is not generally calculated when determining the net worth of a business—a figure that could be used in leveraging outsidefunding. As seen in Table 7.1, fifteen people in the group recounted instances in which they were given space, time, goods, services, or a combination thereof at no cost or in a bartering exchange. These goods and services were provided by a wide variety of people, including family, friends, pastors, vendors, customers,

Table 7.1   Sources of Non-monetary Support

Participant	Source of Support
Wendy	Ma had an empty room, and I used that as my inventory. My fiancée has been to a lot of trade shows and helps lifting boxes, he takes orders . . . his nieces have been my secretaries at trade shows. So I think everybody has chipped in.
Jackie L.	A fellow business owner told me I could . . . do whatever I wanted with [the goods]. . . . They gave me their time. . . . My husband helped me, my friend P. helped me . . . my friends just kept working, and we got the order out . . . the UPS driver helped me.
Efua	The phone system guy comes and does stuff for me that we're supposed to be charged for, and he won't because I have a good relationship with him. And I'll call people and I'll talk to people about getting stuff and I get free things . . . all kinds of things.
Ava	I went into the hospital for surgery. . . . I had some friends work the business for me.
Helen	I had twenty students volunteer. And I get a lot of stuff. . . . I can do fundraising through donation letters.
Sharon	And my friend offered [the space] to me without any cost involved for these three months with an option to rent in January.
Lani	[My business partner's] family helped with remodeling and renovations . . . [I] probably would have had to come up with a lot of money to pay people to put down floors and so on. It was more a bartering kind of thing. We cooked and my partner and I made food and did ironing . . . cooked and cleaned the house. And that's how we paid. It works.
Paulette	And I didn't even have to pay en exhibitor's fee, which is very nice. And I have my girlfriend, an unpaid employee . . . the best kind, really very helpful.
Cheryl H.	When I first took the course . . . I was like, I want to take this class, but how am I going to take this class and everything. And my girlfriend's daughter, she's 15, she would come and fix [her son's] food for me and stuff.
Robin	I have a board person who's been with me from the beginning. And they don't contribute $1,000 or anything, but they give me what they can. They give me time and energy. Which right now is just as important.

Table 7.1 *(continued)*

Participant	Source of Support
Cheryl O.	I've kept my membership there and...you can have an exhibition in their space for nothing and...they'll do your mailing and stuff for you. Again, I have this husband who has good technical expertise, and he's going to help me build and design these things.
Jackie K.	There are some people that I've had contact with over time or at different points in time who have given me helpful information that's been very useful or we've done some kind of barter that's been very useful. Or people have just given me things.

Source: C.A. Smith © 1999.

colleagues, business peers, and community organizations, attesting to the depth and breadth of the social capital networks that facilitated this group's financial growth.

Financial capital accumulation refers to the ways in which the business owners continued to accumulate capital after their businesses were started. In response to questions that asked for their definition of success, the women below answered in terms of one quantitative measure: the level of sales or profits.

> *Jackie L.:* The actual pay was like, wow, I'll never forget the money!
> *Efua:* Money's still coming in.
> *Gina:* The first year...I made $xxx,xxx. They say I'll never get rich but...
> *Sharon:* I think I made the most money I ever made at that two day conference.
> *Nancy:* We have $xx,xxx of equipment. I'm successful...[enough] to buy my equipment.
> *Cheryl:* My bills are paid. Knock on wood. And this year,...I'm making money. I mean not tons of money but it's respectable.

Others talked differently about the value or place of money in their businesses:

> *Frankie:* Money, that's not number one. That's not even two, three, or four.
> *Lani:* I think just, actually seeing a vision to completion, I think....I didn't envision myself making a whole lot of money in opening the business. So therefore the purpose wasn't really to make a lot of money. Incidentally, I make a lot of money if I do well.

Jackie K.: I'm in this to make money. I guess also growth, whether it's well...whether it's just doing something better or having a quantitative difference. And it would be nice if there was some money attached to it.

Sandy: I never focused on how much money I'm going to make. The focus was to just keep working it and make it the best you can. The money will follow.

In answer to a question about their initial goals for the business, making money was a priority in the owners' overall expectations. Several women mentioned making money as their start-up goal. For them money used was for extra income, to gain financial self-sufficiency and freedom to be their own boss. Even though they had all been nominated as successful entre-preneurs, some of the group members reported they did not feel successful because they had not achieved their financial goals. When deliberating their success, they talked about their sense of profitability or lack thereof.

Devya: Yes, yes. I just don't have the numbers I want but yes, I am very, very successful at what I do. Very successful. It's a lot easier if you start out with money.

Efua who reported she had "money coming in" on a regular basis still felt she was not successful:

I don't feel successful. No, I really don't. I'm told that...When I can say I've reached success that I'd like to be bringing in like $xxx,xxx/year.... [and] have a number of clients from other areas, six or eight contracts going on someplace else, that's when I can say I'm successful.

Similarly, Helen, although she measured her success in people not dollars, did not feel successful either:

And the business point of view we're not making money. You know, to be honest, I don't feel successful. I still feel like I have so much to do.

Two others declared that although they felt successful on other levels, they had not achieved the level of profitability they desired:

Deborah: [The business is] increasing sales, but I still have not made the money I want to make....I want to make the money.

Robin: [I'm still] trying to establish myself financially through the school.

Although all individuals quoted above made specific mention of the fact that they did not feel fully successful because they had not reached their financial goals, there seemed to be agreement among them and other participants that they still considered themselves to be successful in other areas, as evidenced by their qualitative definitions of success. They were all determined, however, to be both quantitatively and qualitatively successful.

A small number of women discussed level of sales and profits, not only in terms of asset accumulations but also in terms of use of the profits. These reported uses included achievement of financial self-sufficiency:

Deborah: I want to get out of the need to, I want, when I want something it is accessible.

Efua: Then I wouldn't need another job. I'd be fine.

Jackie L.: A house on the beach in Jamaica!

In addition, an increased ability to help others was an indicator of success—a good use of profits—in keeping with the cultural traditions of Black women.

Helen: We are trying to find money to help people—this business is not measured by how much money you make. So I think for us dollars are measured in terms of how many people we help.

Swantz, who studied female entrepreneurs in Tanzania, believes there is a theory of women's economics in which quantitative success is measured horizontally. A successful business is one in which the number of people supported or the number of other businesses assisted is a measure of success. In the individualistic market economy, these indicators are not taken into account. However, these Market Women supported and helped others start and sustain businesses and used those measures as indicators of their success, in keeping with an Afrocentric worldview.

The size of the business was considered in terms of number of contracts procured, new locations opened, and number of people hired. Approximately half of the owners who have essentially "one-person" operations wanted to make enough money to hire more permanent help because they could no longer run the business alone efficiently; time poverty issues were affecting their successful management. A few others talked about their ultimate goals, which involved having bigger and additional locations for their businesses, ranging from "big work, the big-money contracts" for Efua to a having a chain of stores for Paulette, to having her own catering hall for Cheryl H., and to being on the NASDAQ for Frankie. Sharon simply wanted women to have a good day. Jackie L. wanted to achieve a level of financial success to ensure independence and security for herself and her family:

As a Black person, it is so important to have your own, to own your own, and I just to make sure there would be something there...my friends and I would see...my family, many times they got laid off and want a job, this was a place where they could come and get a job.

Finally, another reported quantitative measure of success was the age of the business, explained in terms of survival. Six women, whose businesses ranged in age from three to ten years and averaged four years of age, defined their success in business in terms of "still being here" or survival:

Wendy: [My success] is that I'll be here tomorrow, the next day, and the next day after that. That I'm still here and I'm still ordering and people are still wanting what I've got.

Jackie L.: No, no I think definitely because I'm still here. I think that is the biggest success is that I'm still here.

Jackie K.: My first thought was it still exists. Longevity.

Sandy: So the main thing is, here in this time...of economic turmoil and everything that we're still,...we're surviving. But we see ourselves as growing, no matter what. Not as fast as we want, but we're growing. We're not going backward but we're going forward.

Traditional Small Business Administration (SBA) statistics indicate that 80% of new businesses fail within five years. This group of entrepreneurs is more than holding their own.

Quality, Commitment, and Excellence: Measures of Success

Whether articulated or not, financial success, or making a profit and sustaining it, was an overarching goal of all the women, because if their businesses did not make money they were no longer in business. The women who did not define success in terms of financial or quantitative measures did so in qualitative terms; all the women added qualitative elements to their definitions of success in business. These women valued their businesses differently than purely quantitative asset accumulation. Some of the qualitative aspects of valuing their businesses had to do with how they did business and were both goals and measures of success. Concern with efficiency of operations, high quality, and commitment to work contracts—elements of McClelland's Achievement Orientation—were included in one of their definitions of success, the achievement of excellence.[3] Concern for their customers and employees was an additional element of the achievement of success and excellence.

Arlene is the owner of a beauty parlor she built from scratch; it is located in a county north of New York City. She had had a dream of opening her own shop for years but didn't do so until she finished her EAP course. Up until that time, she had rented a booth in other shops. I interviewed her ten months after she had opened. The shop was warm, color-coordinated, and welcoming, and she was rightfully proud of it. She talked about how she had to persevere to overcome the obstacles she encountered: being turned down by Fleet Bank for her first loan; jumping through hoops to get the loan from a community-based lender; moving into the space, which was a wreck, and having it renovated; and not being able to officially open until she got her certificate of occupancy, which took six months while paying rent for those six months, even though she could not do business and thus had no income coming in for those six months. This committed woman keeps a full-time job while she also runs her business full-time. But, as she says, the business is exclusively hers. The elements of quality, concern for customers, commitment to the work, and efficiency orientation are evident in her narrative:

[My goals are] pretty clear because I was just looking over my business plan and I'm pretty much on track.... I'm paying my bills and that's pretty good for my first year. I feel really good... it just felt good to be in my own salon... it's really different from all the salons around here. It's been pretty good and people tell me that's good.

I use the best products. I could use a cheap product and charge you a cheap price but I believe in quality. The best thing about my business is that you can come in here and you can get the best product. I enjoy when people come in and tell me that I made their hair grow. I had some customers for like ten, twelve years and still coming.

I like [being the boss]. I was always the boss. I think I'm kind of understanding because I've been in that position, like... my employees. There's a lot of things I'm learning. It is so important to keep your receipts and really get organized. And I'm trying my best to get real organized. I have a computer at home. I'm watching him [her accountant] and then I'm going to put everything on my own computer and try and do good things on my own.

It's just mine... [a]nd I work really hard , I work really hard... to get where I am. To just come here and just open the gate, I mean it feels... it feels good. Sometimes I don't believe it... one day I came in here and I just cried, because you know... tears of happiness!

Other stories reflect the same perspectives on these alternative indicators of success, including efficiency orientation:

Jackie L., the hat designer:

When I do a job I like to do my best and give it my all and then after I've figured out how to do the job well, then I kind of like to do other things, take on other things. Plus, do the other things that keep my business running.

Sharon talked about her empowerment seminars:

I've always taken the position of trying to help people with direction, trying to find the ways to do things effectively. But the most consistent follow-up is me. I develop my own print materials. I develop the seminars myself. I execute them myself. I do evaluation . . . after every conference to find out what people think of it. I'm . . . hands-on throughout every aspect of it. I guess that's the true sign of an entrepreneur.

Patricia, the owner of the day care and learning center:

I mean I really had to come to grips in my head that this is what I had to do. There was just no half steppin'. I had to do it. I had to do everything, and I had to do everything right. I had to bring my building (learning center) up to code. And social service did come to approve us.

Most spoke unequivocally about their concerns with high quality:

Wendy, the bookseller:

It was an amazing feeling. It was like you were providing a service to someone and the person comes back and says you were right or thank you or this is a great book. . . . [T]this was one lady came and she was looking for a book for her child. I was able, you know . . . [B]y asking specific questions, I got to know what the child liked and provided it for her. The next year she came back and said . . . "that book you suggested was beautiful. My child loved it." Things like that in my dark moments, it keeps me going because it makes me feel great doing that.

Efua, who owns the janitorial services company:

I'm very particular about things so . . . in this business I have kind of high standards for how I want my work completed. And how I want it to be seen. . . . I don't believe in half doing something. I don't want it to . . . just be passable. I want it to be exceptional.

Jackie K., who holds shows for Afrocentric products, along with a directory of goods and services:

I've always made a point of at least making it esthetically pleasing...this is another thing in terms of atmosphere...I decided to skip a year of publishing because I knew that I hadn't done a good job with that particular issue and there was no point.

Finally, several individuals spoke about their commitment to the work:

Frankie, the restaurateur: You have to be willing to commit yourself 110 percent.

Deborah, the floral designer: A lot of people have told me, what happened is I never dropped the ball when it is thrown to me.

Cheryl O., the artist: And you, to some extent, but into your enthusiasm until it's three o'clock in the morning and you've got an order you've got to get out.

Efua sums things up: Your business, the buck stops here....I can't say very well somebody will do it. I have to do it.

Concern for others, concern for excellence, willingness, and ability to work hard and to see through a commitment are lessons usually learned at home in the broadest sense. These women survived and prospered in business because they drew on age-old supports: the cultural traditions of the mother–daughter bond, sisterhood, and spirituality.

I'm still here though!

—Wendy

CHAPTER 8

Mothers, Sisters, and Spirituality: Contributors to Success

For I am my mother's daughter and the drums of Africa still beat in my heart.

—Mary McLeod Bethune, in Bell, J., 2002, p. 17.

Hold a friend with both your hands.

—Niger/Nigeria/Chad, Eisen, A.,
Black Folk Wit,
Wisdom, and Sayings, 1994, p. 29.

I've learned to walk out on faith.

—Deborah

Black women scholars have identified themes felt to be distinctive to women of African descent in America, who have experienced unique life situations in their history. They have lived under multiple systems of domination, beginning in colonial days, continuing through chattel slavery, and ending with their "two-fer," Black women get counted twice—as Black/minority and as women—"two for one", status in America in the late twentieth and early twenty-first centuries. For some, their distinction comes about as a result of having been forcefully taken from their homelands, brought over in chains, making "the same trip on the same ship" regardless of where it landed. For others who came voluntarily, the legacy of chattel slavery, the Black Codes, and Jim Crow laws has subjected them to the same institutionalized racism, sexism, and discrimination. This history makes them different from even other women of color—Native Americans, Asians, and non-Black Latinas—who have suffered under similar yet different systems of discrimination based on their own unique histories in this country.

I recognize that Black women are not a monolithic group. Nevertheless, I assumed that at all women of African descent in the study population, even though they were of differing ethnicities and cultures, have had life and business experiences that are more similar than different as they were living and doing business in the United States. Their strengths, coping mechanisms, abilities, and worldviews are the foundation for the themes identified in the literature that are echoed in the words and perceptions of the study participants. The Black Women's Themes, used as a frame of analysis specific to the

Five Generations, Harlem, New York, 1917.
Courtesy of Watson/Joseph/Smith Family Collection, Harlem, NY.

study group, came from the literature in the field, with the exception of trust, which was identified as such because it was mentioned so often by many of the women. The themes used were sisterhood, the mother–daughter bond, spirituality, community, will, trust, and time poverty. The list of themes with explanations can be seen in the Appendix. Peterson, in her study of will and success, identifies Black family relationships, including the mother–daughter bond and Black women as sisters, in addition to deep spiritual awareness and community connectedness, as subthemes of self-will.[1]

Some of those themes overlapped as well as intersected with business behaviors identified by Godfrey and other women economists that are particularly associated with women. Women's business and economic themes include horizontal growth, concern for community and planet, and "doing good and having fun" while making money.[2] However, gender is not necessarily unifying. Although many White women entrepreneurs have similar concerns, behaviors, and issues as Black women entrepreneurs, they have not had to deal with racism as well as sexism while they built their businesses. In fact, over the course of history in the United States, White women have been some of the worst oppressors of women of color. According to Higgenbotham and other Black women scholars, feminism has "failed to see white women's own investments and complicity in the oppression of other groups of men and women."[3] In the past, many White women had inheritances that included enslaved women; many made their fortunes on the backs of Black women. In the present day, White privilege continues to favor White women in the market place, in accessing capital and in achieving recognition. For example, one of the successful African American women in Woodard's study of successful Black entrepreneurs reported that when she went to a bank-sponsored seminar on women in business, she was the only Black female there, and she "quickly found that my set of issues were different from other women there."[4]

As a consequence, to highlight and summarize those indicators that are possibly distinctive regarding Black women entrepreneurs, the use of Black Women's Themes as a framework for a different kind of analysis and a distinctive "angle of vision" is useful. Not surprisingly, given Black women's history and cultural traditions, themes related to family and faith were most outstanding and are significant elements in their social capital accumulation—a major contributor to success. This chapter discusses those contributions: the importance of the mother–daughter bond, the culture of sisterhood, and the significance of spirituality.

The Mother–Daughter Bond

The mother–daughter bond is prominent in the lives of Black women and has been since ancient African days. As Sarah Lawrence Lightfoot writes: "Now I plaited my daughter's brown braids and could feel the sensations of my mother's soothing hands on my head as I laid mine on my daughter's."[5]

The role of mother and daughter and the strength of that bond have been pivotal in sustaining the Black family over time, in passing on survival as well as instrumental skills, and in providing for the continuity of the traditions of service, accomplishment, and resistance to injustice. This powerful bond was a pervasive theme that was apparent throughout the interviews. The connection has also been found to be important in entrepreneurial success for this group of women and was an important part of their social support system. It was the most talked about aspect of the "relationship with other" focus, which was a key element of success. Most of the women talked about their mothers, whom they described as heroes, role models, and sources of support, including emotional, physical, and financial. Those individuals who mentioned this connection felt their mothers were, for the most part, sources of unconditional emotional encouragement, love, and inspiration.

Nancy is a single woman whose business is a music production company that also has a twenty-four-track recording studio, created primarily for the discovery and advancement of young urban Black artists. The story of her mother's influence on her life and business was especially poignant. Nancy had a particularly close relationship with her mother.

> I was a mama's girl. I say that unashamedly. And I believe that all of the positive aspects of my life are directly related to the contributions...the many contributions...that she made to my life.

When her mother died, Nancy was determined to create a legacy in her honor. She opened her business for her mother, even naming the music production company for the strength of the connection.

> My mom basically was the primary reason for my decision to start my own business. My mom was my sole inspiration. So as a testament and in honor of her, I decided to name my company name my company [after our connection]. Because I believe she's always with me.

When asked about her business start-up activity, she answered

> I think for me being that I had been in a partnership with my mom, God bless her soul, we owned rental property together. And my mom, I think from her pearls of wisdom...she always believed in ownership. Whether it was owning you know...your own home, and then once established...go out and invest in something that would generate some kind of long-term revenue. And consequently that led us to get into the rental property market.

Her mother was also her first business teacher and mentor:

> My mother taught me how to balance a checkbook when I was eight.
> I've been fortunate because my mom, again God bless her soul, was
> really the individual that taught me ... how to be disciplined. I've been
> taught to take care of your needs before your wants. My mother had
> always showed me that you had to be self-sufficient. I can honestly say
> that my mom, my mom's instilling that hard work, perseverance,
> tenacity and a belief in God, um that's it.

Nancy's mother was also her source of support:

> My mom was a licensed social worker and an ordained minister and
> was not accepting of secular music. But she was very supportive in
> many ways regarding my decision to go and start my own company.
> And often she would call or I would call her and she would say,
> "How's the business going, what are you doing?"

Nancy identified mother as her main role model in life as well as in business:

> Her life history definitely influences my present today. She hurdled so
> many barriers in her life. And she fought, she won, she lost but she
> kept running the race. I think for all intensive purposes, I never had to
> look for a hero outside of my home. My mother was my hero and still
> remains my hero.

Nancy's perseverance, hard work, will, and determination to succeed are, in
part, a result of her dedication to the memory of her mother. That bond has
fostered success. Her willingness to be interviewed, to have her story told, is
because of her mother:

> I mean I think about my mom and having lost her in the physical
> sense, ... I've often wondered who's going to tell her story. I'm going
> to tell it. I'm going to tell it through my work. Because her story is
> certainly worth being told and had it not been for her story, I
> wouldn't have had a story.

Several of the others talked about this connection. Cheryl O. was also
especially close to her mother, named the business after her, and put her
mother's picture on her business cards:

> I've just begun to think about a name for my business ... my mother
> had probably died three or four years before that and ... that name
> had been in my head for a long time. ... [I asked myself] who you are
> in terms of who you want to be and who you don't and decided that

I'd always been Louise's daughter...I put my mother's face on my business cards.

Others talked about the kinds of support they received from their mothers, including financial help.

> *Wendy*: Ma. I believe I put up the first money for the class. Ma came up with the actual money for the first inventory and then came up with part of the money and I came up with part...we went in half/half together.

Two women reported that their mothers inspired the formation of their businesses, either directly or indirectly. One of them:

> *Deborah said*: And my mother, what made me think about it was my, I wanted to make for my mother for Christmas. And ah, because she has everything and so I figured I'd make her a unique set for herself.

Deborah's gift for her mother was a gift made from Afrocentric cloth, which inspired her to create other gifts for sale.

Another told of an incident in which her mother took an active role in supporting and promoting the business unbeknownst to the daughter:

> *Jackie K.*: I recently found out...my mother got my address book and went through my address book and called my friends. I had no idea. [She said,] "Do you consider yourself a friend of my daughter?" And of course people would say yes and then she would say "Well, I expect to see you at the show today (laughter)."

Robin talked about her mother, who was a role model, supporter, and inspiration.

> But my mother has inspired me throughout my life with dancing. And my mother was like, "Oh, this [business] is great, because she does those organizations and things like that."

Several women also talked about an intergenerational bond among kins-women in terms of their grandmothers, who served a similar function as their mothers. Grandmothers are often part of the mother–daughter bond, over generations. We heard from Helen and Efua about their grandmother's influence on their lives and sense of self, and consequently, on their business as sources of support, influence, and education.

In contrast, there were two women who expressed some ambivalence about the relationships they had with their mothers. Cheryl H. described how her mother had initially discouraged her from starting a business. Only after Cheryl H. had done well in business did her mother become a main source of support and referred customers to her:

> I don't know what she was afraid of but my mother is like that. She's not the type of person that's going to venture out. She's like, "Oh, but don't get too involved [in the business]." She said "I don't really want you to take risks," and I was like...but I left my house when I was twenty-one so I really, I...don't listen to her when she does that. Now...she's the one mainly who would give me customers.

Cheryl H. realized that her mother was merely being protective of her and so was only able to embrace her business venture after she saw it was working.

The strength of the bond and its disruption through the death of the mothers seemed to have had significant effects on the entrepreneurs. Some of the women talked about the loss of their mothers and the effect it had on them and, in several instances, the effect it had on their businesses.

Paulette was especially clear about the impact of her mother's death on her life:

> My mother only had a sixth-grade education, my father third grade. So then...[S]he said "I found out about you can go to college at night." That's what she always said, "You have to go to college at night or you have to come home." I lost my mom like four years ago. And every day, you know...I think about it.

Wendy, in contrast, talked about a support group that helped her in her business began in relation to another woman's loss of her mother:

> [The support group] started with a woman, she had lost her mom and I believe she sort of created a group to interact, you know to talk about different things. And it helped her mourn.

Two women also spoke about a somewhat ambiguous or negative effect the mother–daughter bond had on them.

Ava is solely responsible for her invalid mother and talked about that situation as being difficult as she tried to do business: "Yeah, I had my mother. And knowing the situation at home with my mother. You know?"

Sharon, who considers herself an independent woman, but who had to struggle with the double-edged sword of independent womanhood, as her mother was a role model she felt to be both helpful and somewhat difficult, said:

> That comes a lot from my mother. My mother is very family oriented, very quiet. And I noticed a lot, you know a lot...of her gifts were

unexpressed because she was so quiet and somewhat passive about certain things. She was very active in regard to children and making sure they had what they needed. She created just the right type of world that I needed to grow up and to make me feel...good but not necessarily have a lot of self-esteem or confidence.

The mother–daughter bond is a mutual one, and the women in the group talked about their own daughters and their connections with them, as daughters, as protégés, as business partners, and as keepers of their dreams. The threads pull in both ways. Frankie laughed when she talked about her daughter:

When I see my daughter interacting with her children, she reminds me of déjà vu. I never thought it would happen. [She said,] "I never thought I would become you." Can't help it But you know something...The family is the unit.

She focused on her daughter as a mother and her grandchildren's relationship to her business goals.

This is what I ultimately want to complete. I'm putting this together so that the grandbabies can continue with it. They are going to be involved from the very beginning, okay?.

Patricia was and wanted to be a role model for her daughters:

And my three girls went off to college. And they just want to see me grow. They just want to see mom do these things [the business you know].

In addition, the entrepreneurs who had grown daughters often involved them directly in their businesses, as workers and apprentices. Those mothers were mentors, and some apprenticed their daughters so they would be able to take over the businesses if they so chose.

Efua, whose daughters help her work her cleaning business, is training her older daughter in the art and science of cleaning and maintenance, as her grandmother had taught her.

And my daughter handles the work, which I have to say she's a pretty good supporter of the business. I'm teaching her along the way. Because a lot of things she doesn't understand with business and she thinks she can say certain things and do certain things. You know how young people are, and I was like, "You know, you can't do that in business. You have to keep your professionalism."

She somewhat diffidently admitted that this same daughter considered her to her to be a mentor:

> That's what she tells me. So a matter of fact...[S]he even wrote something. She wrote...for a class or something that I was her mentor, her hero.

Sharon, who runs seminars for women, has employed her twenty-something-year-old daughter in the business:

> My daughter, in fact, is my co-pilot. She assists in a number of ways. If there's a task, a small task, like phoning or checking on a few details or checking on enrollment or registration, she'll do that. I pay my daughter. Because I think that's real important for my daughter to see that her work is worth something, and it's not just a give away. She's very good at what she does. She's very good at customer service. And she was trained well.

Interestingly, there are a growing number of formal business partnerships between mothers and daughters beyond the study group, some of which were found in a recent article in *Ebony Magazine*, a periodical by, for, and about Black people. Entitled "Mother–Daughter Business Buddies," the article profiled five mother–daughter partnerships. One of the enterprises, Blackberry's, an Afrocentric upscale lifestyle emporium located in Macy's Herald Square in New York City and the Pentagon City Mall near Washington, DC, was founded by E. Diane White, a Harvard MBA. White is quoted as saying, "it would have been impossible to achieve such success without my mother's support and insight." Another mother–daughter partnership reported was entertainer Gladys Knight and her daughter Kenya, who have a Las Vegas bakery business, Kenya's Cakes of the Stars, they keep afloat with "love, laughter and respect."[6] Other businesses were as diverse as a the Mayo family's concrete reinforcement business in Raleigh, North Carolina, run by Mary Mayo and her two daughters; Sylvia Woods's New York City soul food restaurant and food service business, cofounded and run by her husband, sons, and two daughters; and Deborah Gilliam's Los Angeles–based twenty-year-old court-reporting business, co-operated by Gilliam and her two daughters, who are employees. Diverse in place and type of businesses, these particular family businesses are complicated as well as enhanced by the bonds between mothers and daughters:

> [D]espite minor disagreements and conflicts, a growing number of Black mothers and daughters have found they share not only a blood tie but also a keen sense of what sells in the marketplace. Genuine love, trust and respect are what set apart these mother–daughter duos

who are courageous enough to branch out in nontraditional partnerships in hopes of building long-lasting legacies together.[7]

Informal learning and teaching through apprenticeship, role modeling,
observation, and mother–daughter family support—financial as well as
emotional—are factors in success that were as present in these modern-day
mother–daughter businesses as they were in the past in the African women's
craft guilds and in the apprenticing by enslaved women of their daughters,
as they taught them the healing arts, textile work, retailing, and the like.
The presence of this aspect of Black women's entrepreneurship in the
popular literature, including the themes of trust and family bonds, may be
an indication that these businesses are beginning to be recognized for their
existence and, ultimately, their contributions to the community and the
economy.

Sisterhood

Sisterhood is another prevailing theme in Black women's lives. As
connections with "sisters" and unconditional support, both emotional and
financial, a growing number of "sister networks" used for both business
and social purposes were apparent and important in the women's lives.
Burbridge reminds us that the effects of time poverty are often mitigated by
the levels of support available from extended family networks—sources of
social capital and non-monetary financial support.[8] In the last few years,
there has been an increase in the number of networking groups and organizations comprised of and organized by and for Black women that promote these sister connections.

The importance of female networks among Black women can be traced
back to the Market Women of ancient Africa and their kinship guilds, the
female slave networks that provided support and care in colonial and antebellum America to the many Black women's organizations formed in the
nineteenth and early twentieth centuries for the purposes of "uplifting one
another and the race."[9] Elements of connections with other women of color
included feelings of trust, support, encouragement, and sources of information. Paramount was the perception of the connections experienced as
being part of an extended family kinship system.

Descriptions of sisterhood also referred to the extended family notion
that recalls the extended family kinship systems prevalent in Africa that
have been retained in Black communities in the United States since colonial
days. Known as "fictive kin," these sisters and their bonds are cultural
traditions that have survived over time. What is striking now is that the
many sister's circles, networks, organizations, and sororities are now focusing on economic development, supporting and encouraging entrepreneurship among and for women.

Whether their focus is around romance, reading, spirituality or investments, sister circles are coming together all over the place. The type of collectives may be new, but not our wisdom in turning to one another; that's always been part of our culture. In Africa, our foremothers pounded grain together, sought one another's counsel, kept an eye on one another's children.[10]

The sisterhood theme illustrates the group's experience with a particular type of support system. Paulette, whose group of sisters pooled their cash so that she could move into new retail space, also talked about how they provided non-monetary sources of support as she was operating the business—serving as unpaid employees in the shop, assisting her at trade shows, and providing a place she could go where she would be welcomed and sustained.

It was because you know...I don't have family here...they are my family. I know that if I call at two in the morning they're going to come. We're like that with each other. And I think that's very important that women do have that sort of support. That sisterhood is like real sisterhood.

Another of Paulette business experiences also graphically illustrates the notion of "sisterhood" in its broadest terms and the value of a fictive kin network in the success of business. She describes an experience she had when went she went from New York to Boston to participate as a vendor in a conference held by the Boston Chapter of 100 Black Women, presently known as the Coalition of 100 Black Women. Paulette had been "discovered" by a member of the organization who saw her booth at the Democratic Convention and invited her to come to Boston to do a show at their conference there. She was a featured vendor there, recognized for her excellence in product and service, and her exhibitor's fee was waived because her contact wanted a "certain type of exhibitor" there. As it was at the beginning of her business life, Paulette had only a small car—not a van like she has now—and she packed it up with merchandise and drove it to Boston. She underestimated the time it would take to get there, however, and arrived too early to check into her room. The desk clerk, maintenance, and back office staff in the hotel, all people of color, helped her by giving her a place to stay in the employee's lounge so she wouldn't have to pay for extra day.

The employees. They fixed coffee for me. They gave me a sandwich. They gave me a blanket and a pillow. And told me to rest until the next day....They were so kind to me. And the next morning...they had unloaded my stuff for me and taken it to the exhibit hall. I never forgot them, you know....They set the whole thing up.

All who helped her were not only women but people of color who recognized that a person of their community was in need and helped. When she went to set up her booth she realized she had quite a bit of merchandise, but not as much as the established vendors who had been exhibiting at these conferences for a while. She said about the vendors

> They received me so well...they were very kind to me. There was none of that competitiveness, none of the cutthroat kind of thing. And the women there received me so well. And those women were like kinship the way they embraced each other. It was like old girl, school-girl type of thing. I mean...[W]e really sort of hit it off with one another.

> And they loved my things. And I didn't have enough because they wanted more. And they were coming to my room. And the next morning when I was leaving they invited me to their own [conference] breakfast. They invited me to come back. It was really, really heartwarming the way it went. I stayed in contact with a few of them. I think I made the most money I ever made at that two-day conference. That was my most successful everything.

Elements of sisterhood, trust, community, and cooperative economics were demonstrated in this event, which resulted in Paulette's most successful vending occasion on many levels. For this reason, the incident stood out for her as one of her most positive significant business experiences.

Paulette's business and personal experiences epitomize sisterhood and her descriptive ability make them compelling manifestations of this theme and worthy of telling. One of the growing trends in sisterhood in action is the creation of a variety of sister circles. Paulette was very involved in the community of vendors in Harlem, and she also joined a "circle of sisters" made up of vendors:

> We have a social relationship as well as business. We share information. We'll each take on a project in terms of going over and taking designs to do your own designs there, to go to the cutting houses. So we share information...Most of these women are single mothers who share information in terms of parenting skills. We do a coop where we buy tee shirts, socks, underwear, wholesale as a group. We do trips together because...I believe you should have your children under a sort of protective umbrella when you're with the same kinds of people that have the same kinds of ideas of education or whatever.

> We sometimes do a show and we let the children get a table. We do a little entrepreneurship program for them, which I'm starting in my son's school this year.

This sister circle story has elements not only of sisterhood but also of cooperative economic strategies, collaborative learning, education, and the protection of their children. Its purpose and function are reminiscent of the women's mutual benefit societies and club movements, whose goals were also social, economic, and educational—"lifting as they climb."

All the other women in the study group also were members of various sister circles and have widespread networks of care. Wendy's group was begun by a woman who was seeking support after her mother's death. Meeting with sisters helped her talk and helped her mourn; later the group began to evolve. Wendy was invited into the group because she met a lawyer at one of her trade shows who invited her and described that experience:

The "Sisters Helping Sisters." It's a group of ladies that just get together some weeks and we talk about what's happening in NYC or around the globe.... [J]ust being there to support one another... you know if we have to do letter writing and stuff to try and get some young people we can mentor.

Wendy was also part of an investment club, a multiethnic group of sisters, the Multi-Ethnic Sisterhood Alliance (MESA), who met monthly

A group of ladies. I believe everyone has a concern about investment and the concept is retirement.

She would bring her books to both groups and was sold out at every meeting. The members also served as referrals to other customers and offered sales opportunities, including inviting Wendy to their places of work to sell her products. The women in these groups were all professionals with upper- and middle-management positions and practices. We see how the nurturing networking also led to commercial success for Wendy.

The narratives exemplify some of the strategies that confirm the value of nonmonetary support and networking. Some microenterprise training programs, usually those generally run for and by Black women, are building on this existing strength in designing their programs and curriculum. One example is the Business NOW (Neighborhood Organization of Women) in Atlanta, Georgia, which has as its specific mission business and sisterhood.[11]

Trust, another Black women's theme mentioned often by the women, is closely related to the notion of sisterhood, both in terms of Black women trusting each other and, to a lesser extent, feeling betrayed when they were cheated or let down by other Black women. In the spirit of sisterhood, many reported automatically trusting other Black women, especially in terms of asking for receiving and using advice and support in their business dealings, and they were not disappointed but "uplifted" and benefited from it.

Jackie L. talked about how she had to search for help from agencies getting her business started:

I saw M. and I saw her brown face ... and I saw a Black woman was telling me this. And I thought OK. Why would I ... not listen to her. So you know ... I just trusted her.

Nancy, who belongs to a group called Sisters in Entertainment, understands that

Black women have been the ones who have given me the most helpful advice. And it's almost been like throwaway stuff, something they just casually mention.

Devya talked about the need to be seen as a trustworthy person by her meditation customers:

They wanted to be able to trust me. And I work that too ... I work at maintaining trust because it's very, very important to the work I do. [Work] felt wonderful that someone could trust me that way.

Lani also felt gaining the trust of her customers was important—that "your customers trust you."

Other indicators of trust were discussed, including being able to trust themselves and in their own abilities. An important aspect of trust included trust in God or in a higher being and encouraging trust within the community, which clearly intersected the themes of spirituality and community.

Cheryl H. talked about trust in her church community:

A lot of people in the church, they don't have confidence in people in the church. I just wanted to show them that you can have something nice, the same thing that you get outside. You should trust people inside to give them the job because this is how you help each other. You have to learn how to trust people.

This aspect of trust, linked to learning and success in business, is related to what Sabel calls a "culture of trust." This way of doing business, reported by some of the study group members, has also been identified as "learning by monitoring":

"Learning by monitoring" or agreeing upon the fairness of interactions in a business deal leads to "cultures of trust" in which the fate of each (firm or actor) is seen as so entwined that no one would think of exploiting the other ... in learning by monitoring, individuals (and firms) are sociable.[12]

Most of the women doing business together, getting advice, and inspiring others formed communities of trust based on shared historical, cultural, and personal experiences. Wiltz discusses the nature of sisterhood and concludes that Black women's relationships with each other "are our succor."[13]

However, there were a few incidents in which women were betrayed by sisters doing business with each others. Findings in the area of distrust illustrate the fact that not all relations among Black women are without conflict, and not all sisters operate in a trustworthy manner. This finding is not surprising because Black women, as with any group, vary along many dimensions, and where there is difference there is the potential for conflict.

Ava's situation, with her past experience with mistrust, was made more difficult by the fact that a member of her church betrayed her trust:

> I bought the business based on the fact that I'm dealing with a believer, an honest person, a considerate person. Lo and behold, when I took over the business that Monday, because she had to clear out some things. And when I came into the store that Monday...I found she had taken over three-quarters of the inventory.

Even though she had been betrayed and was a victim of a crime, Ava's beliefs were so strong she did not press charges because "Believers don't take believers to court." However, bell hooks, an educator and essayist, counters that "We've got to have a better understanding of what sisterhood is.... It's not the absence of conflict, but how successfully you confront and cope with conflicts when they arrive."[14]

Spirituality

Jackie L: So I think there has to be some kind of divine intervention.

Spirituality is defined here as encompassing a general sense of spiritual connection and faith, a belief in a higher being, seen as a source of guidance and strength, and the use of prayer. Spirituality was often mentioned by the women in the study as a solution to the achievement of balance and wholeness and was believed to provide a foundation that contributed to success in entrepreneurship. Therefore, for this group of individuals, spirituality, which goes beyond participation in organized religion, was perceived to be a factor in their success.

The literature is replete with discussions of the place of spirituality in Black women's lives, including a recent study by Ehrhart-Morrison, who profiled thirty-two African American women identified as being successful in many walks of life, including four entrepreneurs: "A goodly number of the women I interviewed for this book grew up in spiritually oriented environments, and many credit their spirituality for their success."[15] A majority of the group talked about some aspect of spirituality during the interviews. Others reported being concerned with the development of their spiritual lives without being connected to any organized religion.

A consistent feeling among the respondents was that spirituality was a key element in their personal and business lives. Yet, the group was not of one accord in their religious beliefs; they were, as self-described, "hardcore, down-home Baptists," Protestant, Catholic, Buddhist, and Muslim. Subthemes of spirituality included faith in themselves as well as in a higher being and the place of spirituality in their business operations and as an essential component in a holistic approach to seeking balance in mind, body, and soul. A few representative stories illuminate both the similarities and the differences among this group of spiritual women.

Figure 8.1 provides a graphic display of the signs of spirituality as they pertain to entrepreneurship and the interactive nature of the relationship. There were four main groupings: belief, behavior, faith, and values and their indicators. Several of the women's descriptions of the aspects of spirituality in their lives and businesses were intriguing.

Helen's story is particularly fascinating. She is a Black woman, born in Barbados, who moved to New York and worked in corporate America before becoming a Buddhist nun. We remember she learned how to be an entrepreneur at her grandmother's shop in Barbados and had degrees in marketing and business. When she became a nun, she accidentally backed into doing business by starting a Buddhist Center that became a community retail store offering classes, tea, books, music, clothing, and comfort to local residents. Interviewed in her store, she made a point of not wearing

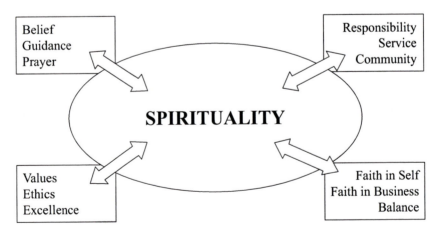

Figure 8.1. Spirituality Indicators in Entrepreneurship.
Courtesy of C.A. Smith © 1999.

her robes and mentioned that when she first moved into the neighborhood she didn't wear them, to ease her way into relating to her neighbors.

She formalized the business as a not-for-profit entity, raised seed money from grants, and used interns, donations, and fund-raising to keep the business going because it barely made enough to survive. Because she is a nun with an active spiritual practice, she is quite clear that her spiritual beliefs affect her business activities positively. She described her business:

I have a business. This is a Buddhist Center. The services...[W]e provide...a space where people can come and do meditation. But the idea of this place is that you don't have to be Buddhist to come in here. It's like a reading room. It has a library. But you could come, you could sit and read and help yourself to a cup of tea...And everything is free. People move into this community, they have the keys to this place. We have CDs. This section is retail. And this clothing rack is for the community. Everything on that rack is $2.

The one thing that helps, I think, is my spiritual life in making things grow. Because you develop other skills that help you in business that you're not even aware of, like listening to people. Because as a nun, you have to do a lot of listening. And you know you develop because you learn to be calm. You learn how much you use your energy in a sort of negative way. So I always say that..... [L]ike having a spiritual edge. It really gives you an edge on people. I think with spiritual practice, you know...you're looking at things. You have a different platform to sit on, mostly, than most people do. You have this other place you're coming from.

And I'm very proud of—of [W]hat I've learned about business, is building relationships. That's the key. And being honest.

Other women's words give expression of a general sense of spirituality and its meaning in their lives and businesses. Devya, whose meditation business provides what can be considered spiritual guidance of sorts, says:

And I think the one thing that overrides all of that is faith. A tremendous amount of faith.

Ava, who has very strong beliefs, thinks spirituality is important:

Because nobody knows where you are going in life. And it's only by the grace of God that we have gotten you know...this far.

Sharon, who describes herself as being spiritual but not religious, says:

Having an idea about, you know...what all of this might mean in terms of this integrating into your life and how it might fulfill you on a spiritual basis.

Sharon's story is presented here because she connects her spirituality to her familial roots and sees it as part of a holistic balancing of mind, body, and spirit, a goal and measurement of success. Sharon has a doctorate in early childhood education. She also has two businesses—a seminar production business for women's personal development and a tea gallery for women—and describes their purposes here:

The seminars integrate certain things that appear in each of the seminars. And that's mutual support, personal development, positive thinking, networking and spiritual unfoldment.... [I]t has a holistic approach to women actualizing themselves.

It doesn't connect people in such a way that they have to rely on the cohesiveness of the group or the group affiliation to acquire these skills or attain the goals they set out for themselves. We have a different niche (from a church setting). We do women's circles, tea parties, an annual conference...and at the end we wrap it up with a circle, which is the spiritual component of bringing it together. Having an idea about what all of this would mean in terms of this integrating into your life and how it might fulfill you on a spiritual level.

She attributes her speaking ability connection to the oral tradition associated with spirituality and her family:

If you go to a family reunion, you've got speakers...and there are preachers in my family and stuff like that. It's from that tradition I grew my art. I wasn't aware of it in terms of the speaking style that I had the ability to conjure things up in people's minds just with the spoken word. I kind of speak from a different pulpit.... It's a different setting but it's kind of the same stuff.

Her method of practicing her own spirituality led her to meditate daily, accessing a number of individuals she considered to be what Daloz calls "unknown mentors"—those she has never met in person but who nonetheless guide her behavior and her journey:

I have a number of people in my meditation that I think about. And most of them are deceased. And that way you can access the spirit a lot quicker.

Bessie Coleman, the aviator. At a time when you could not even conceive of a women flying, this was a Black woman who flew. A

Black woman who went to France to get her skills to do this and who didn't settle for keeping her dreams grounded. She made them airborne literally.

Nat King Cole... when I meditate I ask for his elegance, his sophistication, and his command of his God gifts.

Hattie McDaniel, an actress, who I admire for her personal power and her love of people.

Zora Neale Hurston for her writing ability and insight into people, customs, and cultures.

Josephine Baker for her worldliness, humor, her sophistication, her ability to speak a foreign language.

Mother Hale for her ability and insight into working with mothers and children.

Adam Clayton Powell. I admire him a great deal. I admire his lifestyle and other things that people have found not so great. What I ask for is his charisma, his competence, his oratorical skill, his innovation and originality.

I guess I have a lot of mentors for business.

Sharon's spirituality illustrates aspects of a search for internal balance, connections with her familial and cultural traditions, and her use of meditation to get in touch with her mentors, who "absolutely, absolutely" help with her business development. The latter connection to spirituality is fascinating as it refutes the prevailing myth that Black people, especially women, have few if any mentors or role models in business. Sharon's story tells us mentors for entrepreneurs don't have to be about business but about their character and how they conduct themselves in business and in the world.

One of the aspects of spiritually, belief, was indicated as several of the women stated clearly that they believed in a higher being:

Jackie L.: I thank God and all that because of God and the stability of my parents. I believe in a higher power.

Arlene: I don't want anything that's going to separate me from God.

Cheryl H.: I believe in God.

Others added their belief that God, in whatever form, was a source of guidance and strength, in life and in business:

Frankie: But you know something, the good Lord is in front of me. I can't forget my religion. He's in front, the "Big Guy's" in front, so we're just leaning on him for strength. Like I thought the Lord's in front.

Ava: They gonna think you're crazy, but it's the truth. God and the Holy Ghost . They're team players. But I always believe what God has for me I'm gonna get. But the Holy Ghost is something that can direct your life, if you allow it.

Sandy: I follow my vision and God's guidelines. So I feel very blessed that I had God and my family there to support me.

Of particular note and interest was the perception from the group of how religion, spirituality, and faith affected their business development:

Deborah: So I actually did ask God to help me find something. I mean the idea came to me to start my own business.

Jackie L.: So I think there must be some kind of divine intervention. I don't know, whatever. It's like they put up this divine intervention because I was up in the B. taking those classes.

Ava: Not knowing down the road for a year, God was planning for me to have a business. So he provided me with the business.

A number of women mentioned that they turned to prayer in times of stress and uncertainty as a means of overcoming adversity, persevering, and obtaining strength and guidance. Some illuminating words follow:

Ava: We were meeting for prayer every day. So I went to church that night. And I rolled under the pew (laughter) and you know . . . just cried out before the Lord and said "Well, what a big mess."

Patricia: Last year, strange as it may sound, um, I had this strong urge to pray. And normally I don't get down on my knees and pray but I guess I do pray in my way every day. But this time I took to my knees, and I asked God to please help me with this center. As soon as I got up from this prayer, the phone rang.

The preponderance of feeling in the group about their understanding of spirituality displayed a remarkable degree of consistency both within and across individuals. All reported they believed in a higher power, prayed, or meditated for guidance and strength or saw themselves as living a spiritual life that carried over into their business dealings.

Frankie: The old folks say "You have to worry the Master to death." I'm religious, I'm a religious person. I will give that helping hand because I feel that there's a reason for me to be doing this. Okay, as you can see, my religious values are intact.

Organized religion and church membership were discussed by certain of the women, as were their connections with their church community and their pastors. Cheryl H.'s story helps us understand how faith, church membership in a traditional religious organization, and links to the church community help with business.

Cheryl H., the balloon and cake artist, is a young, thirty-something single mother of an eleven-year-old boy, who helps with the balloon work. She is also an active and committed member of her church community. She talks about how she turned her cake decorating skills into a business.

> Because I was doing the cakes, I started out doing it just for fun and then later on as I was going to church I realized through my pastor this is what God gave me to do, he was the first to tell me that's what God have me do.

> We were in service and he said there's seven people in here that God's getting ready to bless in their businesses. And then he came over to me and said you're one of them young lady.

As she received more and more decorating jobs, Cheryl H. started setting up the tables, and then realized something more was missing; balloon decorating caught her eye but she didn't know how to do it or know anyone who did. She engaged in some self-directed learning activities but first

> I prayed about it and I went back to the library, I went to a business library this time...and found one book.

Cheryl H.'s cakes are masterpieces of creativity, artistry, and skill. She attributed her ability to her belief on God:

> I really just started looking at stuff and just started doing it. Because what happens is God let me see it in my mind. I have to see it in my mind. I am blessed. God is blessing me.

She also talked about several aspects of faith and trust in relation to her church community:

> They [her church group] gave me the faith to believe in myself. And I found the trust in God. God just reveals different things and I used to be so shy. When I first came to that church I was so shy I wouldn't even open my mouth.

Her pastor was her mentor:

> I will have to say my pastor because he's the one who encouraged me...I'd walk past him and I would turn around and I would just look

and he would just smile at me. Then I would just feel like, Okay, I'm doing it right you know.

And she spoke about her faith and its relationship to her success:

> If it was for God my Creator, if I didn't have Jesus Christ in my life it wasn't for him in my life...I don't think I would be successful at all....Because I did not even have confidence in myself to do anything. God will always tell me if I put my trust in him, he will make the way for me.

Cheryl H.'s faith and trust in God and herself and the emotional and financial support and guidance of her pastor and her congregation both propelled her to go into business and helps her continue. She is now contracted by the church to do all their major celebrations, events, and conferences.

Others also found support in their church groups:

> *Frankie*: Last year, when my store was open, you know, when you first started...I had the pastor down. So we dedicated it to my Lord and Savior.
>
> *Arlene*: sing in the choir....I pay my tithes and I've been OK. I've been doing good, you know. I mean church really helps me spiritually.

Church membership was also seen as an important source of social capital and networking opportunities, both in the "giving" and the "receiving," and a growing number of churches and organizations are operating faith-based operations, training, and technical support systems.

> *Deborah*: At that time, I wasn't really active in church. But...now I am. And my church has a business ministry.
>
> *Frankie*: I'm a member of the C. Baptist Church but I go to F. Baptist out here....We, the covenant, [the business'] covenant [is] to always remember those that did not make it, to give them a helping hand, to never forget where we came, and always feed the hungry. At the end of the day, any food that's left cooked...is to be donated to the shelter.
>
> *Ava*: So I volunteered at the church. If somebody helps me, then I should help somebody else. I always have a mission, you know, to provide for the needy.
>
> *Sandy*: A lot of my customer base [is] church goers. We [network] with a lot of other churches too. Um, sometimes you know with

the other churches because I do, um, loan a lot of my items for fashion shows for churches and stuff.

Several women who discussed spirituality but not organized religion, and those who did not refer to spirituality as defined here referred to volunteer community service they did as value-based activities—a spirituality of sorts. Their participation, either on their own or through the auspices of organizations, was based on their personal commitment to others, a cultural tradition of Black women. Some clarifying words:

Sharon: I work with different kinds of groups. When someone needs assistance, they contact me. Sometimes it's church groups. A speaking engagement...sometimes, it's gratis because it depends mostly on the things people approach me about.

Lani: The women's shelter...they have a community initiative to do some gardening in the neighborhood to have some green over here. I don't need a lot of herbs or spices but as part of that network I buy from them. I'll buy the spices from them and I get organic spices grown right here.

Cheryl O.: I donate to the scholastic art show each year. People would ask to donate work...to an auction or this or that and I would always do that....People have been really nice to me...and I try and give back to other people and be encouraging and give advice. You know...[T]he same way that people have done for me.

Thus, there appears to be consistency in values and behavior based on a spiritual worldview reported by a majority of the group, including the commitment to the community, the giving back to others, and responses to requests for help. It was implied that the sense of wholeness that comes from faith in a higher being and faith in their own capability added to the women's ability to persevere and prevail in their business activities.

One of the major findings of the study was the role and importance of spirituality in the life and business experiences of the study group participants. Although most research and writing in both academic and popular literature on Black women in the economy focuses on women in the work force rather than entrepreneurs, some common truths emerge. As suggested by the findings, faith, a component of spirituality, encompasses both faith in a higher being and faith in one's self, closely connected with a strong sense of self.

Robert Guerrero, the Muckleshoot Indian Tribe Director of Education, conducted a study on the strategies of successful American Indian and Native Learners in Adult Higher Education. His findings were stunning in their agreement with the results for these Black women and their spirituality. For example, one of Guerrero's main findings was that a major strategy employed by the successful learners was the embrace of their culturally connected sense of spirituality:

> The role of spirituality was seen as pivotal by the participants in that it provided them with various options for becoming and maintaining themselves as successful learners. Spirituality was viewed as a way to gain emotional strength and grounding and as a way to keep students connected to their culture."[16]

Spirituality was a theme that overlapped the themes of community, sense of self, excellence, and balance. Black women's reported spirituality, belief in God, use of prayer, and church membership was not surprising. What was interesting was the way in which it was perceived to have affected their business. Spirituality was felt to give some women an advantage, a base of support, and a source of guidance, strength, and inspiration that enabled them to get through difficult times in business as well as life.

There was also a connection between spirituality and balance, substantiated by the fact that the women view the achievement of balance as a recognized need, a goal, and a measure of success. Their words bear out the fact that they value balance and that this includes inner balance, achieved by doing things for themselves—be it increased leisure activities, time alone, simple rest, or exploration of their spirituality. Sharon's seminar business provides a venue in which all women, but especially Black women, can have a moment in time for the renewal and refreshment that enables wellness, wholeness, and health:

> It's in a way, it's the time out that women don't generally take for themselves. It's a retreat, it's just the kind of day off you would give yourself perhaps if you had a true day off, where you didn't . . . take the day off to see about elderly parents or go to visit my child's teachers. It's the type of day you'd design for yourself.

The achievement of inner balance and sense of well-being brought about by the holistic integration of mind, body, and soul was universal among the women in this study as they talked about spirituality, regardless of the organized religion or nondenominational spirituality they most identified with. For some of the women in the study, church membership, attendance, and ritual were an important part of their spiritual, social, and business lives. Guerrero's Native American students similarly saw spirituality as a way of helping them get back in touch with their traditional Indian roots and rituals and to reconnect with their heritage, which helped them achieve academically and personally.[17]

This holistic sense of balance was found to carry over among these entrepreneurs, as they were also concerned with achieving a balance between their businesses and their lives. They did not separate the two but blended them, as opposed to the typical Euro-American, market-driven business model, which compartmentalizes work, life, and spirituality.[18]

During the member check focus group I convened in which the women who participated gathered, at my invitation, to hear the preliminary findings and interpretations, the spirituality theme was reported to have been found frequently, as were its reported connections to the values held up by spiritual business people that resulted in ethical, honest, efficient, and respectful ways of doing business. One woman asked if this wasn't in fact a negative in business, because she'd seen many unethical practices and had seen people doing them make more money faster. She asked "Am I the only fool?" for doing business honestly. The others in the group then asked her if she had acted unethically or dishonestly would she be able to "sleep at night." She said no. These responses may indicate that people who are honest in business and who value ethics, balance, and family over asset accumulation and work may, in fact, not do as well quantitatively.

There seems to be a connection between a sense of spirituality and values in business behavior, as expressed by these women. Writing about the "Moral Ambiguity of Entrepreneurs," Stewart addresses this issue. He contends that entrepreneurs are generally highly valued in the United States for their creativity and innovativeness but are not valued in the rest of the world for the way in which they accumulate wealth, through "opportunism and self-seeking behavior."[19] A term that exemplifies an opposing way of doing business is "cooperative economics," based on the Afrocentric principle of community connectivity over individual attainment. The spirituality, ethical outlook, trust, and concern for balance exhibited by this group of Black women entrepreneurs may highlight some of the lessons that can be learned from many ethically challenged corporations and chief executive officers, whose poor behavior and lack of values are rapidly coming to light—and hopefully to justice.

These themes closely associated with Black women have stood the test of time. Grounded in a traditional African worldview, those threads have connected values, strategies, and beliefs that have produced excellence. Social capital or relationships with others provides the backing for all the pieces in this patchwork story quilt. Deborah's words offer an excellent summary of their values:

I'm growing in my spiritual life, which teaches me to think and to believe in myself and what I can do. And if it doesn't go through, it just means that that was not meant to happen for me. If that wasn't in God's plan for me, it's OK it didn't go through.

CHAPTER 9

Social Capital: A New Kind of Quilt

African people are diunital people, seeking richness of meaning in apparent contradictions. They are comfortable bringing together realities which may appear contradictory or in opposition, for example body/spirit, sacred/secular/individual/community. They reach for a synthesis of opposites.

—Sister Thea Bowman, *Lead Me, Guide Me:*
The African American Catholic Hymnal, Preface

As we have seen in the previous chapter, the women in this study were seeking balance between seeming opposites. For our present-day Market Women, relationships with others were evident and paramount in their life and work and epitomized the blending of individual and community goals. Social capital, or the depth and degree of one's social networks based on mutually beneficial relationships, is a strong thread that binds all the patches and pieces of Black women's entrepreneurship together. Lani's story gives us examples of the use and value of relationships in her business development.

Lani is a small woman who repairs shoes in one business and sells healthy food to the residents of her economically distressed neighborhood in her organic food restaurant in her second business. She related the story of her informal social network, which, as we have seen, provided a great deal of nonmonetary support through bartering that reduced the amount of financial capital she had to raise to open the restaurant.

My partner's family was instrumental in helping us get started. In helping me to really put together all the ideas for the business and not just the mental to view...the mental picture but actually helping with the physical labor.

She explained the elements of her informal network of support as:

[S]ort of an informal network. My partner's family are Colombian and some of them don't speak much English and from my association with them they've been so helpful. I've been the one to go to court for them at times. And translate letters and write letters and things like that. And it's been a network; as people have come from abroad they always come to us and to me to first, [to] help them get a job and then get settled. And then being here in NY, some of my customers were from the directors of the women's shelters here. And with the Clubhouse, it's an agency for...mentally challenged individuals. I have an interesting position there...on the board of directors. It's opened up a lot of avenues for me in that people have referred people to me and have come and asked for advice. I've met a lot of people through that.

She went on to clarify the reciprocal nature of her giving to the people and organizations in her community:

Women boiling and washing clothes (1870s). Courtesy of Robert N. Dennis Collection of Stereoscopic Views, Miriam & Ira D. Wallach Division of Art, Prints, and Photographs, The New York Public Library, Astor, Lenox, and Tilden Foundations.

In fact for the women's shelter I get business coming in here simply because some people have said, "We'll go to her because she's concerned about what you eat." And if you want to lose weight or you know you're sick and you need to be on organic food. You need to start eating right. So I get referrals from all over. From all around.

Connection to and concern for community is also apparent, as Lani's business activities promote both her own business success and the common or public good.

I thought there were a lot of nice people in the neighborhood that just didn't have a lot of choices in the neighborhood. It's healthy fast food. It's organic so that it makes different. It's different in that is it here. We've tried to make it as homey as possible as opposed to being commercial. Our prices are very different for...the quality food we put out. Our prices are different, and I believe we're going to see more of these types of business as time goes on. Because I see people beginning to take more control of their health and just...empowering themselves. One of my goals is to see that people over here have a better quality of life.

I didn't envision myself as making a lot of money in opening the business. Incidentally, I make a lot of money if I do well. But the purpose was to have a business that would be different and that would help the community and that would also help me, that I would be true to myself in doing business too.

Maggie Lena and Madame C. J. Walker would have been proud.

Connection with Others

As seen in Lani's account, the quantity and quality of relationship with others is a key factor in social capital accumulation. For these women, critical relationships were with parents, families, and friends. People "skills" or the ability to relate well and work well with others is considered to be crucial in business and involves recognition of the importance of networking and maintaining relationships, including those with customers, vendors and colleagues. Connection to community in a narrow as well as broad sense is essential and operative in Black women's lives. In terms of their themes, giving back to others is an important capital formation strategy in keeping with their historical traditions. In the spirit of those themes and traditions, the mutuality of support means having a strong foundation as well as being supportive of others.

In analyzing the women's social capital networks, I identified two aspects of social capital. One was the traditional business social capital formation activity, bridging gaps and forming "weak ties" through networking for the purpose of information exchange, resource sharing, and obtaining access to markets and financing. The other characteristic reported was the nurturing side of social capital, evidenced by the provision of emotional, familial, and non-monetary and physical support, obtained primarily from traditional bonds: mother–daughter, "sisters," and the community. The former is defined as the "bridging" or connecting function of social capital and is the traditional function of networks recognized in business development literature as contributing to success, especially that of new small businesses, and the latter is the nurturing function of support systems and networks.[1] Putnam, who has written extensively on social capital theory, identified several aspects of social capital including the sociology of friendship, its simultaneous use as a private as well as social good, and its potential negative or positive effects. He contends that social capital, with its networks and "associated norms of reciprocity" and its "conceptual cousin 'community,'" comes in many shapes and forms. He identifies two versions of social capital: bonding, which I call nurturing, and bridging:

> Bonding (or inclusive)... by choice or necessity, are inward looking and tend to reinforce exclusive identities and homogeneous groups [B]ridging (or exclusive) are better for linkage to external assets and information exchange.... The "weak ties" that link to distant acquaintances who move in different circles... are actually more valuable than the "strong ties."[2]

Gittel and Thompson, in their discussion of inner-city business development and enterprise, have identified the "strength of weak ties" as an excellent tool for economic development, including entrepreneurship, especially for communities usually considered to be less than economically successful.[3] Weak ties are functional; strong ties are necessary. Both are needed to succeed.

Jackie L. relates the value of informal networking activity to business success:

> I have a kind of like... an informal type of thing because I speak with other business owners now. I have friends who have their own businesses. And we share stories and we can talk about things and that helps. It just helps to hear other people's stories.

She also talked about how her husband, her friends, and even her UPS driver all pitched in to help her get a major order out, one that established her business on a higher level:

> Just overseeing the order was hard. It was hard from beginning to end but... I really truly saw my friends pitch in.... [P]eople really, really

helped me. They gave me their time because I had two thousand hats and again I'm one person. One person pretty much runs this company. It couldn't have all been done by myself. So my husband helped me, my friend P. helped me, my sisters helped me, another friend C. We all just pitched in and got it done.

For the Black women in this study, participation in traditional networking activities was widely reported, even though, as we know, a number could not take full advantage of all opportunities because of time poverty issues. Some also found lingering evidence of racism and sexism present even in supposedly open forums. Frankie, as we will see, received some benefits from the weak ties she made:

Women out here are seen as homemakers or home technicians. Now they're forming all these wonderful groups and they're making their husbands do various things. . . . Women are more supportive. It's the men that you have to deal with.

She understands that, "in the establishment you can't move by yourself. You need help." But she also recognized that:

[A]s far as them looking on me as an equal. . . . I don't think that it will happen. It's not going to happen yet. A lot of them are waiting to see what will happen.

In addition, certainly by choice and perhaps out of necessity, these women reported a high incidence of participation in "nurturing" social capital activities, among their sisters and with their mothers, families, and communities. Deborah reminisced about how she and her business partner received support from both their families and friends as they were starting up:

My family was very supportive and so was hers because they bought a lot of the stuff and they also would have little parties with neighbors and friends to encourage [us]. And I have friends who are entrepreneurs and we conversate a lot. When one is stuck we'll call each other. . . . So it was good to have that backup support.

It was fascinating to hear the number of groups the women joined. In addition to religious, social, and political groups, many of which have deep roots in the Black community, these women consciously and deliberately found and participated in bridging organizations. They built on weak ties, connecting with people with whom they would not have ordinarily interacted through participation in broad-based entrepreneurship networking groups, trade and industry associations, or community-based lenders such as the Women's Venture Fund and the Bethex Federal Credit Union in the Bronx.

There has been an increase in the number of networking groups and organizations organized by and for Black women that promote connections, sisterhood, and business. Almost all the group members named organizations or groups they belonged to, formal and informal, new and historical, and business and social, that provided networks and systems of support. The full list of nurturing and bridging social and business network organizations and the women who joined them can be found in appendix B. That list also can serve as a resource list for emerging and established entrepreneurs.

Two women, Wendy and Paulette, belonged to more than one organization, and three others, Deborah, Efua, and Patricia, belonged to the same organization, Black Women Enterprises of NYS, which was one of the sites used for focus groups in this study. Black Woman Enterprises is an organization dedicated to the promotion of entrepreneurship for Black women through networking, training, advocacy, contract procurement, and access to markets. The groups with which the women were involved included social organizations, community service organizations, and those concerned with entrepreneurship advancement, financial planning, and health.

The notion of sisterhood can be expanded to include a connection with other women of color and to non-minority women as well. Several participants indicated they also belonged to other mixed women's groups, most frequently those organized around entrepreneurship and small business ownership, providing network support and resource and information sharing. Some also belonged to larger women's business or professional groups; those who did not report membership in either type of networking group reported involvement with informal groups. Jackie L. and Lani were board members for local community-based organizations and not-for profit organizations that focused on providing services to women. Helen and Lani were both involved in women's shelters, prison programs for women and children, and mental health services also geared to the same groups. Arlene worked in an organization that provided services to at-risk adolescent girls. Finally, more than half of the group also reported belonging to wide-reaching organizations and associations felt to be helpful to the businesses. These included networking organizations for entrepreneurs in general and industry-related trade associations.

As noted, all of the women in the group belong to a least one—and many belonged to multiple—networking groups or associations, even if they did not always have the opportunity to take full advantage of the usefulness of these societies. Their business strategies incorporated the recognition of the importance of networking and the ability to act on it, entering both nurturing and bridging networks as they accumulated significant social capital.

Deborah is an excellent networker who has an informal support group and who had joined groups focusing on Black women entrepreneurs, such as Black Women Enterprises, and bridging groups, such as the Women's Venture Fund and a trade association—the Gift Association. Her participation in these groups has benefited her, her business, and those with whom she came in contact.

> I networked going to all of these business classes. I was networking with people...So I feel my social skills played a part because I had the skill to network with these people, talk to people. I wasn't afraid to venture out to let people know what I was doing. What I wanted to do. And because of that all those people helped me. I think it was the networking like I was in different classes. I met lots of people.

She talked about her relationship with the Women's Venture Fund, an organization based on the principles of cooperative economics, peer lending, and networking for the purpose of enabling small business owners to obtain loans and access large markets.

Wendy was also a client of the organization and believes that:

> The Women's Venture Fund opened a lot of doors for me. And I believe it had a lot to do with my going forward also.

Recent studies of other women entrepreneurs of color confirm that for them, social capital formation, especially in terms of establishing networks of support, is significant in becoming successful. The April 1998 study by the National Foundation of Women Business Owners (now the Center for Women's Business Research) states that for many minority women, including Hispanic and Asian women, "networking with others in their own ethnic groups is invaluable."[4] Bonnie Wong, president and founder of Asian Women in Business says that networking is also valuable outside one's own group.[5] Finding emotional support, a commonality of issues, and a level of comfort in one's own group is the function of the "nurturing" social capital networks, and the connection or "bridging" with groups outside of one's own who also have common concerns is the most beneficial way to maximize use of networking opportunities. It is clear that both types of social capital activities are necessary for success, especially for those on the "margins" of business, economic, and academic institutions.

Frankie talked about the benefits of joining groups that were predominantly made up of White women, drawing on the strength of those weak ties:

> The woman who was the founding member of this business group's husband was the commissioner of economic development. She said if I have any problems, don't hesitate....I kept hitting walls. She said "let me make a call." He said my permit would be ready in two days. All this goes back to the center. Networking is powerful.

Wong, along with leaders of Black and Hispanic women business owners associations in New York City, have formed an alliance to share information, conduct mutually beneficial buying and selling, and build a support center, in which teaching and training activities and meeting facilities will be provided to members of the groups. The group has come together in a hybrid network, with members serving both nurturing functions as it evolves. The group was formed because women of color in New York State have been underrepresented in the securing of business financing, contract procurement, and other business development activities that contribute to the growth usually enjoyed by those privileged by race and gender. They felt that such a coalition will begin to correct that imbalance.

Giving as well as receiving emotional support was also a characteristic of this type of social capital, which speaks to the mutuality of social capital accumulation efforts discussed by Swantz in her theory of women's everyday economics. It seems that this aspect of social capital formation is particularly valuable to Black women entrepreneurs or others born of the historical need to provide sensitive and compassionate support in addition to the sharing of information and resources needed to survive and prevail in a discriminatory and hostile climate.

Presence of the mother–daughter bond, sisterhood, community support, group, network, and family support reported by the participants provides evidence of their use as resources for both learning and business activities. Scott, a Black female sociologist who has studied the habits of survival, believes that this viable pattern or web of support, which she calls the "kinship insurance policy," has protected Black people of every economic class throughout history.[6] Thus, retention of the legacy of struggle and connection with each other as well as others engaged in similar struggles is even more important for success and survival in the economic arena. The study participants are good examples of people who continued to struggle and who, even as they become more quantitatively successful, did not forget their connections with others and their communities.

The Importance of Community

In addition to the sense of sisterhood and the mother–daughter bond, concern for and involvement with the wider community is both an enhancement of social capital accumulations and mitigates against the obstacles encountered in business and in life. It is a Black Women's Theme. The women discussed their concern for and involvement with their communities. For the most part, those concerns centered around providing quality services and products to their immediate community, be it a neighborhood or the Black community as a whole, and made those connections part of the women's business operations. We have heard from Lani and Helen about links to their communities. Other voices add to the emphasis on community connections.

Deborah: I wanted to express that I wanted to do something for me, for my people, for my culture. . . . I knew that there was a need in floral design that is not necessarily for our particular group of people, so I knew that this was an area that I could be focused in on, you know . . . using beads and Afrocentric things.

Sharon: My whole approach is to make things accessible to people who have come from a busy day. And they want something that's available in their community.

Arlene: Yes, I did have a customer base already. I thought that there were a lot of nice people [who] just didn't have choices in the neighborhood. They were getting a little something different from what they were used to in the neighborhood. . . . [F]rom just a genuine concern about the neighborhood, that sort of happened.

Identification of one's self as a member of the community was also important to the women, as they clearly articulated their need to stay actively involved. Giving back by giving time, money, or goods to those less fortunate was both a goal of the businesses and a mark of success.

Ava: That's just part of our mission. . . . [D]uring the winter months in crisis situations, you know . . . people buy food or clothing for families in crisis.

Patricia: My goals were to just help children in the community with their homework or study skills. Basically that was my goal . . . [T]o help improve students, give me the opportunity to show families that you can help your children and yourself through study skills.

Robin: My goal was to have an alternative dance school for my race.

Getting and Giving: Role Models and Mentors

There is a story worth telling about an unbroken line of mentors, known and unknown, beginning with Sojourner Truth.

Inspired by the testimony of Sojourner Truth, Mary McLeod Bethune, the daughter of former slaves, became a mentor for a number of civil rights pioneers, among them . . . Dorothy Height.[7]

Height, the long-time president of the National Council of Negro Women, started as Bethune's executive secretary. She said she admired Bethune's deep spiritual qualities and her sense of humor—two Black Women's Themes. She went on to say that:

One of the gifts of Blackness is being connected to a sense of history, so that one's life just isn't for today but it's for hundreds of years that went before and the hundreds of years that come after. When I first started feeling sorry for myself, I remember all the way back to the first slave that jumped ship, to Sojourner Truth, to my mother who scrubbed people's kitchen floors all of her life, and my father who moved us out to Wellington—all those people paid a terrific price so that I can have the opportunities I have. It made me feel like I was directly connected to that kind of genius. When you have that sense of lineage, it is really powerful.

Rosalyn Williams was next in line; she was Height's protégé, and she in turn talked about Height's influence on her:

All those women who were pioneers became invisible people. And to survive being an invisible person is really something. That prepared me for the times when I became an invisible person. . . . I'm in a great line of invisible people.

In the womanist tradition, Williams became the mentor of Roy Matthews, founder of Passages, a placement firm for minority youth.[7] We can assume that Matthews, in his work, mentors many others. The interesting thing about this line of mentors, which bridges centuries, is that the mentors invited their protégés to work with them after observing similarities in ethics, values, and commitment. They taught by modeling, apprenticing, and being role models.

Education has always been a seminal value in the Black community and is part and parcel with community involvement. In economic terms, education is the vehicle for human capital formation and was found to be interwoven with social capital efforts in the business owners' lives and practices. Relationships in learning situations, learning activities, and learning strategies are also vital in human capital acquisition. As a consequence, learning with and from others is an area of overlap between human and social capital accumulation themes. Social capital sub-themes that relate to learning include relationships with parents, families, and friends; the presence and use of role models and mentors; and the presence or absence of support. Indicators include actively seeking and using advice, observation, and listening to learn. The presence of role models and mentors, and collaborative and cooperative learning, is enhanced by relationships with family, friends, and peers. They are also learning strategies associated with success.

Being proactive is a personal characteristic attributed to successful business behavior—being ready and able to receive help in a "teachable moment," as described in adult education, applies to entrepreneurship as well. Actively seeking advice from others about business development and using that advice, whether in the formal entrepreneurship classes or informal settings, was mentioned by a majority of the group members.

Sharon: I'll tell you, I'm ready for help at this point.

Arlene: So I went to Mr. S. and he helped me. He told me that...you have to be strong and that you have to just keep up with her and go. So I went to her and I just sat there and did what he told me to do and I mean everything went very, very well.

People often learn a great deal by observing and watching family members, teachers, or mentors. For example, we know that many successful entrepreneurs come from families in which there are or have been entrepreneurs. We heard from Helen and Efua earlier about how their families helped them understand business so that entrepreneurship became a viable option for them.

Efua: But I [had] experience in that [business] previously when I was younger because that's what my grandmother did for a living.

Many women, including those who worked in their family businesses at a very early age, described observing how people conducted business, related to customers, and approached learning.

Jackie L.: My parents, no job is too small for you to do. Just do it with pride and put your best into it.... I just saw...that [it] wasn't a problem for them to do other things. Because she [her mother] was a nurses' aide and she would do her selling on the weekends.

So then I went to S. and I looked back to them and I started seeing that you know, who's buying...So...I learned through watching them. Seeing them do things, and then I guess observing day-to-day life. Just people.

Frankie: I have been taught many things over the years because my uncle had his own store.... Well, I listen. I listen a great deal to people...helping me learn and to recognize...gotta keep your mouth shut,...got to watch things sometime.

Ava: And what I've observed up to this date, a number of stores are carrying the same things...and I'm noticing their price margins. Informally, that's what I've observed and learned.

Observations of others included learning how to behave in the world by watching; some attributed this learning directly to their desire to become an entrepreneur and how they would behave when they became one. They also reported watching how people conducted themselves in their daily lives, their work habits and ethics, their gender roles, and their attitudes toward money and values. The people most often observed for those attributes and behaviors were parents and grandparents.

Wendy: My dad was . . . very important in the way I see things and the
way I do things. My dad from looking what he's done . . . was
constantly on the go. He would come home and he would work
how many hours and he never gave up. And my dad was always
like, you know, if you're going to do a job, do it the best way you
can, not . . . halfway. And that's me. I do the best I can and that's
the way I am.

We have seen how important role models and mentors are in learning,
especially in learning how to conduct business. They are also important
sources of inspiration. As we have seen, Sharon accesses unknown mentors
and role models through her daily meditation. In a like manner, a high percentage of study group participants reported the presence of role models in
their immediate families—primarily their parents—as well as having other
business owners, bosses, teachers, and friends whom they admired and
respected. Role models have always been present in the Black community,
including those to whom people have turned for business guidance, but they
have not been acknowledged as such in traditional business and education
literature because they have not been recognized as "business people." Most
are unknown to the White community in general, contributing to the ongoing
business myth about the dearth of role models for Black people in business.
However, those role models identified by the women were observed and
emulated not only for their ability to do business but also for their personal
attributes and they way in which they conducted themselves in life. A few
examples follow:

Wendy: She [a teacher] had an aura about her, and she's trained and
she was real positive and she was strong and she was very
forceful in a positive way.

Jackie L.: My professor—she loved what she was doing and she really
made me believe I could make beautiful [things] that people
would want.

Helen: He [her boss] was very fair. And that really impressed me a lot.

Cheryl H.: She [a friend] is a six-year survivor, and she is so strong.
Every time I want to complain I look at her. She will always find
a way. And teach me. She has a business, a lingerie business for
women who've had breast surgery.

Cheryl O.: But for a person for whom, I mean [H]e [her husband] had
his own business. . . . [A] person who was creative for a living
and . . . who doesn't have a lot of material needs.

Cheryl O. also identifies Madame C.J. Walker, the first Black women who
was a self-made millionaire, as a role model and uses her stamp on all her
correspondence because "it is all of a piece."

As previously reported, three women identified entrepreneurs within their families who served as both role models and teachers to them an early age. Two other women give an account of their own mothers or other family members who were their entrepreneurial role models:

> *Nancy*: Well, people in my family have always owned in one way or another, have always owned their own businesses....[M]y uncles owned trucking businesses. Other family members owned rental property....It was pretty much a natural order of progression.

> *Robin*: Well, my mother owned her own business. She's owned it for thirty-five years....[S]o I grew up with her owning, and my father, who I didn't grow up with, is a business owner also. So I guess maybe it's genetic.

Contrary to the prevailing mythology embedded in traditional business literature about Black women, mentors were present and critical in these women's lives. A mentor is defined by Daloz as a guide for a person embarking on a journey through paths the mentor has successfully negotiated.[8] It was not difficult for these women to recognize mentors in their lives, and they were happy to acknowledge and thank them for their help in life and in business. The mentors reported were teachers, bosses, experienced business owners, spouses or partners, and in two cases, church pastors. Some received mentors as part of their formal Entrepreneurial Assistance Program training; most identified and obtained mentors on their own, and usually informally. The mentors were available on an individual basis as sources of information and teaching regarding some skill or aspect of conducting business, both by example and by direct instruction, Most important, the mentors also provided an ongoing source of support, which in some cases was financial as well as emotional. They were clearly seen as guides for the business owners making their journey along the road to business success.

> *Devya*: My teachers, my spiritual teachers. They tell me what to ask.

> *Deborah*: But I find that um a lot of my teachers help me, my mentors...who became mentors later. And then we had mentors [for the specific business] and things like that.

> *Wendy*: She was my boss. I would go to her and say "I'm burnt out" and she would understand and she would kind of walk me through how to get through certain things, like what needs to be done and what needs not to be done. But I did learn from her, the way she worked. Because she gave and she was always like, "Yeah you can do this." She was very, very positive.

> *Jackie L.*: I think the person who teaches to you, to touch you and move you and make you believe in yourself. The guide up in the

Bronx. She made a big change in my life...how you approach
people and speak to people and ask for what help you need.

Efua: [M]y son's father...because he's been in business and he went
through a lot of things with his business.

Sharon: Not for business, I think, but I've had a mentor for my work
in human services. A woman I admire a great deal...a professor
who was a mentor for me in the field of education.

Katherine: [M]y pastor because he's...the one who encouraged me. I
would turn around. I would just look and he would smile at me.
Then I would just feel like, Okay, I'm doing it right, you know.

Cheryl O.: One of the people in the group [networking] who had been
in business for a while, five, six years...he was very helpful...suggesting sources for getting information about doing
shows because he was on the road a lot and making a living from it.

Nancy talked about a teacher she had as a child whom she considered
to be a mentor:

A White teacher who was just wonderful. I mean...[W]hen they say
that teachers are influential in shaping the lives of children, they
certainly are...[she] recognized that I was creative and [she] allowed
me in so many ways to express that creativity....I'll never forget her.

A smaller number of women reported being mentors as well as having
mentors. In most instances they were mentoring or guiding younger women in
their families or communities—their daughters, younger sisters, neighbors'
children, and young people, primarily teens, from their communities. In several instances, the owners had brought their children into the business and
were grooming them to eventually take over. All who were seen as role models
or mentors expressed a feeling of accomplishment and self-satisfaction at
having attained a level of success sufficient to be seen as worthy of emulation.

Adult learning theory identifies cooperative and collaborative learning as
powerful methods of acquiring knowledge and skills. Women's development theory, especially related to cognitive and moral development, understands that growth and learning happen in connection and in relationship,
rather than the in more widely used notion of self-directed, autonomous
learning. These women learned their business and life skills in connection and
in relationship with others, in a womanist, Afrocentric, humanistic tradition.

The most outstanding and overarching finding in the study was the
depth and breadth of social capital possessed by these women. Figure 9.1. is
a graphic that displays how the different kinds of capital intersect and
influence each other. For this group of women, social capital was the most
influential. They possessed every indicator of social capital accumulation
mentioned by Bates, McClelland, and Putnam. Social capital is closely

SOCIAL CAPITAL
Relationships with others

Success Indicators: Being a mentor, role
model, "Giving back," good reputation,
customer satisfaction, wider network, balance.

HUMAN CAPITAL
Collaborative, cooperative learning

Success Indicators: Increased
knowledge, skills, increased self-
esteem, sense of agency, excellence.

FINANCIAL CAPITAL
Non-monetary support

Success Indicators: Increased
social capital account, increased
profits, ability to give back, ability
to empower others financially.

Figure 9.1. Capital accumulations. Courtesy of C.A. Smith © 1999.

related to Goleman's "EQ," or emotional quotient, defined as the posses-
sion of self-awareness, impulse control, persistence, zeal, self-motivation,
empathy, and social deftness (qualities associated with excellence and success in business and life), as well as the self-discipline, altruism, and compassion he feels are necessary for the promotion of a thriving and civilized
society. The findings of the study indicate the group participants also
possessed a high emotional quotient (EQ) associated with business success,
not surprising in this group of successful entrepreneurs.[9]

Butler, an African-American entrepreneurship researcher and scholar,
contends that the collectivist tradition, historically present in the Black
community, stresses relationships in entrepreneurship: "It does not view
entrepreneurship as an individual phenomena. Individualism is replaced
with group self-help and institutional building skills."[10] Swantz, who, in her
theory of women's everyday economics that emphasizes connection to
community, believes that "service activities compliment income generation."[11] We see those elements clearly in this group of women. Their present
affirms the past and guides the future of those who want to come after them.

*I know where I am in the community. I'm in the heart of the Black
community.*

—Sandy

PART III

The Future: The Sankofa Principle—The Wisdom of Learning from the Past

The African symbol of Sankofa is graphically portrayed as a stylized bird looking backward or a mirror-image heart-shaped figure. In the Akan language, a literal translation is to "go back and retrieve" —SAN (return) KO (go) FA (look). The Sankofa principle means we need to reclaim our past to understand our present and plan our future. Black women entrepreneurs, descendants of the ancient African Market Women, have maintained the tradition of connection to the family, the community, and each other as they overcame the constraints of the times in which they lived. Generation after generation has been immersed, whether consciously or unconsciously, in the Sankofa principle, retaining and passing on those values, skills, and attitudes for the betterment of those who followed.

For women of the African diaspora who have been deprived of a great deal of their economic past, these forgotten "patches" in our historical quilt are critical to continued success. This section will connect the past, present, and future of Black women entrepreneurs, highlighting their distinctive gifts and offering inspiration and advice for those who will come after them. The African symbol of Sankofa and the Gullah saying below are part of a continuum of philosophy and values that calls attention to the significance of knowing and understanding history.

If you don't know where you're going, you should know where you come from.

—Gullah Proverb

*Harriet Powers, American, 1837–1911, Pictorial Quilt. Photograph ©
2004 Museum of Fine Arts, Boston.*

CHAPTER 10

Gifts from the Margin

The experiences of these Market Women provide lessons for living and doing business. Living on the "margins" provides gifts. The gifts from the women appear in the form of experience and comfort with life in the edge, resistance, and resiliency; creativity; and determination. The other gift they give is a new vision of success, power, and wealth. This chapter imparts some words of wisdom from the group for those who want to open and develop their own businesses. Each woman was asked what advice she would give to new or would-be entrepreneurs, and each had her own suggestions. They had very specific ideas for would-be business owners, based on their own experiences. The advice they felt would help entrepreneurs along the road to entrepreneurial success touched on strategies for acquiring financial, human, and social capital; and spirituality, as well as establishing a sense of self, following a vision or a dream, and achieving balance. Those thoughts are shared in their own voices.

Deborah, the floral design artist, has been in business for a number of years, going solo after dissolving the partnership that structured the start-up. Her products range from single flower buds made from Afrocentric cloth to large centerpieces, wreaths, and floral arrangements for entire wedding receptions, including the "jumping the broom" motif that was used to formalize weddings in the antebellum era. The materials she uses include cloth as well as dried and fresh flowers; all have an African American motif. Her clients include well-known public figures, a major retail catalog, and individuals and organizations. She is very well organized, skilled in her work, and proficient in her marketing strategies and money management. She is also an entrepreneur with vision and creativity and was planning for a major

Harriet Powers (American, 1837–1911), about 1900. Photograph © 2004 Museum of Fine Arts, Boston.

expansion of her business. Deborah has established a solid customer base and reputation, enhanced by print and media coverage in local newspapers and television. Being a mentor and giving advice in a number of areas was important to her. Because she was one of the graduates of my entrepreneurship class, I often invited her to speak to my new classes. Deborah used this class as well as others to grow her business. Well-known in her local area, she had been interviewed on a television show about her business and talked about her appearance on the show and its outcome:

> After that TV show I got lots of calls from women asking me how I got started. What encouraged me to go forward...and I always talk to them...like in classes that people ask me to speak [to,] I'm always happy to do that. I tell them to stay focused, it's hard work, do a business plan because that teaches you to focus and bring everything together—organize, plan, project, visualize.
>
> One, find something that you like. You have to like it, when times get rough and hard [or] you're not going to stick with it. Two, stay focused and don't be discouraged. Because there were many times when I didn't sell anything. For instance...the very first sale we didn't sell anything. But I did not stop there. You cannot stop there. Because it's very easy to say, "Oh I don't have anything, it's not going to work." And if I had stopped that day I would have never known I could have evolved this far. So stay with it. But first you have to like it. Because if you don't like it you're not going to stay with it.

Deborah's story highlights several themes we have identified earlier, some of which are echoed in the words and thoughts of the other women. These successful women, although probably not recognized as such by the wider world, have shared their stories and the wisdom that ensues from them. Their identification of what they considered to be important sets the stage for newer and broader definitions of success, power, and wealth.

New Definitions

Jill Nelson, in her own journey tale of becoming a grown-up Black woman, feels that Black women have been made invisible because all too often and for too long they have been defined by others.[1] Insidious images have prevailed over time. Names have been created meant to support those images and disempower the named. Accomplishments and contributions have been measured by yardsticks that were meant for others. To take back our power, to understand its presence and persistence, Black women have had to rename ourselves, reclaim our history, and re-present our accomplishments. This section explains how the women in the book have defined themselves as women and entrepreneurs and reshaped the concepts of success, wealth, and power, and by so doing challenged the prevailing negative views of Black women.

Success

Success in entrepreneurship has many definitions, both qualitative and quantitative. The self-definition of success in business as presented by the group is framed by several of the Black Women's Themes. New definitions of wealth, power, and success in business have been documented in the words of the study participants and echoed by others.

Rita McGrath, a traditionalist who teaches at Columbia University's business school, understands wealth creation as the primary goal of new businesses; she writes that success can be construed as "what the organization can muster in terms of finance, manufacturing and marketing," or the extent to which the entrepreneur can recognize and make creative uses of resources.[2] In our women's terms, successful business strategies result in measures of success that include not only making profits but also using those profits in an ethical and meaningful way. In the history of Black women in America, the ability to use the profits of business for freedom for self and others, for resistance, and to fight for civil rights was used in part to gauge the success of their businesses.

The women's own definitions of success reflect the value of alternative and expanded definitions. Table 10.1 summarizes those definitions. In the definitions, social capital elements encompass connections and relationship with others, including defining monetary success. Success in social capital terms as described by the contributors includes an increased ability to do for others—to help, teach, and employ others; the effect of their success on others is also central to this definition. For example, quite a few individuals talked about how their success in business enabled them to give to others through teaching by modeling and mentoring, through providing community service, or through taking leadership positions in their communities:

Table 10.1 Definitions of Success

- Freedom to make own choices and control own lives; empowerment
- Financial self-sufficiency and comfort
- Ability to give back to community and to financially empower others
- Self-satisfaction in achieving own goals
- Balance between life and work; mind, body, and spirit
- Making a living doing what they love to do
- Achieving excellence, obtaining respect
- Being a role model
- "Living the Dream"

Source: C.A. Smith © 1999.

Frankie: I am able to contribute to soup kitchens and still have enough business coming in where it won't make a difference. Because you know something, when you give, and you give with the heart, it's going to come back. I've seen it already. It's been shown to me already.

Paulette: I have to make it, I have to you know…[a]nd now I feel I can. I have to because I know people are watching me. And…I feel I'm representing a group of women.

Patricia: To leave an imprint or philosophy for others to follow. To teach people to be successful, self-satisfied. My success is that I can share a little bit with others.

In addition to having an increased ability to help others, the chance to empower others, especially financially, was offered as a measure and indicator of success:

Lani: I knew part of my purpose here would be to educate people before I could really sell them some of the things.…I wanted to work with people and healing.

Nancy: I paid my student loans back a year, a year and a half before they were due because I wanted some other Black kid to be able to have the same opportunity to go.

Patricia: They were 13 years old, their parents wanted them to do something like junior counselors. I gave them $40 or $50 every other week.…I gave them something at the end, so we help each other.

The market women of the study also offered definitions of success that included a strong sense of self, self-satisfaction, and doing what they loved to do, with customer satisfaction being an element of social capital. One aspect of a strong sense of self involved freedom or independence—being one's own boss—and was included in their definition of success:

Jackie L.: The freedom it gives me, oh my God! What freedom. I don't need to be running around and hanging out and it's the freedom of my mind. It's almost like my soul, you know.

Nancy: But also freedom. Freedom to make choices and decisions. And to work with other people who share the same vision.

Doing what is loved was identified as success by a number of the women. Their words paint a picture of their strong feelings about what they do and how they feel about doing it:

Deborah: I love, I love making something and seeing their face when they see it.

Paulette: I like every day. I just like everything. I like to be able to stand and look and see everything in order.

Cheryl O.: Doing what you love . . . or being able to do what you love. I mean a . . . [A] lot Of people have things they love but they can't do them because they have these other things. I get to do a lot of stuff I really want to do (laughter).

Customer satisfaction, being able to satisfy their customers and meet their needs by providing them with excellent products and services, was mentioned by most of the women. They agreed that the in-person provision of quality products and services combined with the enjoyment and satisfaction of the customers was a hallmark of achievement.

Devya: The tremendous benefit that I see people getting when they allow me to give it to them, a teacher. To see that transformation is phenomenal . . . to see people who are terrifically stressed and tense, to see them come back to themselves . . . they're competent with their health, standing in their normal weight and . . . radiant. It's the most exciting thing!

Ava: The warmth that you feel when you come in here. The communication. And the consideration. Old people love the place because they can get 10% off anytime they walk in. We give away a lot of things free, too. My definition of success is being able to supply the customer's need.

Cheryl H.: I feel like I'm successful by bringing joy to people and making their dreams come alive.

Cheryl O.: I felt wonderful though. It was very exciting and when people oohed and aahed and the first time I got a letter after a show from a customer talking about how much she loved the piece that she bought . . . it's wonderful.

Deborah: I love making something and seeing the person's face when they see it. That's a good feeling for me . . . customer satisfaction is a good feeling for me. I enjoy the customer liking the service or product I've performed for them. And it also makes me feel good to know that I've accomplished what I've set out to do.

Sandy declared that her customers were the most important factor in her achievement of success.

Self-satisfaction or personal satisfaction was also included in the ability to provide exceptional products and services to customers. In addition, personal satisfaction involved the achievement of goals, realization of a vision, work/life balance, happiness with the business, and happiness in feeling the job was well done.

> *Jackie L.*: It was a great feeling. It was so good to go then to go in the store and see the hats. It was a great feeling and having the catalogue it was great. That someone actually wants to buy this product. Right, it came from me and that people want it...That's amazing. I'm flattered people are going to pay for it. To me that's just, that's great, that's great!"
>
> *Frankie*: It's going to be my pleasure to just, know and to see people enjoy my food. You...get that bubbly feeling. You just feel warm and like, I don't know...You get choked up and you can't find the words that are adequate enough to explain or describe. And sometimes all you can do is say "Wow!"
>
> *Sharon*: I think everyone is put here to do something and when you find what you want to do and something you really like, that's good. It's self-fulfilling. And that in itself will give me personal satisfaction and say "Well, I did it!" So the first success in that sense that I got from that was that I actually fulfilled a goal that I set for myself to do it.
>
> *Arlene*: One day I came in here and I just cried because you know it's...tears of happiness.

Finding work/life balance—achieving balance between family, business, social, and personal needs—and achieving an inner balance, including having a sense of happiness and moments of fun, were closely related to personal satisfaction.

> *Ava*: But that stuff (conspicuous consumption of material possessions) doesn't interest me. I just like to have [a]...what do they call it? An even keel life. It's a business. I'm just doing it. But it's a fulfillment for me. Yeah...I have fun.
>
> *Sharon*: As I said, positivity, wellness, wholeness, all the things that women need to support them in their healthy lives.

Excellence is another theme that was noted repeatedly in the interviews and that was composed of several additional components that included concern with efficiency, quality of products and services, commitment to work contract, and work/life balance. Concern with efficiency of operations, high quality, and commitment to work contracts—elements of McClelland's Achievement Orientation—distinguish outstanding entrepreneurs from average entrepreneurs. These elements were included in the women's definitions of success related to the achievement of excellence.

Jackie L.: When I do a job I like to do my best and give it my all . . . after I've figured out how to do the job well, then I kind of like to do other things, take on other things. Plus, do the other things that keep my business running.

Sharon: I've always taken the position of trying to help people with direction, trying to find the ways to do things effectively.

Freedom as success is closely related to control. Internal locus of control—controlling self and not being controlled by others—was another component of success that was related to the sense of self. A number of women talked specifically about having and maintaining this sense of control over themselves and their businesses.

Jackie L.: It's my hell. It's not someone else's hell that I have to participate in. It's my hell.

Paulette: I guess the best thing is that it's my business. It's my energy. It's my dream. And although it's sometimes frustrating, it's overwhelming, it's mine. And it's only going to be what I make it to be.

In all, the women defined success as including an enhanced sense of self, freedom, and independence; an internal locus of control; self-empowerment; and use of power for the benefit of others, especially those who "look like them."

Power

Power is associated with internal locus of control. It is defined in relation to entrepreneurship as the ability to control finances, operations and situations. Traditionally, it is defined as the "ability or capacity to perform effectively" and "the ability or capacity to exert control over others."[3] Camille Cosby, in the foreword of a book entitled *Powerful Black Women*, offers yet another definition of power, one that affirms the groups' perceptions:

Power is the ability to listen as well as act. . . . Power is to live honestly. . . . Power is to have reciprocal trust and love. . . . Power is to be knowledgeable. . . . Power is to accept peoples' ethnic differences as well as human similarities. . . . Power is to be flexible. . . . Power is to speak one's mind.[4]

Her definition of power is less concerned with exerting power over others than over herself in *relationship* to others. In *The Tao of Leadership*,

John Heider defines power as coming "through cooperation, independence through service and a greater self through selflessness," a definition that is in keeping with Black Women's Themes and traditions.[5] Nancy, the music producer, has a very clear view of the value and use of power and talks about both power and control:

> I think although you may have power, power is important but what's more important is how you use that power. And...not to abuse it.... [T]he good thing about power is that you can change things and conditions. To know that I would be in control of my own financial, spiritual, emotional and physical journey.

She went on to relate power and empowerment to being Black and female:

> I think I realized then that it's so important that we as women, that we as Black people not give our power away.... Yes, power in the sense that you set out to do something, you do it, you're making decisions. You're not silent, you have a voice. And that in your having that voice, and your having that power that you give others that look like you and think like you the same opportunity.

Wealth

Power is often inseparable from wealth as one of the uses of power is the acquisition of wealth. Joline Godfrey, a highly successful woman entrepreneur by any measure, offers an alternative definition of wealth, used as the customary measure of success: "wealth is... a complex that includes self-esteem, integrity, quality products, family, friendships and contribution as well as financial achievement."[6]

As we have seen, the women in the group did not focus on money as their primary motivation for going into business for themselves, as is typical for many new entrepreneurs, although wealth creation, the fundamental purpose of traditional entrepreneurship, was one of their goals. Although recognizing they needed to create wealth or profits for their businesses, their expanded definition of success encompasses an additional way of measuring it. Their definition, supporting Godfrey's, included a broader, more inclusive definition, realizing the effect of success on themselves as individuals and others. The success of the participants contributed to their sense of self, reported as an increase in knowledge and improved skills, a desire for continuous learning and growth, a sense of empowerment and agency, and increased self-esteem.

The desire for continuous, lifelong learning was unanimous within the study group. This theme overlaps the theme of excellence, as the women related additional learning to achieving excellence. In addition, the desire to continue to learn was connected directly to success for two of them:

Helen: So my mind is constantly searching. I can say that my mind is very positive but it's not finished. When somebody says to me you're successful, that means—to me—that means that you're done. Not being finished is successful. Absolutely.

Similarly, Nancy felt she was preparing for success:

Right now I don't define myself as successful. I define myself as preparing...in the preparation stage for success.

All of the women in the study reported on the helpfulness of their formal training in their enterprises; most specifically talked about how they were able to transfer that knowledge and increased skills immediately to their business operations. Used in combination with their informal learning strategies, their comments acknowledge the link between learning and success

Wendy: I called [the Entrepreneurial Assistance Program] and I decided to take the classes. That was my real commitment in starting the business. [The best learning experience]...was taking the class and the person who ran the class, the work master....I sat down and listened to what you had to do and that was the reality of how much work I had to put in....It was just, I put myself in a learning situation by wanting to get into business and I got that done.

Lani: I think it's [Entrepreneurial Assistance Program] more purposeful too. Because it's not simply to get a college degree, but it's to...actually utilize it and put it to use within the business that I am doing now...and so that's what I did. I listened to what he [her teacher] said and I used that to build the business.

A good number of the group members reported a sense of personal empowerment as well as a sense of agency, defined as knowing that what they do matters.

Deborah: I'm successful because... I've learned not to let tribulations or disappointments get in my way. So I've learned that ...I am good and I'm a leader. I'm a leader because I'm not following someone. I actually took the initiative to go ahead and do something and I did it. And I didn't need anyone to tell me what to do. I had the drive to go ahead and do it. And stay focused. So in that sense I feel successful. I feel successful as far as developing my skills. I feel positive about it because it's helped me grow as a person.

Jackie L.: It was great. I thought, "Wow, you can do things; when you say you can't do it, it usually means you can. You can do things!"

Women talked about successful events in their business lives that led to increased self-esteem and feeling empowered.

> *Sharon*: That felt great. That felt tremendous. It gave me an even greater sense of integrity about who I am as a person.
>
> *Cheryl H.*: I feel good about myself because I feel like I'm doing something that not only do I like but others like. And I never really felt good about myself before because I had so many obstacles that my self-esteem was very low.
>
> *Sandy*: I feel like, um, I almost feel like I'm at a place I shouldn't be...because I look back on my life and in one point you could feel like you're worthless and then you start feeling good about yourself knowing that there's more to you than what you're exactly doing. That you have a purpose and talent that you can develop.

The theme of respect/recognition, that is, achieving self-respect and receiving respect and recognition for accomplishments, was included as both a measure and effect of success. Respect and recognition are especially significant for Black women, as we are not often respected or recognized for our accomplishments. More than half the group recounted instances in which they received outside validation for their work in terms of awards, scholarships, media coverage, and acknowledgment from customers.

> *Devya*: When people call my name, they call in a good frame of reference.
>
> *Frankie*: At the awards ceremony, where...the politicians came, I spoke impromptu and the rest is history.
>
> *Paulette*: But then I began to see, I began to like the recognition of my product. More people were beginning to recognize me. So it was really very heartwarming, the way it went.
>
> *Robin*: Everybody that I came up with knew that about me, they admired me about that. So those are the personal things that I have about myself and my reputation.

Many confirmed they had some media coverage about themselves and their businesses. They had print coverage, most of which was in local newspapers, as well as broadcast coverage. Devya had radio coverage, and Deborah and Sharon were interviewed about their businesses on local television. Efua appeared on a video about entrepreneurs. Several members of the group also reported they were asked to speak at meetings and classes for new and would-be entrepreneurs. Frankie, Patricia, and Cheryl O. received awards recognizing their accomplishments as entrepreneurs.

Recognizing the value of relationships in business is one of the key
elements in social capital formation and is characteristic of successful entrepreneurs.[7] The group knew the value of developing and maintaining
relationships in business, grounded in respect, with customers, employees,
vendors, colleagues, and people in general. They saw the respect and recognition as being mutual and interactive:

> *Arlene*: If you [the employees] work good and do what you're
> supposed to do I have no problem with paying you. You know I
> appreciate you because you are a big help to me because I used to
> do everything by myself.

They gave examples of how customer appreciation and recognition have
been integrated into their ongoing business practices and procedures,
whether by discounts, special events like a brunch for preferred customers,
or promotional items for regulars.

An increased ability to "give back" or affect the community at large
can be assessed by the leadership positions taken by successful entrepreneurs. Several were involved in their communities, organizations, or
agencies in leadership positions such through board membership, being
committee chairs, and through church committees and ministries. Helen
and Lani confirmed they obtained these positions as a direct result of having
a business that was recognized as being successful and committed to the
community. In the womanist tradition, these women acted on their concern
for the betterment of an entire people.

Swantz's theory of women's economics measures success in business
horizontally; that is, success is assessed by the number of other businesses
an owner helps start or grow.[8] More than half of the group of Market
Women talked about how they helped or tried to help others start businesses by encouraging them, serving as mentors or role models, sharing
information, giving advice, and making referrals.

Ava, in talking with a regular customer, said to him: "Why don't you
open a business? And he established a business. And he didn't even take the
training." And Paulette, who rose to a leadership position in her vendor's
organization, noted that

> I've introduced them to Mr. L. And so some of them are looking into going
> into his program. And I encourage a lot of the women vendors, even if
> they're afraid to open a store on their own, to do a collective venture.

Cheryl H. was vociferous in her desire to help other Black people start
businesses.

> I want to help people because I think that as Black people... I'm
> seeing so many things and I'm not saying I'm doing everything right,

but I talk to people and I'm saying to myself "What is the matter with y'all?" I hate, I really hate . . . I just want to be able to help. I want us to come together. Our businesses should be blooming because everybody else's is.

Sandy added, "I like to help others start little businesses too by being a mentor."

The Best Thing about My Business Is . . .

When discussing success in business, I asked the women to tell me about what they thought was the best thing about their businesses; understanding these answers pointed to what was significant for them. As they shared their feelings, it was clear they knew what they valued and were happy for the chance to share their perspectives.

Jackie L.: Of course the best thing about the business would be . . . the hats themselves. Because I really think that I'm trying to bring some fun, some freedom into the hats. It frees them [her clients] from wearing big, stiff, staid hats.

Frankie: The first thing that jumps to mind immediately is community service. The second is products. It's going to be my pleasure to just, to . . . just know and to see people enjoy my food (laughter). I'm telling you. I think those are the most important two.

Efua: I'd say the best thing about my business is me. Because I know if I get the work I can do the work, I can do it to the person's satisfaction and beyond. I know I can handle it. The best thing that's going for me is that I'm not going to quit.

Wendy: My product and my customers. My customer service. My books. And then I always find other interesting things other than books to bring in. Things like bookmarks, which sort of relates but it's just really different. Being able to send things to people and you call them and they're like thank you I received everything with no problem. You know things like that.

Helen: The best thing is that anybody can come into a busy city, and people can say it's a very peaceful place. Any person can walk in the door and get some kind of spiritual experience. Get information. Take some classes for free. And have some nice friendly people to talk to them and serve them tea . . . some peo- some people get so involved they move into the community. Because this is a definitely a strong community. The community service and the kind of services we have, that's the best thing.

Sharon: Personal experience and knowing what bad service looks like and what it feels like, not only if you're Black and not only if you're a woman because I got it both ways. I had it in the segregated South and I had it in NYC. I've had it all over the place and it doesn't feel good. From all of it, from gender, race, from all those things, I know what it feels like. And it doesn't feel good. I guess what would contribute to the success is having a vision of what good service looks like and creating it for others.

Paulette: The best thing about my business is my energy. It's my dream. Although it's frustrating, it's overwhelming, it's mine! And it's only going to be what I make it.

Lani: The best thing about my business is that it's different. That's the best.

Arlene: The best thing is that people come here and you can get the best product. They come in here and they follow me wherever I go.

Nancy: The best thing about it [the business] is the fact that I'm able to do it…to know I've strategized, I made sacrifices, and I am disciplined enough to stick to it. To be able to put a product out. To know I would be in charge of my own financial, spiritual, emotional, and physical journey.

Robin: The best thing is that what happens is that people come and first of all I attract people that don't know dance school period. The reputation is…that they will come here, they will get trained and they will get into good schools.

Patricia: The best thing about my business is independence, I am able to implement what I think should be done.

Jackie K.: The best thing about my business is that it still exists! The other thing is that is does provide a service to mostly small, start-up home-based businesses. One of the things that I've noticed is that there are a number of people who have been doing their businesses at home but now they have considered doing the show because they don't have to deal with the home party, the advertising. They can come and reach a much larger market.

Cheryl O.: The best things are this year I'm making money, not tons of it, but respectable. And I get a lot of positive feedback which is always good for you. And I have all these pretty things around me. I get to have my own and I get other people's stuff because I have things people want to work with.

Sandy: The best thing about my business is first, number one, working with my family because without them there would not be a successful business. Because they have sacrificed a whole lot too.

Another area is being able to supply the people with what they need and to have it on hand and to be able to see their needs and fulfill them.

The women were easily able to identify the best things about their businesses. When I asked a follow-up question about how they felt being successful Black women entrepreneurs, they said smilingly, "exciting," "bubbly," "blessed," "happy," "scared," "strong," "wonderful!"

Strategies for Success: Advice Given and Taken

In redefining success, the women also talked about commonly used approaches to business development and management. When asked about any advice they would give to new entrepreneurs, the women offered many words of wisdom and concrete strategies that they found had worked for them. The organization of those strategies, using the frameworks of McClelland, summarizes the advice given by the women in Table 10.2.

The advice falls into the broad categories of personal characteristics, capital formation, and management strategies; spirituality; and the development of a strong sense of self. Presented in the words of the group, the authenticity of the advice is unmistakable.

Personal Characteristics: Vision, Learning, Love, and Commitment

Devya, our meditation mentor who provides services for healing, suggests:

It's easier if you start out with money. It's a lot easier. But the most important thing is that you have a vision. It's the vision that carries you through when things are rough, when the money is low, when it looks like you've made one too many mistakes. It's the vision that keeps you going. If you have a picture of what it is you want to have happen, everything that happens you take as a learning experience.

Wendy, the bookseller who had a dream of running her business from her own bookstore, encourages dreaming and perseverance:

When you dream, dream big, but also to know that you have to take little steps to get to that dream. And be prepared to take those steps as well as the hurdles that will come up. Just one, one step at a time and you'll get there.

Table 10.2   Business Strategies Associated with Entrepreneurial Success

McClelland	Market Women
Proactivity:	Human Capital:
• Increase communication skills, both written and verbal, become assertive • Ask for what you want, need • Reach out to others	• Learn you business, get training, train your employees • Be clear about what you want to do, make lists • Know your business and be committed to it 24/7, 100% • Take calculated risks • Have a vision, dream big, do it
Efficiency Orientation:	Financial Capital:
• Recognize opportunity and act on it • Operate business efficiently and have excellent products/services • Plan your business/write a plan	• Make a personal investment of money • Develop a cash flow, put savings back into the business, watch your money • Write a business plan
Commitment to Contract:	Social Capital:
• Make a commitment to work respectfully with others—customers, clients, vendors, family • Make a commitment to work contract	• Surround yourself with professional, knowledgeable people • Network with people who have the same vision • Build relationships in and outside of the industry • Be true to yourself

Source: C.A. Smith © 1999.

Jackie L., the hat designer, was and is very clear and focused about her goals. She also loves what she does and is very good at it, believing both things are necessary:

> To be clear. To know what it is you're doing and why you're doing it. To be clear in the way that you want out of what you're doing. Because there are so many things that can sidetrack you and pull you and drag you off in different courses.

Efua, a third-generation entrepreneur, understands that

> If you're not committed to your business, don't go there. Because this is not a nine to five—it's a twenty-four hour. It never stops. Even when your so-called job is finished for the day it's not finished. It's

your business, the buck stops here. You know you can't say well somebody will do it. I have to do it. It you're not going to be committed, if you're not going to raise it like it's a child—that's what it is, it's a baby then don't bother. Because that's what it is.

Financial Capital: Making and Managing Money

Sharon knew money and determination were connected:

It sounds like the same old thing if you've been exposed to any of this stuff on starting your own business... to say don't think about the money. But... initially I wouldn't encourage people to think a lot about the money. What is your gift to the world? If you have enough determination you've got to test it first. You've got to test the idea and see if you have enough determination to follow through on it. You've got to have a kind of acid test score whether or not and then be willing to take the chance... [T]hat follow through means a lot, not giving up.... Staying with it.

Robin, who is strong, determined, and talented, considers money management a critical skill for business people to cultivate. She believes they should

Make a personal investment of money, get training both... for running the business, both classroom and informal.

Sandy, the founder of her family business, did not start it primarily for the money:

I never focused on how much money I'm going to make. The focus was just to keep working it and make it the best you can. The money will follow.... I feel if you focus on the money then that's all you're going to see. You're going to get discouraged because when you first start you're not making it, but you've got to learn your business for your business to make money. The first advice I would give... is to have confidence in yourself and make sure that whatever ideal or dream you have it can come through. But always surround yourself with professional, knowledgeable people.

Social Capital: Building Relationships with Others

Nancy, for whom the relationship with her mother was her most important, understands the value of building all kinds of relationships in business:

Network. Work with other people who share the same vision. Have a business plan. Learn as much as you possibly can about [your] industry. Be resourceful. Build relationships....I've heard people talk about building relationships with those individuals who are in those industries they are attempting to pursue. I say build relationships with people that you come into contact with. That you know...[W]hether it's a banker, whether it's the postman. Why? Because you'd be surprised how anybody can be helpful to what it is you're doing. If you're of the mindset to only network and just build relationships with people that are working in the industry...I think what happens is you miss. I believe you have to be a risk-taker.... Keep your eyes and ears open because opportunities arise in the strangest places.

Human Capital: Building Knowledge and Skill

Ava, who had been running her business for a long time on innate skill, logic, common sense, and wit, suggests that people take classes specifically for entrepreneurship training:

To get the blueprint for establishing a business. You've got to know the inner nucleus of operating a business. You know, establishing a business. Definitely...Do your business planning. You do not do what I did. Do the complete opposite. A lot of areas I've been able to correct. Develop a cash flow, you can put a little money in the bank each month.

Helen, the Buddhist nun, has some management advice:

You can't do everything. You can't micromanage. Watch your money. Train your people...train your people...very well, because your people represent you.

Cheryl H., the self-taught balloon decorator, cake artist, and ex-banker, thinks:

I would tell them they have to obtain the knowledge of the business. Because so many people say, "Oh. I want to have a business," and they don't even do any type of research. You've got to take some kind of class or something. Because I feel it's important to get the knowledge of something to perfect your business. Like even...I have the creativeness but even the Bible says you got to study to show yourself approved. If you don't get the knowledge you're going to be destroyed. If you don't get the knowledge you're going to fail.

Knowing your business is what you really do. I know my business inside and out.

Paulette, who has her own retail space, is a mentor to other vendors, and gives back to her community, is also very well organized. She makes lots of lists and would ask new business owners to

[M]ake a list of questions as to what they want to do in a business, why they want to do it, how many sacrifices are they willing to make. And to answer those questions truthfully. See what support systems you have. And if they can answer those questions honestly, then they'd know whether or not they want to go into business. I'd ask them to take some kind of formal instruction, be it through a Business Outreach Center or seminar. And to speak with other people they trust, other business mentors. People who are in business, who have been in business for a while.

Patricia, the educator, not surprisingly believes in the value of lifelong learning:

Get more training! Grow yourself, be willing to grow. Have patience. Just do it!

Jackie K., who completed her doctorate while starting her business, which was totally separate from her academic discipline, reflects on her experience:

One of my first thoughts was to get to do something like the EAP [Entrepreneurial Assistance Program]. I found that useful. If you are going to do a business, you should probably do a business about something that you know.... [I]t shouldn't be something that you pick out of left field and decide, OK, this is something I want to do a business in. Because you have to put too much energy in it. I would encourage people to get some experience in, with ... what you want to do before you jump out there.

Spirituality

Frankie, the self-described hard-core, bible-thumping Baptist/cook/accountant says:

You have to be willing to commit yourself 110%. You have to be willing to put everything on the line and go for broke. When you make that commitment and stick with it. Stay focused—no matter what stay focused. It will come to pass. It will come to pass. You got to pray a lot. That's very important. Because everything else will come to pass, even the money, okay?

Sense of Self

Lani, the shoemaker and restaurateur, is very strong, physically, emotionally, and intellectually. She tells business owners to

> [B]e true to yourself. If you have a good business idea and you feel it's worth developing, be honest with yourself on whether or not you'd be willing to put in the time and energy and be ready to give up... a lot of things that you might be quite complacent with. And when you see it beginning to work, stay with it. Stay with, stay with it.

Arlene, who loves her business so much it brings tears to her eyes, says

> It's going to be a hard way to go but don't give up because everything will be all right.... [Y]ou've just got to keep trying.... [T]here's so many things that come in your way and you're going to think it's not possible. Plenty of times I thought it was not possible. But you have to be patient and just keep on trying.

Cheryl O., the artist and sculptor who is on her feet a lot and has to be physically strong, brings things down to basics:

> Get some really comfortable shoes. There's that whole physical thing that is going to make a difference for you. If you're not pretty healthy you're going to have a hard time. You've got to be willing to work long hours and not taking money out of the business. Reinvesting when you begin to make a little money. It goes back into the business... If you're going to do this, you have to focus on doing it because if you don't it's gone. There are plenty people out there, you know... who are as smart, as talented as you... many are called but few are chosen. There's no way around hard work. And, never turn down an opportunity for free publicity. Talk to anyone who asks you.

Get focused and stay focused, stick with it, network, talk, build relationships, keep learning, recognize opportunities, organize, plan, and pray. Those are the key words and recurrent themes that appear in the advice given from the Market Women. Those strategies are the very ones found to be helpful for all entrepreneurs. However, they are expanded and enhanced in the light of the cultural traditions and life experiences of these Black women.

In sum, the women in the study have shown, in their own words, that they have defined themselves as entrepreneurial women, have reshaped the concepts of success, wealth, and power. By showing their stuff—hard work, determination, intelligence, excellence—they have also challenged the stereotypical views of Black women and, by extension, other marginalized groups in American society. Thus, they empower themselves and others. As was true of the entrepreneurs in the far and near past, these twentieth- and twenty-first-century Market Women have achieved success as they define it. With their accomplishments, they unleash the "wonderful stuff" that comes from being a Black woman.

I am at peace with myself and with the business. I feel there is no failure in me.

—Sandy

CHAPTER 11

The Wonderful Stuff: Empowerment through Reframing, Reconstructing, and Redefining

I am phenomenal...charming...smart...strong...stubborn... blessed.

—The Market Women

There is wonderful stuff in all of us, and one of the ways we discover it is by telling our stories. The power of story is well known: it informs, inspires and sustains us. Story provides a window into different times and places, into the inner lives of people we know and don't know. Story sustains history and tradition. We need to tell our own stories, because as women of the African Diaspora, so much of the richness of our narratives and thus our lives has been lost. This verbal story of the economic lives of Black women entrepreneurs in the United States reminds us of who we are and why we're here.

The Calendar Sisters' Story

In Sue Monk Kidd's novel, *The Secret Lives of Bees*, a young White girl comes of age and finds herself through her mother's history while living with a trio of Black, middle-aged sisters who, as it turns out, are successful entrepreneurs. The story demonstrates how the tenor of a given time and place is reflected in business activities, and those activities are in turn reflective of the economic, social, and political realities of the day. As we read, we discover the nature of relationships between men and women,

Blacks and Whites, and children and adults in the South on the cusp of the Civil Rights movement. We understand the power of time and place in people's lives.

As with other works of fiction, this book is in part about Black women's entrepreneurship and economic lives, although it is not generally recognized as such. By viewing the book through an entrepreneurial lens, we realize how the Calendar sisters' business, Black Madonna Honey, served as a vehicle for preserving history, culture, ritual, and in the case of one sister, sanity. We see how the business empowered the family by providing financial freedom and self-sufficiency, satisfying work, and a safe space for the women and their kin, both blood and fictive. The themes we have come to know through the Market Women—the mother–daughter bond, sisterhood, family, community, spirituality, and empowerment—shine through this well-told tale.

The success of this book, written by a White Southern woman, comes about because of its universal themes of coming of age, finding one's self through history, family, and social relationships, and unique responses to gender and social inequities based on the characters' particularities. In a like manner, the uniqueness and universality of the Black Women's Themes raised as the Market Women seek success provide lessons and inspiration for many. Discovering one's history and culture—creating one's own story

From the series "Women of Color in Color" monoprints. © Cheryl Louise Olney. Courtesy of Louise's Daughter: Three-Dimensional Art and Contemporary Craft.

quilt—is an enlightening and powerful approach to achieving self-defined success.

The Kalideoscope: History, Culture, Tradition, Race, Gender, and Class

How we see things depends on the lens we use and the angle of vision we view them through. As in a kaleidoscope, the patterns we see change as we change lenses and angles when we turn the scope. Similarly, the patterns of entrepreneurial activity and success look different depending on the lens and angles we use to examine it. We see that history, culture, and tradition had an effect on the ways in which these present-day Market Women operated in the world of business and defined success. The Black Women's Themes worked well for them. Their stories revealed connections to African traditions that enabled them to survive and prevail in a business climate characterized by fierce competition, dishonesty, and privilege, further tainted by the legacy of sexism and racism. This dominant economic worldview is in some ways antithetical to the Afrocentric model embraced by these women and articulated by George Fraser in his discussion of race and success:

> We believe in the Afrocentric principles of cooperation and community. Afrocentricity promotes the oneness of all things. Cooperation, collectivism and sharing are the essential elements. Community is considered before the individual.[1]

The retention of those principles can be a double-edged sword: A belief system that can advance success in business can also reduce the competitive edge associated with the search for profits at all costs. We recall Jackie L.'s concerns that her ethical behavior would reduce her profits.

History and culture provide links to the relationship between race, gender, and class, which are present in all people's lives. They factor in the business outcomes of this group of entrepreneurs in a unique way because of how they have been perceived and treated in American society. On the basis of the reported experiences and perceptions of the successful Black women in the study group, race and ethnicity seem to have made more of an impact on entrepreneurship outcomes than did gender. In spite of being connected with community and family as sources of support, Black women, more than all males and even other women of color, are described as being the most time impoverished when it comes to running their businesses. We know they are more likely to start their business alone, meaning without partners who can contribute capital and expertise to their businesses—a factor in the level of time poverty experienced by Black women entrepreneurs.[2]

It is true that most of the businesses run by Black women are structured as sole proprietorships.[3] Usually their business revenues, which rank the lowest of all entrepreneurial groups even though they are among the fastest-growing segment of new business owners, is the sole assessment measure of their success or, by implication, lack thereof. However, as seen in the findings of this study, most Black women have extensive sources of support, including non-monetary financial capital infusions. Additionally, the study group members had high levels of human capital and emotional intelligence, more than the general community at large, and more than the general entrepreneurship population. They also have equal if not better survival rates than majority-owned small businesses and a self-defined assessment of success. Conclusions drawn from these seemingly contradictory outcomes suggest that other explanations for the disparity in revenues are probable.

One factor may be differences in earning power. A study was conducted by Catalyst, a not-for-profit organization that researches women in business, that reports that "For every $1 white male managers earn, minority male managers earn 73 cents; white women managers, 59 cents, and minority women managers 57 cents."[4] These wage differentials, which hold for non-managerial positions as well, mean that Black women have to work more hours to make the same money as males or, to a lesser extent, White women. The women in this study have "income patched" their businesses, most working part or full-time while they ran their businesses. Thus, Black women engaged in running their own businesses usually have less time available to put into those businesses, resulting in lower revenues and profit margins, reported in the economic data on entrepreneurship. These other factors are ordinarily not considered in economic data; the stories behind the numbers have not often been told. For the most part, race, gender, and class differences are reported but not analyzed in the economic data collected.

Race and gender are not always unifying, and the business chances of women of color are different from those privileged by race or gender. Robert Woodard profiled eleven Black successful entrepreneurs, three of whom were women who founded, owned, and operated their own businesses; they were deemed "successful" by both quantitative and qualitative standards, as the criterion for inclusion in his study was gross annual revenues of $1 million or more. Financial success not withstanding, he concluded that gender indeed did make a difference in entrepreneurship, even among people of the same race:

To deal with gender-based barriers is an additional burden for black women doing business. To their credit, black women entrepreneurs consider this a moot issue and see any bias, regardless of the source, as just another impediment to navigate before conducting business.[5]

The words and lives of our group of Black women confirm his conclusion that "African American women are adroit at turning negative situations into positive outcomes for their businesses." My evidence as well as his reveals that they do so with "integrity and professionalism."[6] This group of willful, determined Market Women experienced the challenges and benefits of being Black women as positives in their lives. As precisely put by Sharon, the Ph.D.-holding tea gallery owner, in describing the value of being a Black woman, "But on the positive side it unleashes so much wonderful stuff!"

Recommendations for the Black Women Entrepreneurs

Successful Black women entrepreneurs, the chosen study population, have through their own words shared their wonderful stuff, offering advice to other new and would-be entrepreneurs. By telling their own stories, they made recommendations for life and business. In this section I offer my own recommendations, based on the experiences of these Market Women, my historical research, the insights gained from other scholars, and my own lived experiences as an entrepreneur.

My foremost suggestion for Black women entrepreneurs and anyone else seeking success is that they put into practice the African principle of Sankofa—the wisdom of learning from the past. I hope that Black women entrepreneurs get in touch with their heritage as it relates to entrepreneurship, which began with the powerful Market Women of ancient Africa. This heritage provides the foundation for the entrepreneurial activities of Black women in America. By knowing their history they can know that entrepreneurship is in their tradition, that as a group they are not new to it, and that they are not alone. The first step would be, then, for the entrepreneurs to learn about that legacy and reflect on how it can be used in their present business practices.

The Afrocentric philosophy described by Fraser includes the sense of community and connectivity in entrepreneurship, which is at the base of much of the economic activity within the Black community. The Seven Principles of Kwaanza, created as a distinctly African American holiday ritual, are based on retention of this worldview; their essential element is cooperative economics, which can be used to build on the strengths inherent in the Black community: the mother–daughter bond, sisterhood, extended family/kinship support networks, and the connection with community. Building organizations like those described in history—the market and craft guilds of Africa; the Colored Females's Free Produce Society that operated in antebellum days; the Female Trading Association of NYC, a cooperative grocery store owned and operated by Black women in the early 1800s; and the early-twentieth-century women's club movement—offer historical business strategies that can be applied to modern-day economic practices. In this new century, the emergence of new "sister circles" whose focus is on economic development and self-sufficiency attest to the fact those lessons have been learned.

However, Black women entrepreneurs should also integrate some effective practices from present-day market economy strategies, including use of technology, research, innovation, and ethical competitive practices. As we know, most enterprises owned and operated by Black women are structured as sole proprietorships; they are easy to form and are very cost effective. However, they do not offer the protection of the individual owner's assets and make it more difficult to raise outside capital. I suggest that more Black women avail themselves of relatively newer business structures such as limited liability companies or limited liability partnerships. Those entities provide protection of personal assets and also lend themselves more easily to forming cooperative and collaborative ventures. Formation of business cooperatives, interfirm networks, joint ventures, and strategic partnerships with other Black women or other entrepreneurs from nurturing or bridging networks is a strategy that would enable larger and more financially lucrative ventures, supported by partnerships that often occur naturally. Of course, establishing trust, a Black Women's Theme, both personally and legally is essential.

Participation in programs such as Joline Godfrey's An Income of Her Own Program, a mentoring program for young female entrepreneurs, and the Kauffman Foundations Buddy program, which provides funding for mother–teenage daughter businesses partnerships, can build on the mother–daughter bond and provide opportunities for accessing training, mentors, and role models for future successful entrepreneurs. Although many such programs already exist in some communities, if they are absent in a given locality, the leadership abilities, proactivity, and sense of community of Black women entrepreneurs can be used to create such programs, if they have the time.

Financial capital formation strategies can also be built on the naturally occurring social capital networks by forming "susus," or cooperative savings societies that have their origins in Africa. Susu is derived from the Yoruba word "esusu," which roughly translates to "pooling the funds and rotating the pot."[6] Many groups within the Black community have formed susus to advance their ability to save; however, much of that money has been used to finance special occasions and major purchases. In addition, some family groups have reported they use the susu money to acquire the down payment for home ownership. I learned recently from a young doctoral student from Africa that young women are active in susus, using the money for tuition and other educational purposes. I think more Black women should form susus for business development purposes, similar to that of the Korean "kee," a cooperative of businesspeople who collect money monthly that is paid out to the member whose business needs the money the most in any particular month.

There are also other cooperative financing methods that can be accessed and that include "peer lending circles" modeled on the Grameen Bank of Bangledesh, which are cooperative, self-help financing tools for microbusinesses that have trouble raising capital from majority lenders. Recently, traditional lenders such as banks are acknowledging the legitimacy of these ethnic savings societies in the formation of capital that can be leveraged as collateral in business financing.

I also that recommend that Black women who are successful be mindful of the need for apprenticeship and mentoring opportunities for new and would-be Black women entrepreneurs. Although many already do, including some of the Market Women, I propose that more successful Black women take on apprentices in their businesses, whether formally or informally. The same is true for mentoring. Organizations such as the Women's Venture Fund and Black Women's Enterprises, Inc., both New York based, offer peer lending, business training, mentorship, and access to markets as well as networks of support for small, women-owned businesses.

In keeping with the Sankofa principle, which can also be viewed as a symbol of resistance to relinquishing one's culture, Fraser suggests that Black entrepreneurs emulate the example of Underground Railroad, which he views as a quintessential network that brought about social change.[7] The Railroad Network was based on the strength of weak ties and formation of both nurturing and bridging networks. It is therefore suggested that successful Black women entrepreneurs form a modern-day umbrella Underground Railroad Network, based on existing organizations, aimed at bringing about economic, social, and political change in the Black community and the larger society. To this end, the network could form strategic alliances with others both like and unlike themselves, building on the theory of the "strength of weak ties," which can heighten success.

Black women entrepreneurs, who are natural leaders, already take leadership positions in their existing social and business networks, both with a view to growing their businesses and improving their communities, but we need more, as the ranks of successful Black women entrepreneurs grow. As leaders, they can continue to take as many opportunities as possible to make themselves and their businesses visible by taking on speaking engagements and participating in conferences—again, if they have the time.

One of the almost unanimous characteristics bestowed to themselves by the group members was their vision. Wallace, a teacher of minority small business owners who have moved beyond the microenterprise stage of business development, quotes the bible in relating the value of vision in business: "Where there is no vision, the people perish."[8] He encourages Black entrepreneurs to use that vision to hold on until they get their "first hit." Wallace theorizes that there is a "First Hit Phenomenon"[9] in Black business development. It is his position that after persevering for a seemingly long while, businesses get a first major hit in their business growth, be it a major contract, a major strategic alliance, or the like. After the first hit, which may be years in coming, the second, third, and subsequent hits come more frequently and often produce greater financial rewards, resulting in rapid business growth.[9] The women, who reported having visions of their businesses that enabled them to persevere, held on or are holding on for the major first hit. To date, they have held their visions and they have not perished. Last, but certainly not least, I recommend that Black women entrepreneurs continue to laugh, love, and celebrate themselves!

The Women: Role Models, Mentors, and Historians

The women's feelings about the interview were very important to me, so I asked an unplanned question about how they felt about the interview experience. Their answers confirmed they were appreciative of the opportunity to talk about themselves because as Black women, they were not often asked. Some recognized that the opportunity to reflect on their experiences helped them in their business planning, while others mentioned that talking about their own business history reminded them of how far they had come. Most important, they felt comfortable, relaxed, and respected.

Jackie K.: It was good. Good...because I think we Black women don't always get included in things. I don't think we get to talk about ourselves and be listened to.

Arlene: It was fun. It was real interesting. I mean...I'm real comfortable with you. It was good.

Ava: It was so nice. This was great for me...it keeps me focused on where I'm going.

Sharon: You've been easy to talk to. It was great. It helped me crystallize a lot of where I am. I appreciate the opportunity.

All thanked me for being interested—I thank them

This is an extraordinary group of women—funny, feisty, determined, willful, resilient, visionary, creative, and caring. They used the interviews to give voice to their hopes and dreams, efforts and triumphs. They describe and define who and how they are—in short, their humanity. They have much to teach others; their stories are inspirational. They are compelling role models on many levels and in many areas. It was a pleasure and privilege to get to know them. Knowing them strengthened my mission—to tell their stories and give them their "propers"—respect, recognition, and acknowledgment.

Final Reflections: The Process of Making the Story Quilt

I loved doing this research. I became part of the continuum of African women as I immersed myself in the stories of ancient African queens, warriors, and rulers; in the biographies of women such as Eleanor Eldridge and Mammy Pleasant; and in the newspaper articles and advertisements in the newspapers such as the *Colored American* and the *Douglass Papers*. I reveled in the photographic images of Black women from the nineteenth and early twentieth centuries. The historical patch began to take shape. The next step was to connect this patch to the present-day Market Women.

I loved meeting this vibrant, smart, and energetic group of women, who graciously gave of their precious time to participate in the study. I accommodated them to the best of my ability, holding the interviews in places most convenient for them, including hotel lobbies, cafeterias, their homes, their places of business, and over the telephone. All the interviews were characterized by a great deal of laughter, comfort, and recognition of shared experiences. Nikki Giovanni rightly says Black women's humor transcends all dimensions of their individuality, providing immediate connections with each other. I became connected to these women through my "sisterhood" with them and, through them, to the community of Black women entrepreneurs, the wider Black community, and the world of entrepreneurs. I vowed to tell their stories with honor and respect. Their stories add a vibrant patch to this verbal story quilt.

I learned and confirmed some truths along the way as I worked on this verbal quilt. I am clearer than ever about the need for us as Black women to become our own storytellers by writing our memoirs and autobiographies, as well as biographies of unknown women whose stories may not yet have been fully told. We need to become archivists of our photographs and family objects, looking into our desks, attics, and basements. We need to decide what to do about collections of art and artifacts we have acquired over time. At a recent conference on Black women's history, Black women archivists raised my awareness of the need to have the historical bits and pieces of our lives preserved and handled by professionals in museums and libraries.

I recently discovered a place where family collections and memorabilia were gathered and displayed, the Family Heritage House Museum in Bradenton, Florida. Located at Manatee Community College, the museum was founded by the husband-and-wife team of Fredi and Ernest Brown, Jr. They started in 1990 with their collection of African art and family mementos for the purpose of preserving the history and culture of people of the African diaspora in general, and those in Florida in particular. The museum is operated by Mrs. Brown with the assistance of volunteers and interns. In recognition of its importance to the community, the president of Manatee Community College had an extension built on the school's library that houses the museum, at this time a gallery and resource center for the study of African American achievements, and that is included on the Florida Black Heritage Trail. Much of the artwork and many items in the expanding collection are donated by Black Floridians and Black retirees living in Florida who come from many places around the country. I plan to donate some of my own family photos and objects to that collection.

As we expand our foundations by tapping into family and local histories, we should also continue to collect oral histories from the oldest members of our families and communities, from every walk of life, documenting them on both audio and videotape, on paper, and online. The upsurge in family reunions provides ample opportunities to do so as well as creating family histories for each member, ensuring that history is not lost. Happily, scholars and researchers, and especially Black women, continue to do service by studying original personal documents and public sources and writing books and articles that celebrate Black women and their history. As a scholar, researcher, and educator, I am amazed and gratified by the interest generated so far about this topic. As I move about in my classes (I have developed a course based on my research for this book), at conferences and in places of business, entrepreneurial women of color want to tell me their stories. White students want to explore their family and cultural economic histories. Colleagues and friends tell me about women entrepreneurs I should interview. My work is far from over—rather, it is just beginning.

Finally, as a Black woman, I believe we need to reflect on who we are as part of the African diaspora, connecting to women like us around the world, strengthening and lengthening our nurturing bonds. As citizens of the world, we also need to strengthen our bridging bonds, using those threads to connect and reconnect the patches of our ever-growing quilt. My goal in writing this book was to connect the past with the present, the unique with the universal, and the realities of the time with the dreams of the future. This book is my service to all my communities.

In any given room everyone from blonde to redhead to silverhaired to bald can be a Black woman. Who wouldn't want to be a Black woman knowing nothing can defeat the indomitable spirit that is determined to love and laugh? And when things are not going well with you, why not gather a few friends, fry a chicken or two and sit around a table saying: I am a Black woman. I am the best thing on earth.

—Nikki Giovanni, in D. Dance, ed., *Honey Hush: Anthology of African American Women's Humor*

APPENDICES

APPENDIX A

Black Women's Themes

- Sisterhood: having, feeling, and acting on a sense of connection with other Black women and women of color
- Mother–Daughter bond: bond with mothers and with daughters
- Spirituality: sense of faith, belief in higher being, use of prayer, values
- Community: concern for and involvement with community
- Will: determination, strength, and force of will
- Trust: Ability to trust others and being trustworthy
- Time Poverty: social, familial, and economic factors that are more compelling for Black women than for other women in general.[1]

APPENDIX B

Networks

Nurturing Social and Business Networks

Deborah: Black Women's Enterprises of New York State

Wendy: Sisters Helping Sisters and Multi-Ethnic Sisterhood Alliance (MESA) Investment Club, Circle of Sisters

Efua: Black Women's Enterprises of New York State

Paulette: New York and Boston chapters of 100 Black Women, Jack and Jill, The LINKS, Circle of Sisters, Sister's Health Coalition

Robin: Jack and Jill

Patricia: Black Women's Enterprises of New York State

Jackie K.: Delta Sigma Delta Sorority, Association of Black Women in Higher Education

Bridging Social Capital Networks

Devya: American Women's Economic Development Corporation, Women's Venture Fund

Deborah: Women's Venture Fund

Wendy: Women's Venture Fund

Frankie: County Women's Business Enterprise Coalition

Sharon: Women Incorporated, National Association of Female Executives

Nancy: Women in Music, American Business Women's Association

Trade and Professional Organizations

Deborah: Gift Association and Quilting Association

Efua: Le Tip, C.M.I.

Helen: Brooklyn Economic Development Center Alumni Association

Sharon: National Association of Educators of Young Children

Cheryl H.: Qualitex Balloon Network

Arlene: Beauty Culture Association

Robin: Harlem Venture Group, Harlem Merchant's Association

Cheryl O.: Artists' CO-OP, Empire State Craft Alliance, Pyramid

Jackie K.: Chamber of Commerce, Small Business Council

Sandy: African-American Retail Association, Fashion Association.

APPENDIX C

Resources for Entrepreneurs

- Entrepreneurial Assistance Programs, Empire State Development Corporation, Division of Women's and Minority Business Development
- Small Business Administration, http://www.sba.gov
- Small Business Development Centers (technical assistance and training located on college campuses; state based)
- Black Women Enterprises of New York State (networking, training, procurement)
- Women's Venture Fund (peer lending and training), http://www.womensventurefund.org
- Trickle-Up Program (microlender), http://www.trickleup.org
- Count-Me-In (online microlender), http://www.count-me-in.org
- Accion International, http://www.accionnewyork.org
- Online Women's Business Center (Small Business Administration), http://www.onlinewbc.org
- Center for Women's Business Research, http://www.womensbusinessresearch.org
- Enterprising Women, http://www.enterprisingwomen.org
- American Women's Economic Development Center, http://www.awed.org. Minority Business Development Association, http://www.mbda.gov
- The Kauffman Foundation, offering entrepreneurship training and education programs for children, adolescents, and adults, http://www.emkf.org

- Camp $tart-up, part of Joline Godfrey's Independent Means, Inc., which provides training, resources, and opportunities for adolescent entrepreneurs, http://www.anincomeofherown.com

American Women's Economic Development Center has a resource link that provides contact information for many of the organizations listed above. Although many resources are New York based, there are several national organizations and federal government resources listed as well.

APPENDIX D

Descriptions of Businesses Studied

1. The Businesses

List of Market Women and Their Businesses

Table A.1   Types of Businesses Owned

Owner	Business
Devya	Meditation services and products
Deborah	Floral arrangement design services and products
Wendy	Multiethnic bookstore
Jackie L.	Accessories designer
Efua	Cleaning/janitorial services
Frankie	Restaurant/catering services
Ava	Health food/herbal products store
Helen	Retail "gently used" books, clothing, videos
Sharon	Tea gallery/consulting services
Paulette	Retail accessories
Cheryl H.	Balloon/cake artist
Lani	Organic restaurant/shoe repair
Arlene	Beauty salon
Nancy	Music production company
Robin	Dance school
Patricia	Learning center
Cheryl O.	Artist
Jackie K.	Marketing/promotion company
Sandy	Clothing retail/manufacturing

Source: C.A. Smith © 1999.

2. Names, Locations, Contact Information

Devya
Devya & Associates
Meditation, Stress Management, Counseling
P.O. Box 20655
New York, NY 10025-1515
http://www.DevyaWorld.com

Deborah St. Clair
D'Works
Fabric and Fresh Floral Design
32B Debs Place
Bronx, NY 10475

Jacqueline Lamont
Jacqueline Lamont Millinery
470 Broadway, 2nd Floor
New York, NY 10013

Ava Selby
Adonijah Health Food
206 Utica Avenue
Brooklyn, NY 11213

Sharon Cadiz, Ph.D.
Timeless Tea Salon and Gallery
12-21 35th Avenue
Long Island City, NY 11101

Paulette Gay
The Scarf Lady
408 Lenox Avenue
New York, NY 10029

Cheryl Hinton, Owner
Revelation
Decorator/party consultant
192 E. 8th Street, #4C
Brooklyn, NY 11218

Arlene Santos
Exclusively Yours Hair Salon
405 Riverdale Avenue
Yonkers, NY 10705

Robin Williams
Uptown Dance Academy, Inc.
P.O. Box 1569
New York, NY 10035

Cheryl Louise Olney, Artist
Louise's Daughter
1237 E. Main Street
Rochester, NY 14609
http://www.louisesdaughter.com

Jacqueline Kane, Ph.D.
JAK Productions
Black Mail Order Directory
30 Limerick Drive
Albany, NY 12204-1742

The businesses listed are those whose owners gave permission to include their locations and contact numbers.

Notes

Chapter 1

1. West 1999.
2. Godfrey 1992; Levinson 1997.
3. Butler 1991.
4. Drachman 2002, 5.
5. Center for Women's Business Research 2002.
6. Walker 1999, 612.
7. Mullings in Zinn and Dill 1994, 265.
8. White 1985, 199-200.
9. Ibid., 159-160.
10. Herskovits 1941; Walker in Hine 1993.
11. Bundles 2001; Bell and Nkomo 2001; Harley 2002.
12. Scott 1991, 9.
13. Walker in Hine 1993, 397.
14. Brown in Hine 1993, 1276.
15. Sterling 1984, ix.
16. Lerner 1972; White 1985.
17. DuBois in Mullings 1994, 283.
18. Radford-Hill in Scott 1991, 2.
19. National Foundation of Women Business Owners 1995, Center for Women's Business Research 2002.
20. Nelson 1997, 8.
21. Fraser 1994; Godfrey 1992; Levinson 1997; Swantz 1994.

Chapter 2

1. Schwarz-Bart and Schwarz-Bart 2001.
2. Dodson in Schwarz-Bart and Schwarz-Bart 2001, vi.
3. Madden 2000, v.
4. Schwarz-Bart and Schwarz-Bart 2001, 10.
5. Ibid., 18, 22.
6. Ibid., 29, 30-41.
7. Ibid., 44-47.
8. Ibid., 48-50.
9. Ibid., 68.
10. Ibid., 76.
11. Ibid., 102, 104.
12. Ibid., 108, 113.
13. Ibid., 149, 152-154.
14. Ibid., 164.
15. Ibid., 176, 184.
16. Ibid., 260.
17. Ibid., 268.
18. Ibid., 239.
19. Williams 1972, 29.
20. Davidson 1969.
21. Williams 1972, 173–187.
22. Williams 1972; Herskovits 1941; Meier and Rudwick 1968.
23. Herskovits 1941, 62.
24. Walker in Hine, Brown, Terborg-Penn 1993, 394.

Chapter 3

1. Hine and Thompson 1998, 10, 11.
2. Walker 1997.
3. Turner in Haynes 1963.
4. Walker 1997, 207.
5. Hine and Thompson 1998, 11.
6. Whitaker 1990, 4; Hine and Thompson 1998, 14.
7. Walker 1998, 55.
8. Hine and Thompson 1998, 31-33.
9. Sheared 1994.
10. Kwolek-Folland 2002.

11. Hine and Thompson 1998, 37–38.

12. Kwolek-Folland 2002, 14–15.

13. Fisher 1881, 390; Hine and Thompson 1998, 23; Sterling 1984, 91.

14. MacDougal in Sterling 1984, 91.

15. Walker in Hine, Brown, Terborg-Penn 1993, 396; Hine and Thompson 1998, 22.

16. Peiss in Hine, Brown, Terborg-Penn 1993, 104.

17. Birmingham in Hine and Thompson 1998, 21–22.

18. Hine and Thompson 1998, 47.

19. Hine and Thompson 1998, 47

20. Butler 1991, 44; Walker 1997, 208; Walker in Hine, Brown, Terborg-Penn 1993, 396.

21. Mills in Walker 1997, 395.

22. Walker in Hine, Brown, Terborg-Penn 1993, 395–396.

23. Walker in Hine, Brown, Terborg-Penn 1993, 395.

24. Sterling 1984, 48.

25. Walker in Hine, Brown, Terborg-Penn 1993, 396; Hine and Thompson 1998, 115.

26. Drachman 2002; Keckley 1898; Sterling 1984, 251.

27. Katz 1995, xii.

28. Katz 1995, ix-x.

29. Hess 2004.

30. Hudson 2003; Norling in Hudson 2003, 22; Pleasant in Hudson, 2003.

31. Hudson 2003, 2.

32. Kwolek-Folland 2002.

33. Scott 1991, 9.

34. Drachman 2002, 130–136; Weare in Hine, Brown, Terborg-Penn 1993, 831.

35. Drachman 2002, 121.

36. Suggs in Drachman 2002, 135.

37. Marlowe in Hine, Brown, Terborg-Penn 1993, 1219.

38. Butler 1991.

39. Bundles 2001; Sterling 1984.

40. *Colored American*, n.d. in Sterling 1984, 218.

41. *The Anglo-African*, September 17, 1859.

42. *The Weekly Advocate*.

43. *The Frederick Douglass Papers*, 1855?

44. Hine and Thompson 1998, 245.

45. Hine and Thompson 1998, Jones in Hine and Thompson 1998, 245–247.

46. HBO Home Video, 2003.

47. Hine and Thompson 1998, 166.

48. Hunter 2003.49. Sterling 1984, xv.

Chapter 4

1. Hine, Brown, Terborg-Penn 1993.

2. Walker 1993, 397.

3. Lesbock in Hutton 1993, 60.

4. Giovanni in Dance 1998, xx.

5. Wilson 1983, xii; Gates 1983.

6. Gates 1983.

7. Wilson 1983, 41, 124.

8. Jacobs 1861.

9. Hine and Thompson 1998.

10. Cooper 1991, 110,117.

11. Walker 1982, 214.

12. Schomburg Center for Black Culture Database New York Public Library.

13. Hutton 1993, 57.

14. Hutton 1993, 75.

15. Hutton 1993.

16. Hine and Thompson 1998, 226.

17. *The Anglo-African*, Weekly December 17, 1859, 18.

18. *The Anglo-African*, September 17, 1859.

19. Calloway-Thomas; in Hine, Brown, Terborg-Penn, 1993, 224–226; Hutton 1993, 63.

20. Hine and Thompson 1998, 227.

21. Hine and Thompson 1998; Hutton 1993.

22. Stewart in Hine and Thompson 1998, 106.

23. Hine and Thompson 1998, 106.

24. Hunter 2003, 75, 88.

25. Hunter 2003, 97.

26. Hine and Thompson 1998, 123.

27. Kwolek-Folland 2002.

28. Hine and Thompson 1998, 74.

29. Hine and Thompson 1998, 123.

30. Hine and Thompson 1998, 123.

31. *Frederick Douglass Paper*, July 11, 1854.

32. Hutton 1993, 72; Jerrido in Hine et al. 1993, 426.

33. Smith in Hine, Brown, Terborg-Penn 1993, 114.

34. Fleming in Hine, Brown, Terborg-Penn 1993, 128.
35. Gilkes in Hine, Brown, Terborg-Penn 1993, 968.
36. Isreal in Hine, Brown, Terborg-Penn 1993, 1073.
37. Gilkes in Hine, Brown, Terborg-Penn 1993, 971.
38. Weare in Hine, Brown, Terborg-Penn 1993, 831.
39. Lewis 1925 in Hine, Brown, Terborg-Penn 1993, 1258.
40. Hine and Thompson 1998, 182.
41. Cash in Hine, Brown, Terborg-Penn 1993, 52.
42. Hine and Thompson 1998, 138
43. Hine, Brown, Terborg-Penn 1993.
44. Ringgold in Hine and Thompson 1998, 314.
45. Hine, Brown, Terborg-Penn 1993; Hine and Thompson 1998.
46. Hine, Brown, Terborg-Penn 1993.
47. Hine and Thompson 1998, 211.
48. Green in Hine and Terborg 1993, 272.
49. Hine and Thompson 1998, 189.
50. Hine and Thompson 1998, 231.
51. Hine and Thompson 1998, 224.
52. Hine, Brown, Terborg-Penn 1993, 923.
53. Hine, Brown, Terborg-Penn 1993, 923.
54. Hine, Brown, Terborg-Penn 1993, 222, 223.
55. 365 Days of Black History.
56. Freydberg in Hine, Brown, Terborg-Penn 1993, 263.
57. 365 Days; Thompson in Hine, Brown, Terborg-Penn 1993, 1042.

Chapter 5

1. Small Minority-Owned Business Enterprises and Small Women-Owned Business Enterprises, U.S. Census Bureau 2002.
2. Center for Women's Business Research, http:/www.womensbusiness-research.org, December 2001.
3. Center for Women's Business Research 2002 Fact Sheet, 2001.
4. http:/www.womensbusinessresearch.com, 2003.
5. Kerka 1988 in ERIC Digest 1993.
6. National Foundation of Women Business Owners 1998, in *Black Enterprise* August 1999, 8, 60.
7. Scott 1991, 10.
8. Bates 1996, 1989; Small Business Administration in Nespor 1994
9. Marsick and Watkins 1990.

10. Marsick and Watkins 1990.
11. Lewis and Williams 1994, 5.
12. Burbridge in Boston 1997.
13. Nelson 1997.
14. Hine and Thompson 1998.

Chapter 6

1. Sheared 1994.
2. McClelland 1986; 1992.
3. Scott 1991.
4. Morrison cited in Herndl 1995.
5. Herndl in Leavitt 1995, 142.
6. Belenky et al. 1969.

Chapter 7

1. Levinson 1999.
2. Center for Women's Business Research 2002.
3. McClelland 1986.

Chapter 8

1. Peterson 1992, 95-108.
2. Godfrey 1992; Swantz 1994, 1995.
3. Higgenbotham 1992, 255.
4. Woodard 1997, 64
5. Bell 2002, 11.
6. Townsel, June 1997, 92.
7. Ibid., 90.
8. Burbridge 1997, 117.
9. Hine and Thompson 1998; Johnson 1999; White 1998.
10. Johnson 1999, 126.
11. Williams et al 1998.
12. Sabel 1994, 138, 152.
13. Wiltz 1999, 194
14. hooks in Wiltz 1999, 194.
15. Ehrhart-Morrison 1997, 191.

16. Guerrero 1999, 131.
17. Ibid., 131.
18. Brush 1992; Hawken in Godfrey 1992.
19. Stewart in Hagan et al. 1989, 123.

Chapter 9

1. Aldrich 1989; Bruderl 1998; McGrath 1996.
2. Putnam 2000.
3. Gittell and Thompson 1998.
4. Nelton 1998, 47–49.
5. Wong in Nelton 1998.
6. Scott 1991, 162.
7. Daloz et al. 1996, 97–99.
8. Daloz 1999.
9. Goleman 1995.
10. Butler 1991, 79.
11. Swantz 1994, 2.

Chapter 10

1. Nelson 1997.
2. McGrath 1996,11.
3. *Webster's American Heritage Dictionary* 1998, 913.
4. Cosby in Smith 1996, xiii.
5. Heider in Fraser 1994, 43.
6. Godfrey 1992, xxv.
7. McClelland 1986.
8. Swantz 1995.

Chapter 11

1. Fraser 1994, 34–35.
2. National Foundation of Women Business Owners (FWBO) 1998.
3. U.S. Census Economic Report 1997, 2002.
4. Harrigan and Feigenbaum 1997.
5. Woodard 1997, 234.
6. Ibid., 234.

7. Ardener and Burman 1997, 32.

8. Fraser 1994, 36.

9. Proverbs 29:8.

10. Wallace 1993, 164, 254.

Appendices

1. Smith 1999.

Bibliographic Essay

1. Higgenbotham 1992, 255; Clarke 1974.

2. Malson, Mudimbe-Boyi, O'Barr, Wyer 1988.

3. Malson, Mudimbe-Bovi, O'Barr, Wyer 1988, 1; Humber-Faison 1988, 2.

4. White 1985, 22.

5. Burbridge 1997, 104.

6. Walker in Hine, Brown, Terborg-Penn 1993; Walker 1997, 1998.

7. Walker 1999, xiii.

8. Williams in Harley 2002.

9. Schumpter in Bygrave 1989; Kent 1990.

10. Bates 1989, Fratoe 1998, Sowell in Y. Jones 1985.

11. Butler 1991, Fraser 1994, Scott 1991, Stack 1974.

12. Scott 1991, 162.

13. Godfrey 1992; Levinson 1997; Swantz 1994, 1995.

14. Amott and Matthaei 1996, 9.

15. Kwolek-Folland 2002; Oppedisano 2000; Walker 1999.

16. Merriam and Cunningham 1991, 9, 234.

17. Chambers 2003; Erhardt-Morrison 1997; Harris 1996.

18. Butler 1991, 324.

19. Daloz 1999.

20. Wellington in Port 1999, A41.

21. Butler 1991, 79, 324.

22. Kitchen 1998, F10.

23. Capowski 1998; Lavalle 1999.

24. Braham 1999.

25. Guerrero 1999, 130-131.

26. Hawken in Godfrey 1992, v, 5.

27. Mason-Draffen 1997.

28. Cole and Guy-Sheftall 2003.

29. Collins 1990, Higgenbotham 1992, hooks 2000.

30. West 1999.

31. Hambrick 1997, 70.

32. Zinn and Dill 1994, 11.

33. Crafts 2002.

34. Fisher 1881.

Bibliography

Aldrich, H. Networking among Women Entrepreneurs. In *Women-Owned Businesses*, edited by O. Hagan, C. Rivshun, and D. Sexton. New York: Praeger, 1989.

Amott, T. L. and Matthaei, J. A. *Race Gender and Work: A Multicultural Economic History of Women in the United States*. Boston, MA: South End Press, 1996.

Ardener, S. and Burman, S. (eds). *Money-go-rounds: The importance of rotating savings and credit associations for women*. Westport, CT: Bergin and Garvey, 1996.

Auster, E. Owner and Organizational Characteristics of Black- and White-Owned Businesses: Self-Employed Blacks Had Less Training, Fewer Resources, Less Profits, but Had Similar Survival Rates. *Journal of Economics and Sociology* 1998;4(3):331–344.

Background Paper on Women's Business Development. Jamaica, NY: Subcommittee on Women's Business Development, New York State Legislative Roundtable, York Small Business Development Center, 1997.

Bates, T. The Changing Nature of Minority Business: A Comparative Analysis of Asian, Non-Minority and Black Owned-Businesses. *The Review of Black Political Economy* 1989 18(2):25–44.

———. Entrepreneurship Human Capital, Endowments and Minority Business Viability. *Journal of Human Resources* 1985;20:540–554.

Bates, T. and Sevron, L. Why Loans Won't Save the Poor. *AEO Exchange*, June 1996.

Belenky, M., Clincy, B. M., Goldberger, N. M., and Tarule, J. M. *Women's Ways of Knowing: The Development of Self, Voice and Mind*. New York: Basic Books, 1969, 2nd edition, 1996.

Bell, E. and Nkomo, S. *Our Separate Ways: Black and White Women and the Struggle for Professional Identity*. Boston: Harvard Business School Press, 2001.

Bell, J. *Famous Black Quotations on Mothers*. Kansas City, MO: Andrews McMeel, 2002.

Bennett, L. *Before the Mayflower: A History of the Negro in the United States, 1619–1964*. Chicago: Johnson, 1961.

Berlin, I. *Slaves without Masters: The Free Negro in the Antebellum South*. New York: Pantheon Books, 1974.

Biennial Update on Women-Owned Businesses Documents Substantial Economic Impact [e-mail Web report]. Center for Women's Business Research, 2004. Available from www.womensbusinessresearch.org.

Birley, S. Female Entrepreneurs: Are They Really Different? *Journal of Small Business Management* 1989;27(1):32–37.

———. The Role of Networks in the Entrepreneurial Process. *Journal of Business Venturing* 1985;27(1):107–117.

Boston, T. D., ed. *A Different Vision: African-American Economic Thought*. Vols. 1 and 2. London: Routledge, 1997.

Braham, J. The Spiritual Side. *Industry Week* 1999;Feb. 1 (on-line abstract).Brimmer, A. Preamble: The Economic Cost of Discrimination against Black Americans. In *A Different Vision: African-American Economic Thought*, edited by T. D. Boston. London: Routledge, 1997.

Brookfield, S. Adult Learning: An Overview. In *International Encyclopedia of Education*, edited by T. Husen and N. Postwhite. Oxford: Pergamenon Press, 1994.

Brown, A. The Myth of the Universal Adult Educator: A Literature Review. Paper presented at the Adult Education Research Conference, Oklahoma State University, May 1997.

Brown, K. D. Womanist Theology. In *Black Women in America: An Historical Encyclopedia*, edited by D. C. Hine. New York: Carlson Publications, 1993.

Bruderl, J. Network Support and the Success of Newly Founded Businesses. *Small Business Economics* May, 1998 (on-line abstract).

Brush, C. Research on Women Business Owners: Past Trends, a New Perspective and Future Directions. *Entrepreneurship Theory and Practice* 1992;16(4):5–20.

Bundles, A'Lelia. *On Her Own Ground: The Life and Times of Madame C.J. Walker*. New York: Scribner, 2001.

Burbridge, L. Black Women in the History of Economic Thought: A Critical Essay. In *A Different Vision: African-American Economic Thought*, edited by T. D. Boston. London: Routledge, 1997.

Butler, J. S. *Entrepreneurship and Self-Help in the Black Community: A Reconsideration of Race and Economics*. Albany: State University of New York Press, 1991.

Bygrave, W. "The Entrepreneurship Pradigm (I): A philosophical look at its Research Methodologies." *Entrepreneurship Theory and Practice*. Fall, 1989, pp. 7-25.

Campbell Jr., Edward D. C., ed. *Before Freedom Came: African-American Life in the Antebellum South*. Charlottesville: The Museum of the Confederacy and the University Press of Virginia, 1991.

Capowski, G. "Much Ado About Culture" *HR Focus*. 75(10):16 (on-line abstract).

Carby, H. White Women Listen! In *Women's Studies: Essential Readings*, edited by S. Jackson. New York: New York University Press, 1993.

Carter, C. J. *Africana Woman: Her Story through Time*. Washington, DC: National Geographic Society, 2003.

Cassara, B., ed. *Adult Education in a Multicultural Society.* New York: Routledge, 1990.

Cash, F. Associations for the Protection of Negro Women. In *Black Women in America: An Historical Encyclopedia.* Edited by D. C. Hine, E. B. Brown, and R. Terborg-Penn. New York: Carlson, 1993.

————. White Rose Mission, New York City. In *Black Women in America: An Historical Encyclopedia.* Edited by D. C. Hine, E. B. Brown, and R. Terborg-Penn. New York: Carlson, 1993.

Center for Women's Business Research Reports. Washington, DC, 2001, 2002. (www.womensbusinessresearch.org).

Chambers, Veronica. *Having It All: Black Women and Success.* New York: Doubleday 2003.

Clarke, J. H. The Meaning of Black History. In *Blacks in White America before 1865: Issues and Interpretations,* edited by R. V. Haynes. New York: David McKay, 1972.

Clarke, R. Sisters Inc.: Successful Black Women: Making It Happen. *Black Enterprise* August 1999 59–63.

Cole, J. B. and Guy-Sheftal, B. Gender Talk. *Souls: A Critical Journal of Black Politics, Culture, and Society: Black Feminism* 2000;2(4):91.

————. *Gender Talk: The Struggle for Women's Equality in African American Communities.* New York: One World, 2003.

Collins, P. H. *Black Feminist Thought.* New York: Routledge, 1990.

Cooper, J. C. *Family.* New York: Doubleday, 1991.

Cosby, C. Foreword. In *Powerful Black Women,* edited by J. C. Smith. Detroit: Visible Ink Press, 1996.

Crafts, H. *The Bondwoman's Narrative.* Edited by H. L. Gates Jr. New York: Warner Books, c. 1850. Reprint 2002.

Curry, L. P. *The Free Black in Urban America, 1800–1850: The Shadow of the Dream.* Chicago: University of Chicago Press, 1981.

Dallafar, A. Iranian Women as Immigrant Entrepreneurs. *Gender and Society* 1994;8(4, December):541–561.

Daloz, L. P. *Mentor: Guiding the Journey of Adult Learners.* 2nd ed. San Francisco: Jossey-Bass, 1999.

Daloz, L. P., Keen, C., Keen, J., Parks, S. *Common Fire: Lives of Commitment in a Complex World.* Boston: Beacon Press, 1996.

Dance, D. C. *Honey Hush: An Anthology of Black Women's Humor.* New York: W. W. Norton, 1998.

Davidson, B. *The African Genius: An Introduction to African Social and Cultural History.* Boston: Little, Brown, 1969.

Davidson, B., Buah, F. K., and Ajayi, J. F. A. *The Growth of African Civilisation: A History of West Africa, 1000–1800.* London: Longmans, Green, 1965.

DeCarlo, J. F. and Lyons, P. R. A Comparison of Selected Personal Characteristics of Minority and Non-Minority Female Entrepreneurs. *Journal of Small Business Management* 1970;17:22–29.

Denizin, N. and Lincoln, Y., eds. *Collecting and Interpreting Qualitative Materials.* Thousand Oaks, CA: Sage, 1998.

————. *Handbook of Qualitative Research.* Thousand Oaks, CA: Sage, 1994.

Drachman, V. G. *Enterprising Women: 250 Years of American Business.* Chapel Hill, NC: The Schlesinger Library, Radcliffe Institute of Advanced Study, Harvard University, and the University of North Carolina Press, 2002.

Ehrhart-Morrison, D. *No Mountain High Enough: Secrets of Successful African-American Women*. Berkeley, CA: Conari, 1997.

Eisen, A. *Black Folk Wit, Wisdom, and Sayings*. Kansas City, MO: Ariel Books, 1994.

Entrepreneurial Assistance Program. Albany: New York State Department of Economic Development, 1996.

Feigenbaum, R. Minorities Strive for Equal Footing: Despite Success, Networking and Financing Still Remain Major Obstacles to Growth. *Newsday*, June 14, 1999, C18.

Feiner, S., ed. *Race and Gender in the American Economy: Views from across the Spectrum*. Englewood Cliffs, NJ: Prentice Hall, 1994.

Fisher, A. *What Mrs. Fisher Knows about Old Southern Cooking: Soups, Pickles, Preserves, Etc.* San Francisco, CA: Women's Cooperative Print Office, 1881.

Fleming, S. Bethune Cookman College. In *Black Women in America: An Historical Encyclopedia*. Edited by D. C. Hine, E. B. Brown, and R. Terborg-Penn. New York: Carlson, 1993.

Fraser, G. *Success Runs in Our Race: A Complete Guide to Networking in the African-American Community*. New York: William Morrow, 1994.

Fratoe, G. Social Capital of Black Business Owners. *Journal of Black Political Economy* Spring 1988:33–50.

Freyberg, F. Coleman, Bessie (1896–1926). In *Black Women in America: An Historical Encyclopedia*. Edited by D. C. Hine, E. B. Brown, and R. Terborg-Penn. New York: Carlson, 1993.

Garwood, A. *Black Americans: A Statistical Sourcebook*. Boulder, CO: Numbers and Concepts, 1991.

Gates, H. L., Jr. Introduction and Notes. In Wilson, H. *Our Nig; Or, Sketches from the Life of a Free Black*. Boston: Rand and Avery, 1859. Reprint, New York: Random House, 1983.

Giddings, P. *When and Where I Enter: The Impact of Black Women on Race and Sex in America*. New York: Quill William Morrow, 1984.

Giovanni, N. Foreword. In *Honey Hush: Anthology of African American Women's Humor*, edited by D. Dance. New York: W. W. Norton, 1998.

Gilkes, C. Religion. In *Black Women in America: An Historical Encyclopedia*. Edited by D. C. Hine, E. B. Brown, and R. Terborg-Penn. New York: Carlson, 1993.

Gite, L. Black Women Entrepreneurs on the Rise. *Black Enterprise* August 1998: 92–82.

Gittell, R. and Thompson, P. Business Development and Entrepreneurship in the Inner City: Frontiers for Research and Practice. In *Research Frontiers in Community Development* edited by W. Dickens and R. Ferguson. Washington, D.C.: Brookings Institution, 1998.

Godfrey, J. *Our Wildest Dreams: Women Entrepreneurs Making Money, Having Fun, Doing Good*. New York: HarperCollins, 1992.

Goleman, D. *Emotional Intelligence*. New York: Bantam Books, 1995.

Green, M. Composers. In *Black Women in America: An Historical Encyclopedia*. Edited by D. C. Hine, E. B. Brown, and R. Terborg-Penn. New York: Carlson, 1993.

Guerrero, R. The Strategies of Successful American Indian and Native Learners in the Adult Education Environment. Paper presented at the Adult Education Research Conference, DeKalb, IL, May, 1999.

Gurley-Highgate, H. *Sapphires' Grave*. New York: Doubleday, 2000.

Gutman, H. *The Black Family in Slavery and Freedom*. New York: Vintage Books, 1997.

Hagan, O., Rivchin, C., Sexton, D., ed. *Women-Owned Businessess*. New York: Praeger Publishers, 1989.

Hambrick, A. "You Haven't Seen Anything Until You Make a Black Woman Mad." In *Oral Narrative Research with Black Women*, edited by K. Vaz, Thousand Oaks, CA: Sage Publications, 1997a.

Harley, S., ed. *Sister Circle: Black Women and Work*. New Brunswick, NJ: Rutgers Univsersity Press, 2002.

———. Working for Nothing but a Living: Black Women in the Underground Economy. In *Sister Circle: Black Women and Work*, edited by S. Harley. New Brunswick, NJ: Rutgers University Press, 2002, pp. 48–66.

Harrigan, S. and Feigenbaum, R. Management Minority: A Study on Women in the Corporate Sector. *Newsday* October 25, 1997, A55.

Harris, F. *About My Sister's Business: The Black Woman's Road Map to Successful Entrepreneurship*. New York: Simon and Schuster, 1996.

Hartigan, L. Lewis, Mary Edmonia "Wildfire", (b.c. 1843). In *Black Women in America: An Historical Encyclopedia*. Edited by D. C. Hine, E. B. Brown, and R. Terborg-Penn. New York: Carlson, 1993.

Hayes, C. Business Dynamos: Women Business Achievers. *Black Enterprise* August 1998:58–64.

Haynes, R. V. Black Americans and Africa. In *Blacks in White American before 1865: Issues and Interpretations*, edited by R. V. Haynes. New York: David MacKay, 1972.

Herndl, D. P. The Invisible (Invalid) Woman: African-American Women, Illness, and 19th Century Narrative. *Women's Studies* 1995;24:553–572.

Herskovits, M. J. *The Myth of the Negro Past*. Boston: Beacon Press, 1941.Hess, K. in *News from the Schlesinger Library*. Cambridge, MA: Radcliffe Institute for Advanced Studies, Harvard University. Spring 2004, 6.

Higgenbotham, E. African-American Women's History and the Metalanguage of Race. *Signs* 1992;17(21):251–274.

———. Black Professional Women: Job Ceilings and Employment Sectors. In *Women of Color in US Society*, edited by M. Zinn and B. Dill. Philadelphia, PA: Temple University Press, 1994.

Hill, R. E., ed. *Women of Courage: An Exhibition of Photographs by Judith Sedwick Based on the Black Women Oral History Project*. Cambridge, MA: Radcliffe College, 1984.

Hine, D. C., Brown, E. B., and Terborg-Penn, R., ed. *Black Women in America: An Historical Encyclopedia*. 2 vols. New York: Carlson, 1993.

Hine, D. C. and Thompson, K. *A Shining Thread of Hope: The History of Black Women in America*. New York: Broadway Books, 1998.

Hirsch, J. Women Entrepreneurs: Problems and Prescriptions for Success in the Future. In *Women-Owned Businesses*, edited by O. Hagan, C. Rivchun, and D. Sexton. New York: Praeger, 1989.

Hirsch, J., Brush, C., DeSouza, G. Performance in Entrepreneurial Ventures: Does Gender Matter? In *Frontiers in Entrepreneurship Research*. Babson Park, MA: Babson College Center for Entrepreneurial Studies, 1997, pp. 238–239.

Hogan, S., Robinson, S., and Schell, D. Black Entrepreneurs and the Small Business Curriculum. *Journal of Education for Business 1993: Jan/Feb 93,Vol. 68, Issue 3, p 152.*

hooks, b. *Where We Stand: Class Matters.* New York: Routledge, 2000.

Horton, J. O. Free Black Women in the Antebellum South. In *Black Women in America, an Historical Encyclopedia*, edited by D. C. Hine, E. B. Brown, and R. Terborg-Penn. New York: Carlson, 1993.

Howell, D. W., ed. *I Was a Slave: The Lives of Slave Women.* Washington, DC: American Legacy Books, 1995.

Hudson, L. M. *The Making of Mammy Pleasant: A Black Entrepreneur in Nineteenth-Century San Francisco.* Urbana: University of Illinois Press, 2003.

Huggins, N. I. *Black Odyssey: The African-American Ordeal in Slavery.* 2nd edition. Vintage Books, 1997.

Humber-Faison, J. No Flowers Please: The Black Female Educator and the Education of Adult Freedmen. Unpublished doctoral dissertation, Teachers College, Columbia University, 1988.

Hunter, T. W. *To 'Joy My Freedom': Southern Black Women's Lives and Labors after the Civil War.* Cambridge, MA: Harvard University Press, 1997.

Hutton, F. *The Early Black Press in America 1827 to 1860.* Westport, CT: Greenwood, 1993.

Ihle, E. L. Education of Free Blacks before the Civil War. In *Education of the African American Adult: An Historical Overview*, edited by H. Neufeldt and L. McGee. Westport, CT: Greenwood Press, 1990.

Innovative Banking for Microenterprise. New York: Women's World Banking, 1995.

Jackson, S., ed. *Women's Studies: Essential Readings.* New York: New York University Press, 1993.

Jacobs, H. *Incidents in the Life of a Slave Girl, Written by Herself,* 1st edition. Edited by L. Maria Child. Boston: Published for the author. Re-issue edited by J. Fagin Yellin, Cambridge, MA: Harvard University Press, 1987.

Johnson, A. Ferguson, Catherine (Katy) (c. 1774-1854). In *Black Women in America, an Historical Encyclopedia*, edited by D. C. Hine. New York: Carlson Publications, 1993.

Johnson, P. Sister Circles. *Essence* May1999:126–128.

Jones, J. *Labor of Love, Labor of Sorrow: Black Women, Work and the Family from Slavery to the Present.* New York: Vintage Books, 1985.

Jones, Y. Afro-American Urban Life: New Directions for Research. Paper presented at the Central States Anthropological Society. April, 1985.

Katz, W. L. *Black Women of the Old West.* New York: Atheneum Books, 1995.

Keckley, E. *Behind the Scenes, or, Thirty Years a Slave, and Four Years in the White House (the Schomburg Library of Nineteenth Century Black Women Writers)* . New York: G. W. Carlson, 1868. Reprint, New York: Oxford University Press, 1988.

Kent, C. A. (ed). *Entrepreneurship Education: Current Development, Future Directions.* New York: Quorum Books, 1990.

Kerka, S. Women and Entrepreneurship. ERIC Digest. EDO-CE-93-143). Washington, DC: Office of Education Research and Improvement (EDD00036), 1993.

Kitchen, P. "Hints From on High: Work & Spirituality." *Newsday*, September 13, 1998, F10.

Kwolek-Folland, A. *Incorporating Women: A History of Women in Business in the United States.* New York: Palgrave, 2002.

Lavalle Jr., J. The Spirituality of Work. *Life Association News* Feb. 1999. (on-line abstract).

Lennon, T. and Bell. E. Unchained Memories: Readings from the Slave Narratives. 75 minutes. HBO Home Video, 2003.

Lerner, G., ed. *Black Women in White America.* New York: Vintage Books, 1972.

———. *Why History Matters: Life and Thought.* Cambridge: Oxford University Press, 1997.

Levinson, J. C. *The Way of the Guerilla: Achieving Success and Balance as an Entrepreneur in the 21st Century.* Boston: Houghton Mifflin, 1997.

Lewis, J. and Williams, C. "Experiential Learning Past and Present" in *Experiential Learning: A New Approach.* New Directions in Adult and Continuing Education, edited by L. Jackson and R. Cafferella. San Francisco, CA: Jossey-Bass, No. 62, Summer 1994, pp. 5-16.

Livesay, H. Entrepreneurial History. In *Encyclopedia of Entrepreneurship*, edited by C. Kent, D. Sexton, and K.Vesper. Chicago: Englewood Cliffs, NJ: Prentice-Hall, 1982.

Madden, A. *In Her Footsteps: 101 Remarkable Women from the Queen of Sheba to Queen Latifah.* Berkeley, CA: Conari, 2000.

Malson, M., Mudimbe-Boyi, M., O'Barr, J., Wyer, M., ed. *Black Women in America: Social Science Perspectives.* Chicago: University of Chicago Press, 1988.

Marsick, V. and Watkins, K. *Informal and incidental learning in the workplace.* New York: Routledge, 1990.

Mason-Draffen, C. Out on Her Own. *Newsday*, August 3, 1997, F8.

———. Women Used as "Fronts" in Minority Contracting. *Newsday*, October 23, 1997, A55.

McClelland, D. Characteristics of Successful Entrepreneurs. *Journal of Creative Behavior* 1986;21(3):219–233.

———. *Motivating Economic Achievement.* New York: Free Press, 1969.

McGee, L. and Neufeldt, H. *Education of the Black Adult in the United States: An Annotated Bibliography.* Westport, CT: Greenwood, 1985.

McGrath, R. Does Culture Endure or Is It Malleable? Issues for Entrepreneurial Economic Development. *Journal of Business Venturing* 1992;7:441–458.

———. Options and the Entrepreneur: Towards a Strategic Theory of Entrepreneurial Behavior. Paper presented at the Entrepreneurship Division, Academy of Management Meetings, January, 1996.

McKee, K., Gould, S., Leonard, A. Self-Employment as a Means to Economic Self-Sufficiency: Women's Business Development Program. *SEEDS* 1993;15 (ERIC #36J5774).

Meier, A. and Rudwick, E. *From Plantation to Ghetto.* New York: Hill & Wang, 1968.

Merriam, S. and Cunninghan, P. *Lifelines: Patterns of Work, Love and Learning in Adulthood.* San Francisco: Jossey-Bass, 1991.

Merriam-Webster's Collegiate Dictionary, 10th Edition. Springfield, MA: Merriam-Webster Incorporated, 1998.

Minority-and-Women-Owned Businesses: Summary of Findings. Washington, DC: Census Bureau Economic Census, 1997.

Moody, F. B. Entrepreneurship Concepts for Minorities: Considerations for Voca-
    tional Education Personnel Developers. Paper presented at the American
    Vocational Association, Anaheim, California, December, 1984.
Morgan, D. L. *Focus Groups as Qualitative Research.* Newbury Park, CA: Sage
    Publications, 1988.
Morgan, J. When Chickens Come Home to Roost: My Life as a Hip-Hop Feminist.
    Essence May 1999:94–95.
Mullings, L. Images, Ideology and Women of Color. In *Women of Color in U.S.
    Society*, edited by M. Zinn and B. Dill. Philadelphia, PA: Temple University
    Press, 1994.
———. *On Our Own Terms: Race, Gender, and Class in the Lives of African
    American Women.* New York: Routledge, 1997.
Nelson, G. Factors of Friendship: Relevance of Significant Others to Female Busi-
    ness Owners. *Entrepreneurship Theory and Practice* 1989, Summer:7–18.
Nelson, J. *Straight No Chaser: How I Became a Grown-up Black Woman.* New
    York: G. P. Putnam's Sons, 1997.
———. *Volunteer Slavery: My Authentic Negro Experience.* New York: Penguin
    Books, 1994.
Nelton, S. Minority Women on the Rise. *Nation's Business* July1998, 46, 747 –49.
Nespor, V. Learning Processes that Contribute to the Effective Decision-Making
    Processes of Small Business Owners. Unpublished doctoral dissertation,
    Teachers College, Columbia University, 1994.
Neufeldt, H. and McGee, L., ed. *The Education of the African American Adult: An
    Historical Overview.* Westport, CT: Greenwood, 1990.
New Economic Realities: The Rise of Women Entrepreneurs: A Report of the
    Committee of Small Business, 2nd ed. Washington, DC: US House of
    Representatives, Government Printing Office, 1998.
NFWBO. Women-Owned Businesses: Breaking the Boundaries: A Report.
    Washington, DC: National Foundation of Women Business Owners and
    Dun & Bradstreet Information Services, 1995.
Oppedisano, J. *Historical Encyclopedia of American Women Entrepreneurs, 1776
    to the Present.* Westport, CT: Greenwood, 2000.
Padilla-Orasel, M. Entrepreneurial Assistance Program Overview. Albany, NY:
    Empire State Development, Annual Directors Meeting, 1998.
Padilla-Orasel, M. and Smith, C. A. Long Range Evaluation of Impact of Micro-
    enterprise Training: Lessons from "Failures." Paper presented at the Eighth
    Annual Conference, Association for Enterprise Opportunity, Washington,
    DC, April 1998.
Painter, N. I. *The Exodusters: Black Migration to Kansas after Reconstruction.* New
    York: W. W. Norton, 1986.
Palmer, T. Adult Education and Human Capital: Lessons from the Fortune 500.
    Adult Learning 1992 Nov./Dec.22–30.
Patton, M. Q. *Qualitative Evaluation and Research Methods.* 2nd ed. Newbury
    Park, CA: Sage, 1990.
Peterson, E. *African-American Women: A Study of Will and Success.* Jefferson, NC:
    MacFarland, 1992.
———, ed. *Freedom Road: Adult Education of African Americans.* Malabar, FL:
    Krieger, 1996.
Port, S. Women of Color Cite Barriers at Work. *Newsday,* July 14, 1999, A41.

Putnam, R. *Bowling Alone: The Collapse and Revival of American Community.*
New York: Simon & Schuster, 2000.
Ross-Gordon, J. Needed: A Multicultural Perspective for Adult and Continuing
Education. *Adult Education Quarterly* 1991;42(2):1–16.
Sabel, C. Learning by Monitoring: The Institutions of Economic Development. In
Handbook of Economic Sociology, edited by N. J. Smelser, and R. Swed-
burg. New York: Russell Sage Foundation, 1994.
Schwarz-Bart, S. and Schwarz-Bart, A. *In Praise of Black Women: Ancient African
Queens.* Translated by R-M. Réjouis and V. Vinokurov. Madison: The Uni-
versity of Wisconsin Press, 2001.
Scott, K. Y. *The Habit of Surviving.* New Brunswick, NJ: Rutgers University Press,
1991.
Sexton, D. Research on women-owned businesses: Current status and future di-
rections. In *Women-owned businesses.* Edited by O. Hagan, C. Rivchun, D.
Sexton. New York: Praeger, 1989, 185-187.
Sheared, V. Giving Voice: An Inclusive Model of Instruction: A Womanist Per-
spective. *Confronting Sexism and Racism: New Directions for Continuing
and Adult Education* 1994;61:27–38.
Sheared, V. and Sissel, P., ed. *Making Space: Bridging Theory and Practice in Adult
Education.* Westport, CT: Bergin & Garvey, 2001.
Silver, D. *Enterprising Women: Lessons from 100 of the Greatest Entrepreneurs of
Our Day.* New York: American Management Association, 1994.
Smith, C. A. The African-American Market Woman: Her Past, Our Future. In
Making Space: Bridging Theory and Practice in Adult Education, edited by
V. Sheared and P. Sissel Westport, CT: Bergin & Garvey, 2000.
———. 'If You Only Knew': Lessons Learned from Successful Black Women En-
trepreneurs. *Journal of Pedagogy, Pluralism and Practice,* (5). Fall/Spring,
2000/2001. Cambridge, MA: Lesley University On-line Journal. (ERIC/
AVE: CE084301).
———. *Market Women: Learning Strategies of Successful Black Women Entre-
preneurs in New York State.* Unpublished doctoral dissertation, Teachers
College, Columbia University, 1999.
———. Summative Evaluation of the Entrepreneurial Assistance Program from
1991-1997. New York: Empire State Development Corporation, Division
of Minority and Women's Business Services, 1998.
Smith, E. L. Sow Entrepreneurship, Reap Profits. *Black Enterprise* 1997:222–230.
Smith, E. M. Bethune, Mary McLeod (1875-1955). In *Black Women in America, an
Historical Encyclopedia,* edited by D. C. Hine. New York: Carlson Publi-
cations, 1993.
Smith, J. C., ed. *Powerful Black Women.* Detroit: Visible Ink Press, 1996.
Stack, C. *All Our Kin: Strategies for Survival in the Black Community.* New York:
Harper & Row, 1974.
Sterling, D., ed. *We Are Your Sisters: Black Women in the Nineteenth Century.* New
York: W. W. Norton, 1984.
Survey of Minority-Owned Businesses. Washington, DC: Department of the Census,
2002
Swantz, M. L. A Personal Position Paper on Participatory Research. Paper pre-
sented at the Third International Conference, University of Bath, March
1994.

————. Women's Economics: Do Women Really Need Another Economic Theory? Paper presented at the Third International Conference on Development and Future Studies. Keynote Address, Hawken, July 31 to August 2, 1995.

Tan, W. Entrepreneurism: It Is Now Time for a Clearer Definition. *Journal of Small Business Management* 1996;13(1):5–9.

Taylor, S. A. Colored Females Free Produce Society. In *Black Women in America: An Historical Encyclopedia*, edited by D. C. Hine. New York: Carlson Publications, 1993.

The Anglo-African, New York, NY, September 17, 1859.

The Colored American, New York City, NY. In Sterling, D., *We are Your Sisters: Black Women in The Nineteenth Century*. New York: W.W. Norton, 1984.

The Frederick Douglass Papers, Rochester, NY, 1855.

The Weekly Advocate, May 28, 1829.

Townsel, L. Mother-Daughter Buddies. *Ebony*, June 1997:90–135.

Tucker, P. T. *Cathy Williams: From Slave to Female Buffalo Soldier*. Mechanicsburg, PA: Stackpole Books, 2002.

Turner, L. D. African Survivals in the New World with Special Emphasis on the Arts. In *Blacks in White America before 1865: Issues and Interpretations*, edited by R. V. Haynes. New York: David MacKay, 1972.

Vaz, K. M. Introduction: Oral Narrative Research with Black Women. In *Oral Narrative Research with Black Women*, edited by K. Vaz. Thousand Oaks, CA: Sage Publications, 1997a.

————, ed. *Oral Narrative Research with Black Women*. Thousand Oaks, CA: Sage, 1997b.

Wahlman, M. S. *Signs and Symbols: African Images in African American Quilts*. Atlanta, GA: Tinwood Books, 2001.

Walker, A. *The Color Purple*. New York: Pocket Books, 1982.

Walker, J. K. Entrepreneurs in Antebellum America. In *Black Women in America: An Historical Encyclopedia*, edited by D. C. Hine, E. B. Brown and R. Terbong-Penn. New York: Carlson Publications, 1993.

————. Racism, Slavery and Free Enterprise: Black Entrepreneurship in the United States before the Civil War. *Business History Review* 1986, Autumn, 60, 343(4).

————. Trade and Markets in Precolonial West and West Central Africa: The Cultural Foundation of the African-American Business Tradition. In *A Different Vision: Race and Public Policy*, edited by T. D. Boston. London: Routledge, 1997.

————. (ed.). *Encyclopedia of African American Business History*. Westport, CT: Greenwood, 1999.

Wallace, R. *Black Wealth through Black Entrepreneurship*. Edgewood, MD: Duncan & Duncan, 1993.

Weare, W. Mutual Benefit Societies. In *Black Women in America: An Historical Encyclopedia*, edited by D. C. Hine, E. B. Brown and R. Terborg-Penn. New York: Carlson Publishing, 1993.

West, C. Lecture, African-American Studies 10. Cambridge, MA: Harvard University, December 10, 1999.

————. *Race Matters*. New York: Vintage Books, 1993.

Whitaker, L. Black Adult Education before 1860. In *Education of the African-American Adult: An Historical Overview*, edited by H. McGee and L. Neufeldt. Westport, CT: Greenwood, 1990.

White, D. G. *Arn't I a Woman? Females Slaves in the Plantation South*. New York: W. W. Norton, 1985.

———. *Too Heavy a Load: Black Women in Defense of Themselves 1894–1994*. New York: W. W. Norton, 1998.

Williams, C. *The Destruction of Black Civilization: Great Issues of Race from 4500 B.C. To 2000 A.D.* Chicago: Third World, 1972.

Williams, E., McVay, M., Pearson, J., and Reed, Q. *Assessing the Life Skills and Learning Needs of Urban Black Single Mothers*. Paper Presented at the Eighth Annual Meeting of the Association for Enterprise Opportunity, Washington, DC, April, 1998.

Williams, R. Getting Paid: Black Women Economists Reflect on Women and Work In *Sister Circle: Black Women and Work*, edited by S. Harley. New Brunswick, NJ: Rutgers University Press, 2002, pp. 84–102.

Wilson, H. *Our Nig; Or, Sketches from the Life of a Free Black*. Introduction and Notes by H. L. Gates, Jr. Boston: Rand & Avery, 1859. Reprint, New York: Random House, 1983.

Wiltz, T. When Sista Ain't Nothin' but a Word. *Essence* 1999:193–194.

Woodard, M. *Black Entrepreneurs in America: Stories of Struggle and Success*. New Brunswick, NJ: Rutgers University Press, 1997.

Young, N. The Road Less Traveled: A Survey of Research on African Americans in Entrepreneurship. Working Draft of unpublished paper. Department of Sociology, University of Chicago. Chicago, 1998.

Zinn, M. and Dill, B., ed. *Women of Color in US Society*. Philadelphia, PA: Temple University Press, 1994.

Bibliographic Essay

The overall conclusion I drew from my research is that Black women entrepreneurs may in fact have distinctive life experiences that have affected their business activities and strategies. Their worldviews, their ways of acting in and on the world, while displaying many commonalities with entrepreneurs in general, possess some unique aspects resulting from their historical and cultural traditions as well as from the singular intersection of race, gender and class in their lives. The overarching finding of my research was that the depth and breadth of social capital possessed by the Market Women contributed to their success. Relationships with others, including those from the past and those in the present, were key. These women's spirituality, their concern for balance, their integrity, their will, their coping mechanisms—including their use of humor, and their connections with family, notably their mothers and their "sisters," their communities, and the larger society, are distinct. Different perhaps more in degree than in kind, these particular ways of viewing and doing business can serve to inform a wide audience, those who seek empowerment for self and others, and especially those who strive to do good and do well in their businesses and in life.

Much of the work in this book has been informed and inspired by the work of scholars and academics who have researched lives, histories, and experiences that provide for a more complete understanding of Black women entrepreneurs. To investigate my topic as fully as possible, I had to glean information from a number of sources, across disciplines. This interdisciplinary stretch provided a breadth and depth of knowledge that, when patched together, provided a more holistic and complete view of the story of Black women entrepreneurs, past, present and future. Scholarship and research provided a significant patch in this story quilt, and this essay is intended to credit those scholars and researchers and their work.

They include but are not limited to scholars such as Burbridge (1997) and R. Williams (2002) in economics; Butler (1991) and Woodard (1997) in entrepreneurship; Collins in Black feminist theory (1990); Giddings (1984), Hine et al. (1993, 1998), Hudson (2003), Hunter (1997), Jones (1985), Lerner (1972), Painter (1986), Sterling (1984), and White (1985, 1998) in history; Malson et al. (1988) in sociology; Humber-Faison (1988), Peterson (1992, 1996), Scott (1991), Sheared (1994), and Sheared and Sissel (2001) in adult education; Ross-Gordon (1991) and Vaz (1997a,b) in research; Mullings in anthropology (1994, 1997); Zinn and Dill (1994) in multicultural women's studies; J. K. Walker (1986, 1993, 1997, 1999) in Black business history; and Cole and Guy-Sheftall (2003) in gender/Black women's studies. These scholars represent a diverse and growing group who are all working toward "correcting the record of history" and "reclaiming" histories lost from official records in North America.

The Literature

I strongly agree with Higgenbotham and Clarke, who contend that race is a social construct based on power, control, and money and is also a "metalanguage," as it "speaks about and lends meaning to a host of terms and expressions, to myriad aspects of life that would otherwise fall outside the referential domain of race."[1] Race can also be defined as a matrix of shared group experiences, cultural traditions, and similarities of encounters in social systems and institutions based on biological similarities. As such, race can be applied as a frame of analysis for other societal and power relations, such as gender, class, geography, age, and sexuality that affect life and, as used here, success in entrepreneurship.

Malson and her co-editors, in their work *Black Women in America: A Social Science Perspective* (1988) contend that the work of teaching information about Black women is just beginning. They recognize that the job is not new, but they feel there is still much to do and learn.[2] Like Malson et al., the above mentioned scholars believe that a major purpose of research and teaching information about Black women is the unlearning and prevention of transmission of erroneous material about subcultures.[3]

An example of the transmission of insidious information is the work done by Black and White male "experts" E. Franklin Frazier and Daniel Patrick Moynihan (in Stack 1974), who perpetuated the stereotypical figure of the strong, dominating matriarch as the destroyer of Black men and Black families. They argued that the effect on the dysfunctional nature of Black families stemmed from days when Black people were enslaved, families did not exist, and women took over. Deborah Grey White, in her 1985 study of enslaved women in America, has found evidence that disputes every aspect of this flawed theory. White found there was a complementarity of gender-related roles in the slave community that was rooted in the

African tradition and necessitated by the historical and social context of the times. This custom was related to an egalitarianism within both slave and free Black families that was crucial to the survival of the family as a whole. [4]

However, Moynihan and Frazier's pernicious analysis further established the basis for one of the worst, most inaccurate and, most long-lasting stereotypes about the Black woman, that of the "Welfare Queen." Moynihan and Frazier's view of the Black woman was the basis of the "benign neglect" U.S. government social policy in the 1970s that institutionalized modern racism, sexism, and classism in the United States. That image persists to this day; "she" again is the focus of public economic policy, political agendas, and racist and sexist behavior that continues on both individual and societal levels, illustrated by the move to "end welfare (and welfare queens) as we know it."

Hidden History

The economic realities and contributions of Black women have been diffused and disparaged by economists, sociologists, and historians, especially some in the "Academy" who believe that only the canon comprising Euro-American systems of thought provide sources of knowledge, scholarship, and behavior worthy of note and emulation. Women of African descent do not fit into their version of history or economics unless they behave like White men. In addition, Lynn Burbridge, a Black woman economist, notes that even among "Black scholars there have been gaps in the treatment of Black women in economic thought."[5] Many historians, scholars, and researchers are, for the most part, just beginning recognize the entrepreneurial aspects of Black women's lives, either past or present. There are notable exceptions. One is Juliet E. K. Walker, the premier historian of Black business in the United States. Her histories of Black businesses not only trace Black women's legacy of entrepreneurship to Africa but also acknowledge their presence and contributions throughout the course of U.S. history.[6]

In addition, according to Walker, Black business history, like Black educational history, has been relegated to the periphery of scholarship in studies of the African American experience in part because of the so-called informal nature of the documentation of business and learning activities of Black people. Similar to the necessity for surreptitious teaching and learning, much of the business conducted in the Black community had to be hidden in the antebellum era, during Reconstruction, throughout the Jim Crow era and beyond.

Success in business often resulted in violence perpetuated by Whites jealous of the achievements of people of color, such as the race riots in the South that effectively destroyed Black tradesmen, artisans, and retail and service market dominance, the latter being the purview of Black women; the destruction of Black Wall Street in Tulsa, Oklahoma; and the creation of the Trail of Tears of the Cherokee Nation in the South. As a result, Walker contends that "the oral black history tradition and the black press have contributed more to sustaining collective memories of black business activities and leading black entrepreneurs than the scholarly record."[7] This necessity for "informal" scholarship, coupled with the systemic discrimination in academia against both people of color and women has resulted in significantly fewer publications than those by, for, and about White men, who continue to strive to preserve their canon.

In discussion of the lives of enslaved Black women, Deborah Grey White talked about the cooperative nature of interchanges and relationships between bondwomen, including examples of non-monetary social capital contributions, and Dorothy Sterling used letters, diaries, and oral histories that presented the women's activities in their own words, but neither talked about the economic nature of those exchanges. Hine and Thompson recognize many entrepreneurs in their history of Black women in America, yet do not fully connect many of the accomplishments noted to economic activities and motivations. Tera Hunter began to recognize the "wage work" of laundresses and domestic servants in Post–Civil War Atlanta as "independent contracting" and "home-based" entrepreneurs in a continuation of the hiring-out process that prevailed in antebellum America. Yet, even within these excellent histories, the import and prevalence of entrepreneurism in the lives of Black women are not fully acknowledged, the usual focus being on what is termed wage work rather than "creative self-employment."

Given the dearth of information about the history of Black women's economic activities in traditional entrepreneurship history, I had to search across disciplines, often hitting walls. In all disciplines, however, there are noteworthy new books and encouraging movements. Interdisciplinary approaches to research, the coming together of scholars from many disciplines, contribute to a fuller picture of the lives and work of Black women. *Sister Circle: Black Women and Work* (2002) is a sterling example of the power of collaborative inquiry across disciplines. Written by a circle of sister academics from the University of Maryland and edited by Sharon Harley and the Black Women and Work Collective, the book offers chapters that describe and analyze Black women in work, past and present, in areas ranging from the Professoriate, in slavery, in tourism, and as artists, activists, and mothers. The late Rhonda Williams, a political economist, has a chapter in the book that reviews the work of four prominent Black women economists whose writing in the 1980s confirms the necessity of including Black Women's Themes in any discussion of the economic lives and status of Black women. Their recurrent themes include class, race, gender, and community. Those scholars, who "foregrounded" Black women and work in their own research, acknowledge the womanist approach to their analyses, understanding that Black women's economic lives are intricately and centrally connected to those of Black men and children and the community as a whole.[8] This cooperative scholarship is a model that is in keeping with our traditions of collectivism and collaboration and is one worth emulating.

A Different View of Entrepreneurship

In standard entrepreneurship theory and practice, taught in schools of business and management, success is measured solely by profits, rate of growth, size of the business, and destruction of the competition.[9] These calculations do not take into account the many factors that affect business behavior, the value of microenterprises in the economy, and the differential experiences of distinct groups in the marketplace. Some traditional social economists such as Bates, Sowell, and Fratoe do not seem to take into account the unique history and contexts of Black women when assessing their economic worth.[10] In contrast, Stack, Scott, Butler, and Fraser contend that the social capital aspects of their lives, including networks of support among Black people, and most especially Black women, are rooted in a history, and tradition has often been historically ignored or denigrated: "This social system, supported by and composed of a network or relatives, friends, neighbors and boyfriends is one of the strongest in the Black community."[11] Scott calls that nurturing network a "kinship insurance system."[12]

This restricted and limited vision of entrepreneurship has resulted in a set of exclusionary criteria that identifies many Black women's businesses as being unsuccessful, and therefore uninteresting and unworthy of note. Happily, those traditional views are being challenged by entrepreneurs from other countries, including Europe, Asia, and Africa, and by researchers and writers such as Godfrey, Levinson, and Swantz.[13]

One of those works that poses a challenge is Amott and Matthaei's (1991) multicultural economic history of women in the United States. Two non-minority women investigated the differences in women's work and economic positions within the conceptual framework of gender, race/ethnicity, and class. Although primarily focusing on wage work experiences of many cultural and ethnic groups, including poor Whites, one of their goals was to "help compensate for the disproportionate focus on European-Americans in economic history."[14] Another is Kwolek-Folland's 2002 history of women and business in the United States, *Incorporating Women*. She does a better job than most in identifying women of color, including Black women, but they remain on the periphery of the work, and with the exception of Madame C. J. Walker and Maggie Lena Walker, their overall effect is not fully acknowledged. Yet work another is Oppedisano's *Encyclopedia of American Women Entrepreneurs*, which includes a number of women of color, including Black women. Walker's *Encyclopedia of African American Business History*, which compiles a great deal of information about Black women entrepreneurs against the larger backdrop of Black business history in the United States, presents the best picture so far of the depth and breadth of Black women's contributions to the economic sphere.[15] Sharan Merriam and Phyllis Cunningham, an adult educator, investigated the attempts of women learners to achieve balance in their lives in their book, *Lifelines: Patterns of Work, Love and Learning in Adulthood* (1991). While they identified three interaction patterns between work and love, they acknowledged that work and love were culturally defined and, as used in their work, were defined from a White, Western Euro-American sociocultural construction of gender based on a Protestant ethic. The authors eventually recognized that the two domains, love and work, were bound by culture; women of color have always combined both work and love, making a case for the careful investigation of differences in outcomes in a variety of settings.[16]

Finally, it is heartening to see that the number of books written by, for, and about Black women and success appearing in popular literature has also increased: Veronica Chambers's brand-new book *Having It All: Black Women and Success* (2003), and Ehrhart-Morrison's *Ain't No Mountain High Enough* (1997) are but two. In addition, an increasing number of "how-to" books written by, for, and about Black women entrepreneurs are on the shelf—all of which are necessary as we increase the number of visible role models and alternative ways of doing business, viewed through our unique lenses and angle of vision.[17]

Role Models and Mentors

The importance of role models and mentors in successful business development programs is well documented in entrepreneurship education literature. Butler, who writes about economic self-sufficiency in the Black community, supports the historical perspective in entrepreneurship because he believes the preponderance of positive role models for the "entire American business landscape" that have been buried in African American life need to be resurfaced.[18] Daloz (1999) discusses mentors or guides, especially of adults, as educational as well as business mentors who assist learners to become competent travelers on the road to success.[19] Using Daloz's journey metaphor, role models and "unknown mentors" can assist in guiding would-be entrepreneurs in their quests, in which success is defined as the journey, not only the destination.

A Catalyst study article highlighted the difficulties Black women have in overcoming barriers in work situations, which can be extrapolated to entrepreneurship. According to Catalyst, "few women of color had help in improving their careers. Almost half cited the lack of a mentor as a barrier to their progress...29% said they lacked visible role models from their racial or cultural group."[20] Although their findings were based on working women, this perception and experience has prevailed in entrepreneurship theory and practice regarding Black women and other women of color. As revealed in the study, Black women have not had much help from White male mentors in improving their businesses. However, the findings have also disputed the assumption about the lack of role models and mentors that are "visible" to the White world. Butler offers another perspective and explanation regarding the reasons for the "invisibility" of role models and mentors, known and unknown, in the Black community:

> No other racial or ethnic group had had to face the total constitutionally sanctioned exclusion from the larger society that African-Americans have experienced.... [Yet] [t]his group (Black Americans) provides some of the best role models of any group in America—overlooked by both scholars and African-Americans.[21]

Spirituality

One of the areas in which Black women are acknowledged is in their spirituality, but not usually as it pertains to business. "Integration" is a new "buzzword" in business; corporations are now just beginning to understand that workers who are balancing or "integrating" work and life well are more productive. Debates about the role of spirituality in work, in business, and in education are increasingly finding their way in the literature. Kitchen (1998), in her article entitled "Hints From on High: Work & Spirituality," referred to a workshop in New York City, entitled "Integrating the Creative Body, Mind, and Spirit in Work," that focused on helping people put meaning into their lives and work. The stated goal of the workshop was to enable people to tap into their "whole selves" to bring more creativity and productivity to the workplace.[22]

Recent articles in business journals discuss the position of spirituality in the place where business is conducted; its role in "stewardship," or doing the best for all concerned; and "corporate spiritualism," or putting the needs of their people, customers, and employees first to run a profitable business.[23] These positions echo those of the study group participants, who believe the respectful and honest business practices—"good" business—would result in profits. Furthermore, their universal concern with others and their connection to community, their stewardship, was felt to have contributed to a loyal customer base, word-of-mouth advertising, and mutually beneficial networking, resulting in increased sales and profits. One study reported that eight corporate chief executive officers, like many of the women in the study, follow spiritual guidelines to run their businesses.[24] Parallels were evident in the findings of another study of the relationship of spirituality to success among minority populations mentioned earlier.

Guerrero (1999), an adult educator, found that strategies for success included the reconnection with Native-American adult learners' religious traditions and rituals, the establishment of cross-cultural mentoring relationships, the creation of Native American–based support systems, and a sense of determination motivated by the need to give back to the community, all of which added to their increased success rates.[25]

Spirituality is closely related to values. In discussing business values, Paul Hawken, chairman and chief executive officer of Smith & Hawken, a large majority-owned corporation, insists that "A change in values is important because business is destroying our world. And the ways modern corporations harm themselves and others are particularly male." As he relates this behavior to entrepreneurs, who often are often "corporate tycoon wannabes" he continues with his premise that "If business economics is the study of how we add value to raw materials and processes, I suggest that you cannot add values unless you have them."[26]

The connection between spirituality and values and ethics in business is clearly drawn by the study population. The notion of spirituality, integral to the business lives of this and other populations such as Native Americans and, to a certain extent, women, presents a viable model worth following. We need to challenge the notion that spirituality is the sole purview of the so-called "moral majority" and articulate that most people are moral, ethical, and spiritual in their lives and business dealings, whether they participate in organized religious rituals or not. Members of the study group who have dealt with these issues and have found some solutions to them in their spiritual approach to life and work could contribute a great deal to those in the business world and to the general population seeking to achieve the same. Alternative ways of knowing and doing business, guided by spiritual traditions that embrace a sense of spirituality and a related sense of community, have the potential to be very helpful to those individuals and businesses seeking to find balance, integration, and meaning in their work and lives.

Race versus Gender versus Class

The world is rapidly becoming a global village, united in this postmodern information age by mass media, technology, and cheap transportation. In addition, the U.S. population is becoming browner, older, and more sophisticated. Wage work as we know it is rapidly disappearing, and those who do it and control its economic institutions are increasingly female and people of color. To remain competitive in the global economy, American business must become aware of the diversity that is its strength and to use it. To do so effectively, however, business must acknowledge the effect of race, gender, and culture on business behavior. It must also recognize and celebrate the past and present contributions of those on the "margin" to take advantage of the contributions they have made, are making, and will make in the future.

We know that gender and race are not unifying and that other explanation for the revenue differential between White and Black women-owned businesses is not based on management skills but, rather, on differences in race, class, and gender and the power and privilege relationships that accrue from their intersection. For example, the average annual sales and average size of loan secured by members of the Entrepreneurial Assistance Program program are clearly different when examined along the lines of race and gender. Sales of male-owned firms continue to outstrip females across race and ethnic lines, and Whites continue to have higher revenues and obtain bigger loans than minorities. In the study group, it is interesting to note that although Black and White women reported almost exactly equal average sales, White women who took the same training were able to secure larger loans. The fact that these differential outcomes are still apparent, even among clients of the same training program, indicate that issues other than business skills are operating. White women are also securing larger numbers of government contracts than women and men of color. In addition, White men are actually benefiting from the set-aside programs because, as reported by Mason-Draffen, "more than half of the white female federal government contractors in the manufacturing and wholesale industries are 'fronts' for white men."[27]

Intraracial gender issues were raised in the study responses, as they related to an occasional lack of support for the Black's women's efforts in business from their Black male spouses and partners; a few reported intraracial issues in terms of reported experiences with Black males trying to "take over the businesses." One participant experienced the latter so strongly she reported she preferred not having a Black male mentor. Cole and Guy-Sheftal (2000) raised the issue of intraracial sexual politics that affect relationships among Black men and women in many aspects of life.[28] Among the women in the group, reports of negative intraracial gender experiences were occasional, however, as most women in the study reported almost unanimous support and encouragement from the men in their lives. Conclusions can be drawn, therefore, that the women in this study, although having had some negative experiences, for the most part had few intraracial gender issues.

Class issues are not often raised in the discussion of Black's people lives, but intraracial class differences are real and evident; the gap between the growing Black upper and middle classes and those at the lower end of the economic spectrum is widening. Issues of class did not arise often in the findings, and when they did, they seemed to be related to early experiences of some of the women, who may have been low-income at some point in their lives. All of the women could be defined as middle-class at the time of the study, indicated by their education and employment levels. Their concern with not forgetting where they came from and their desire to give back to those less fortunate than themselves indicated their recognition that they may have been of a different class than many in the Black community. Yet issues of class do arise in the community of Black women, though they are not often addressed, because it is uncomfortable, according to Collins, Higgenbotham, and hooks.[29] Those issues need to be addressed, however. Cornel West (1999) reminds us that we need to be careful of being divided because as

> Black people gain more access to academic, occupational, financial and societal institutions, there appeared to be a "thinning out" of the legacy of struggle which heretofore contributed to the viability of Black communities, resulting in a loosening of bonds with each other, paucity of public life and a continued voicelessness, powerlessness and marginality.[30]

In addition, there are two conflicting schools of thought regarding public policy positions related to entrepreneurship training and financing programs that directly affect Black women entrepreneurs, one saying we should only fund high-achieving new entrepreneurs, with others believing that entrepreneurship is a method of alleviating poverty and should be encouraged and supported in low-income individuals who want to start businesses of their own. We must be careful to retain our collective spirit and our connection to each other, for given the reality of life in a society in which we are not dominant, if we all don't do well, none of us do well.

The Research

Race, ethnicity, class, and gender are but a few of the areas that should be further investigated when assessing the economic worth of Black women and other underresearched populations. We must do our own research, moving our work from margin to center and infusing it with respect and honesty. White scholars and researchers often contend that research done by Black women about Black women is biased and unscholarly, as though their own research on their own people as well as with those different from themselves is not. Many Black women who engage in dissertation research, such as Jackie K. in our study, report that their White dissertation committees often restrict them in their work, saying there are not enough Black women to be researched on certain topics, or that they must be compared to White women. This bias is related to an "if a tree falls in the forest" approach to research; that is, if I don't know, it must not exist or be important.

Therefore, we must tell our own stories, approaching the research with our usual care, rigor, and respect. I readily acknowledge that I bring a perspective and a possible bias to the study based on my own personal experiences as a successful Black woman entrepreneur, former Entrepreneurial Assistance Program center director, teacher, and counselor. However I also bring an "informed subjectivity" framed by my distinctive "outsider-within" angle of vision, which serves to sharpen and clarify the words and feelings of the study group. I also have an inherent sense of respect for the women, their lives and their worldviews.

In addition, being a Black woman entrepreneur enabled me to establish an immediate level of trust and comfort with the participants, respond to nuances of language, intonations, and gestures found among Black women, and establish a feeling of "sisterhood." This comfort and trust enabled the participants to relax and speak freely in the interview, possibly more than they would have with another researcher not of the same race or gender. Vaz (1997b), in her work on narrative research with Black women, came to similar conclusions. Hambrick, another Black woman researcher, discussed the research process involved when Black women are both researchers and subjects:

> Over the years of talking with and listening to Black women, I have discovered that the more relaxed the atmosphere, the more intimate I'm able to become with them, and the more open each becomes about her story.... I poignantly acknowledge the rules of objectivity in research, but I didn't want to be objective. I saw no reason for neutrality. Here we were, black women, lives entwined, needing to weave our webs adroitly, bringing truth, enlightenment and healing to ourselves and future generations.... But I was black and I was a woman and I did care. I had gained their trust.[31]

So did I.

Directions for Future Research: New Questions and New Directions

I believe that good research should raise as many questions as it answers. In my opinion, the descriptive empirical research that is at the core of this book has done that. This research had limitations, as does all research. They include the small sample size, commonly used in qualitative research, and retrospective recall issues that may have occurred as respondents had to think back over time. The limitations were recognized and controlled for to the extent possible, using a variety of reliability and validity safeguards standard in qualitative research. They also raise the following questions as areas for future research:

- Are the distinctive themes identified in the study regarding Black women entrepreneurs present among other women of color, non-minority women, Black males, and White males?
- Are there class differences among Black women entrepreneurs, and if so, what are they and to what extent do they impact business development?

- How might the findings agree with or differ from those found regarding Black women entrepreneurs in other parts of the country—the South, West, Midwest, and rural areas?
- What are the entrepreneurial histories of other groups of women—Native Americans, Latinas, Asians, and nonelite Whites, as well as other groups (the disabled, religious orders, non-for-profits)—that have engaged in unrecognized entrepreneurial activities over time?
- What are the differences, if any, among women entrepreneurs in other cultures and countries? Are there any global commonalities or differences in the presence or absence of the identified themes?
- What are differences among Black women entrepreneurs who have become "financially" successful by standard small business standards (i.e., those whose businesses have passed the $1 million mark in business revenues)? What strategies were used to make the transition from microenterprise to small and midsized business levels of development?

Finally, Zinn and Dill (1994) raise another more encompassing question, related to further investigation of a larger issue related to all people: "How do the existences and experiences of all people, women and men, different racial-ethnic groups, and different classes, shape each other?"[32]

New Work

It is very exciting to see the new work that has been emerging in the form of new books and articles by, for, and about Black women. Newly discovered works written by Black women are being unearthed as more and more of this hidden history is brought to light. Gates's discovery of *The Bondswoman's Narrative* establishes Hannah Crafts as the author of the only known novel written by an enslaved African American woman who was enslaved, and possibly the first Black woman who was published anywhere.[33] Most recently, a rare book believed to be the first cookbook written by an African American woman was purchased by the Schlesinger Library at the Radcliffe Institute of Advanced Study at Harvard.[34] I had an opportunity to examine this book firsthand: It was exciting to handle the book and see Mrs. Fisher's inscription in her own hand in the flyleaf. Abby Fisher was an entrepreneur, a successful Market Woman who ran a company that manufactured pickles and preserves. She, indeed, knew her business, and to our benefit, she wrote her thoughts and recipes down.

My book, *Market Women*, is my "first hit." I hope Wallace's theory holds true for me, as I have two or three other books swirling around in my head. There is much more work to do. There are many more stories to be told. The hem of this story quilt has been left open!

Index

White Rose Mission of New York
   Street, 57–58
Wilkerson, Margaret B., xix
Will, strength of, 100–104
Williams, Chancellor, 19, 20
Williams, Rhonda, 250
Williams, Rosalyn, 172
Wilson, Harriet, 45–46

Women of Gee Bend, 61–62
Women's Venture Fund, 168–69
Wong, Bonnie, 169–70
Woodard, Robert, 205
Working Girls Home Association, 58
Work-life balance. *See* Balance

Yennenga, 17

About the Author

CHERYL A. SMITH is Associate Professor in the School of Integrative and Experiential Studies, Lesley University, and a member of the university's Academic Technology and Center for Academic Technology's Advisory committees. In addition, she is a member of the Advanced Graduate Council, which oversees the doctoral program in Educational Studies, and a member of the Women's Studies task force of the Women's Resource Group at Lesley.

DATE DUE

Breinigsville, PA USA
02 October 2009

225149BV00002B/5/P

9 780313 361838